PEACE AND CONFLICT 2010

J. Joseph Hewitt

Jonathan Wilkenfeld

Ted Robert Gurr

Center for International Development and Conflict Management
University of Maryland

Paradigm Publishers
Boulder • London

Published in the United States by Paradigm Publishers, 3360 Mitchell Lane Suite E, Boulder, CO 80301 USA.

Paradigm Publishers is the trade name of Birkenkamp & Company, LLC,

Dean Birkenkamp, President and Publisher.

Library of Congress Cataloging-in-Publication Data

Hewitt, J. Joseph.
    Peace and conflict 2010 / J. Joseph Hewitt, Jonathan Wilkenfeld, and Ted Robert Gurr.
        p. cm.
    Includes bibliographical references.
    ISBN 978-1-59451-715-0 (hardcover : alk. paper)
    ISBN 978-1-59451-716-7 (paperback : alk. paper)
1. War. 2. Social conflict. 3. Violence. 4. Conflict management. 5. Self-determination, National. 6. Pacific settlement of international disputes. 7. World politics—2005–2015. 8. Democratization. 9. Terrorism. 10. Postwar reconstruction. I. Wilkenfeld, Jonathan. II. Gurr, Ted Robert, 1936- III. Title.
    JZ6385.H493 2009
    303.6—dc22
                                                                        2009016071

Printed and bound in the United States of America on acid-free paper that meets the standards of the American National Standard for Permanence of Paper for Printed Library Materials.

CONTENTS

1   Introduction   **1**
Ted Robert Gurr, J. Joseph Hewitt, and Jonathan Wilkenfeld

Regular Features

2   The Peace and Conflict Instability Ledger: Ranking States on Future Risks   **7**
J. Joseph Hewitt

3   Trends in Global Conflict, 1946–2007   **27**
J. Joseph Hewitt

4   Trends in Democratization: A Focus on Minority Rights   **33**
Amy Pate

5   Self-Determination Movements and Their Outcomes   **39**
Monica Duffy Toft and Stephen M. Saideman

6   Trends in Global Terrorism, 1970–2007   **51**
Gary LaFree, Laura Dugan, and R. Kim Cragin

The Challenges of Post-Conflict Transitions

7   State Failure and Conflict Recurrence   **65**
Anke Hoeffler

8   Democratization and Post-Conflict Transitions   **79**
Håvard Hegre and Hanne Fjelde

9   Women and Post-Conflict Settings   **91**
Mary Caprioli, Rebecca Nielsen, and Valerie M. Hudson

10   The Impact of Tribunals and Truth Commissions on Post-Conflict Peace Building   **103**
James Meernik, Rosa Aloisi, Angela D. Nichols, and Marsha Sowell

11   Conclusion   **117**
J. Joseph Hewitt, Jonathan Wilkenfeld, and Ted Robert Gurr

Appendix—Major Armed Conflicts   **123**
References   **143**
Peace and Conflict Editorial Advisory Board   **153**
Acknowledgments   **153**
About the Authors   **154**
About the Contributors   **154**
About the Center for International Development and Conflict Management   **156**

A Note on the 2010 Publication

Peace and Conflict is the flagship publication of the Center for International Development and Conflict Management at the University of Maryland. Its purpose is to make current academic research on conflict, democratization, terrorism, and international development more accessible and interpretable for people in the policy community and especially for an academic audience that wants to better understand how such research informs policy discussions.

This publication continues coverage of several topics that appeared in earlier volumes: the Peace and Conflict Instability Ledger, trends in global conflict, the spread of democracy, and self-determination movements and their outcomes. A chapter analyzing trends in global terrorism has now been added to the set of features in recognition of the importance of tracking this issue regularly. Finally, the volume includes four chapters on a special theme: "The Challenges of Post-Conflict Transitions."

The publication is committed to the principle that analyses should be fully transparent and replicable by other interested researchers. To that end, all analyses use data sources that have been released to the public and are available for further analysis and replication from the *Peace and Conflict* companion Web site.

The partnership between CIDCM and Paradigm Publishers facilitates wider dissemination of *Peace and Conflict* to the academic and policy communities, providing the opportunity for researchers, policymakers, and students to understand, replicate, and extend our analyses. CIDCM will continue to make its findings available to the policy community; an executive summary can be found on the CIDCM Web site (**www.cidcm.umd.edu**) and is available from the Center upon request (cidcm@cidcm.umd.edu).

The *Peace and Conflict* companion Web site continues to feature a suite of data analysis tools (**www.cidcm.umd.edu/pc**). Users will be able to explore data used for analyses reported in this issue by manipulating the data and making modifications to produce their own customized analyses. For the first time, a complete PowerPoint presentation is available featuring all of the key graphics offered in the book. This resource will prove to be a convenient and valuable resource for instructors who adopt the book in their courses and wish to make use of its appealing graphics in classroom presentations.

We continue to benefit from the advice and guidance offered by our Editorial Board, chaired by Ted Robert Gurr, the founding author of the *Peace and Conflict* publications. The board members played a leading role in shaping the contents of **Peace and Conflict 2010**, helping to bring focus to our desire to address issues related to post-conflict reconstruction. As the various chapters came together, they provided careful reviews of each one, making the final collection a more cohesive whole. And, in the near future, they will participate in several consultations to advise us on the content and shape of the 2012 volume. We are very grateful for their valuable contributions to this book. The members are identified at the end of this volume.

The first edition of *Peace and Conflict* in 2001 documented a global decline in armed conflict from its peak in the early 1990s. We linked that decline to the ascendance of democratic regimes and the rising success of international efforts at containing and negotiating settlements to many serious armed conflicts, most of them civil wars. The evidence we assembled for *Peace and Conflict 2008* showed that both the subsidence of armed conflict and the surge in democracy had stalled and begun to reverse. We pointed to a persistent "conflict syndrome" of instability and state failure that cripples the poorer regions of the world despite all efforts of the advanced industrial democracies and international organizations to take remedial action.

The armed conflicts and mass atrocities of the last 15 years left in their wake weakened states, economies in shambles, and human suffering and dislocation on a large scale. *Peace and Conflict 2010* examines more closely the legacies of wars within states and the prospects for rebuilding them. Although much has been written in the four previous volumes of *Peace and Conflict* about active conflict, several chapters in this volume emphasize the challenges countries face as they enter the period immediately following the cessation of armed violence—a period widely referred to as the post-conflict transition.

While the overall number of active conflicts worldwide was declining in the early 1990s—a result of many conflict terminations in that period—other conflicts were becoming active. Joseph Hewitt (Chapter 3) takes a closer look at those that became active and reveals why a focus on post-conflict transitions is especially warranted. Strikingly, of the 39 different conflicts that became active in the last 10 years, 31 were conflict recurrences—instances of resurgent, armed violence in societies where conflict had largely been dormant for at least a year. Only eight were entirely new conflicts between new antagonists involving new issues and interests. These sobering numbers serve as a reminder that many of the destabilizing dangers of the conflict syndrome initially highlighted in *Peace and Conflict 2008*—now reinforced in *Peace and Conflict 2010*—continue to pose serious challenges during the post-conflict phase, underscoring the urgency for identifying appropriate policy responses during post-conflict reconstruction.

Much has been learned by researchers about the prospects of democracy in the aftermath of civil war, the costs and challenges of rebuilding broken economies, how to reestablish the rule of law, and social issues such as the status and representation of women and minorities in governance. It is clear from the evidence seen here that the challenges of rebuilding war-damaged states are greater and often less tractable than ending the fighting itself. There is no certainty that they can be overcome. Nonetheless, the chapters in *Peace and Conflict 2010* offer a full slate of findings that will prove helpful in informing how policies and programs should be constructed to address post-conflict transitions.

- How well do democratic governments ameliorate the hazards of post-conflict risks? Democratic institutions have a limited impact on the risk of conflict recurrence in post-conflict societies because they are vulnerable to the same forces that drive conflict recurrence— poor economic growth, lingering disagreements about power-sharing arrangements, and continued opportunities for insurgencies to organize (Håvard Hegre and Hanne Fjelde, Chapter 8). More encouraging is Amy Pate's report (Chapter 4) that democracies have lower levels of political discrimination toward ethnic minorities than have non-democratic societies, which potentially lowers the risk of conflict recurrence in post-conflict democracies.

- What are the costs and challenges to rebuilding broken economies? Anke Hoeffler (Chapter 7) reports that more than one billion people live in some 50 failed and failing states whose direct and spillover economic costs of $270 billion are more than three times annual global development aid of $80 billion. The largest share of those costs is borne by countries neighboring failed states, which experience significant reductions to economic growth as a result of negative spillover effects (an estimated average loss of 0.6% per neighbor per year).

- Where are future conflicts most likely? Hard evidence about the sources of past armed conflict and instability provides the basis for the Peace and Conflict Ledger presented by Hewitt in Chapter 2. All but three of the twenty-five countries with the highest risk of new failures are in Africa—the exceptions are Afghanistan, Iraq, and Nepal. More worrisome, the average risk scores for these 25 states are significantly higher than the scores for the top 25 at-risk states reported just two years ago in *Peace and Conflict 2008*.

- What do the most recent data suggest about trends in global terrorism? Contrary to some public perceptions, the peak level of worldwide terrorist activity was during the early 1990s, not today (Gary LaFree, Laura Dugan, and R. Kim Cragin, Chapter 6). The greatest number of events in the twentieth century came in 1992 followed by a substantial decline that lasted until 2001, and then a sharp increase that seemingly peaked in 2006. In addition, the locus of terrorist events has shifted among world regions: Western Europe had the highest rates in the 1970s, Latin America in the 1980s, and the Middle East after 2003.

- What specific policy recommendations follow from analyses of post-conflict transitions?

  o Targeted international aid programs should be increased, or at least sustained, for five to ten years after the end of war and should aim at promoting social programs as well as economic growth.

- o UN peacekeeping missions are shown to have a positive effect on sustaining peace and development (Hoeffler, Chapter 7).

- o Preliminary evidence suggests that explicit efforts to incorporate women in the peace process in the stages after the termination of violence improve the prospects for more durable peace agreements (Mary Caprioli, Rebecca Nielsen, and Valerie M. Hudson, Chapter 9)

- o Truth commissions and international criminal tribunals also help reinforce peace and promote economic recovery, though with the important qualification that their positive effects depend on political context (James Meernik, Rosa Aloisi, Angela D. Nichols, and Marsha Sowell, Chapter 10).

Trends in Conflict, Democracy, and Reconstruction

A downward trend in armed conflict seems to have leveled off in the last two years. In 2007, 26 armed conflicts were being fought within states, down by two from the previous year (Hewitt, Chapter 3), but up from a low of 20 in 2004. These 26 armed conflicts include three that had been dormant: Democratic Republic of the Congo restarting in 2006, Somalia restarting in 2006, and Peru restarting in 2007. Four major armed conflicts have terminated since the publication of *Peace and Conflict 2008*: Nepal, Burundi, Indonesia, and Azerbaijan. The risk is that civil wars thought to be contained will eventually resume. Over the past few years, this is precisely what has happened. The rates of conflict recurrence since the end of the Cold War are up substantially. If we look only at the 20 armed conflicts that ended in the most recent decade, two-thirds had a history of recurrence. Since 2000, conflict recurrences outnumber the onset of new conflicts by a ratio of five to one (Hewitt, Chapter 3).

Post-conflict states face great challenges of reconstruction, political and social as much as economic. The implication of increased risks of recurrence is that the internationally brokered settlement or containment of many armed conflicts since the early 1990s did not deal effectively with root causes. Our contributors show, for example, that slow economic growth, badly timed international aid, and lack of attention to social reforms are key factors that lead to recurrence.

A focus on post-conflict transitions is especially warranted. Strikingly, of the 39 different conflicts that became active in the last 10 years, 31 were conflict recurrences—instances of resurgent, armed violence in societies where conflict had largely been dormant for at least a year.

How important is democracy to post-conflict rebuilding and sustainable peace? About half of all post-conflict countries today have some form of democratic governance. But many are semi-democratic regimes in which, typically, electoral processes and legislatures are at the whim of autocratic executives. In 2008, a total of 86 countries had consistently democratic regimes, 28 were autocracies, and the remaining 45 were anocracies, a term we use for hybrid regimes (Pate, Chapter 4). The empirical evidence is compelling that factional, semi-democratic regimes are fragile and subject to failure, whether through armed challenges or institutional failure or both. In fact competitive elections in such regimes often precipitate armed violence and massacres, as happened in Kenya in 2008.

The implication of increased risks of recurrence is that the internationally brokered settlement or containment of many armed conflicts since the early 1990s did not deal effectively with root causes. Slow economic growth, badly timed international aid, and lack of attention to social reforms are key factors that lead to recurrence.

Consistently democratic regimes are unlikely to be challenged by civil wars in the first place. If fully democratic institutions can be established after wars, economic redevelopment is more rapid, the risks of conflict recurrence are less, and transitional justice is more effective (Hegre and Felde, Chapter 8; Meernik et al., Chapter 10). Democracies also have a relatively good track record of reducing political discrimination against minorities, thereby reducing the salience of one major source of grievance around which anti-regime movements coalesce (Pate, Chapter 4). And democratic regimes have a better record of incorporating women into the political process (Caprioli et al., Chapter 9). Yet women seldom are recognized participants in peacemaking or societal reconstruction. So opportunities are lost that might give women more leverage to minimize the risks of war recurrence.

Where Are Future Conflicts Most Likely?

The Peace and Conflict Ledger ranks states based on their estimated risk of future instability or armed conflict. Countries with the poorest performance on five risk factors are at greatest risk for instability in the near-term. These five factors are: the institutional consistency of a regime (democracies and autocracies are consistent, anocracies are not); openness to international trade (international linkages minimize risks); infant mortality rates (a key indicator of socioeconomic well-being); the extent to which a country is militarized; and its proximity to other countries with armed conflict (neighborhood security).

The analyses indicate that the largest concentration of at-risk states is in Africa and South Asia. As noted above, for states that had been previously identified with high risk in *Peace and Conflict 2008*, average risk scores have significantly increased. A similar drift upward in scores is evident in countries at medium risk. Part of the upward shift in risk scores can be traced to worsening neighborhood security. The recurrence of violence in the

Democratic Republic of the Congo, for example, has adverse implications for the risk scores of numerous neighboring states. So there is no basis for complacency about a peaceful future—neither in Africa nor in the Middle East and in Western or Southern Asia, where many of the medium-risk countries are situated.

The dynamics of the African conflict region are of particular concern. Several conflicts of extended duration have coalesced there, including civil wars and genocide that began in Sudan in the 1960s and the deadly Hutu-Tutsi rivalry in Rwanda, Burundi, and the eastern Congo. These are violent communal and political rivalries that feed on one another. Most states in the region are weak and anocratic, infrastructure is minimal, peacekeeping is ineffectual, and rebels move easily across notional borders. One great risk now in the region, in addition to the unchecked genocide in Darfur and its spillover into Chad, is a breakdown of the comprehensive peace accord of 2005 that ended Sudan's north-south civil war. The international community has a very high stake in preventing recurrence but—except for the Chinese—little leverage over a militantly Islamist regime in Khartoum.

A recurring feature of *Peace and Conflict* has been an inventory of movements that aim at secession or self-determination. There are over 1,000 distinct ethnic groups in the world, any and all of which might seek a disruptive break from existing states.[1] In fact, according to this edition's expanded and updated analysis by Monica Duffy Toft and Stephen M. Saideman (Chapter 5), organizations claiming to speak for 132 minority groups now seek self-determination, but only some use either protest (99 groups) or violent means (18 groups). It is true that independence-minded groups are more likely to fight wars than groups with other objectives. The protagonists of the six most deadly wars were the Chechens in Russia, Kashmiris in India, Kurds in Turkey, Tamils in Sri Lanka, and Karens and Shans in Burma. But the international trend has been toward settling such disputes with autonomy and power-sharing agreements rather than with protracted secessionist wars.

Terrorism and the Global Future of Conflict

Many observers think that terrorism, especially by Jihadists, will be the most destabilizing source of conflict in the next decade. We have in this edition the first published assessment of long-term trends in terrorism based on a comprehensive database that includes both domestic and international incidents, a total of 77,000 events world-wide from 1970 to 2007 (LaFree et al. Chapter 6). Analyses of these data show there is no distinct long-term trend, only episodic peaks and declines.

The trends and locale of terror attacks roughly parallel the larger trends and regional upsurges in armed conflict over the last 30 years. This is not surprising since terror is often used as a tactic in larger conflicts fought by

---

1 Recent research by the Minorities at Risk Project at the University of Maryland has identified 896 socially recognized minority groups worldwide in addition to the 274 politically relevant groups profiled by the MAR project.

other means. The increases in global terrorism in the 1980s and 1990s were linked to increased armed conflict in South Asia and Africa. Since 1998 the main locus has shifted to the Middle East, where the top two terror attack sites have been the West Bank and Gaza and Iraq. Terror, especially suicide bombings, has become the Jihadists' main tactic against their sectarian and Western opponents and will continue to make life insecure for many in and on the periphery of the Islamic world, and deadly for a few. But civilian deaths from terrorism have been and will continue to be far overshadowed by deaths due directly or indirectly to armed conflicts in which warlords, militias, government forces, and rebels fight over, among, and against civilian populations.

Armed conflict will be a persistent feature of the geopolitical landscape for the foreseeable future. Risks are especially high in Africa (south of the Sahara) and in the Middle East and West Asia. The conflict syndrome applies to many of the states in these regions, challenged simultaneously by incoherent regimes, militarized societies, poverty, and weak economic links to the global system. When wars do break out here their spillover effects increase conflict risks in neighboring states. The cumulative effect is a protracted conflict region in which cycles of warfare and retribution, intervention and counter-intervention generate an ascending spiral of regional instability.

International actors can have significant influence on this process. High-risk situations can be anticipated with ever-greater accuracy and should trigger an array of preventive diplomatic, political, and economic responses. New and recurring civil wars with centrist or separatist objectives will be fought nonetheless; but the UN, major powers, and regional organizations have growing expertise and success at containing them by brokering negotiated settlements and using peacekeepers to enforce stalemates. Economic and political reconstruction requires sustained and concerted international action but is certainly possible. The wars of Yugoslavia's dissolution in the 1990s were eventually checked by international peacekeeping and diplomatic initiatives, followed by major investments in institution-building. The region's proximity to Western Europe and the active engagement of the European Union's democracies have facilitated reconstruction and stability—an instance of positive spillover. If core regimes can be strengthened in the protracted conflict regions identified in our analyses, they can play a leading role in future stabilization.

Ted Robert Gurr
J. Joseph Hewitt
Jonathan Wilkenfeld

2. THE PEACE AND CONFLICT INSTABILITY LEDGER: RANKING STATES ON FUTURE RISKS

J. Joseph Hewitt

Over the past two years, the risks of instability and conflict have increased significantly in the regions of the world where these dangers were already very high. This is one of the most important conclusions to be drawn from the most recent analyses that produce the 2010 Peace and Conflict Instability Ledger. The heightened risks are not the result of worsening government effectiveness in delivering services to the population or deteriorating economies. The heightened estimated risks are associated with a development that is normally welcomed—the initial steps toward democratic governance. Additionally, since the last publication of rankings, new armed conflicts have outnumbered those that have terminated, driving up estimated risks of instability in many regions of the world where neighborhood security has now worsened. This chapter presents country rankings based on newly calculated risk estimates and discusses some of the key results from the analysis, including the pivotal relationship between democratization and risk of instability.

The Peace and Conflict Instability Ledger ("the ledger," for short) is a ranking of 162 countries based on their estimated risk of experiencing major bouts of political instability or armed conflict in the three-year period 2008–2010. The estimates are obtained from a statistical forecasting model that uses 2007 data (the most current data available) for several variables that correlate strongly with the onset of political instability or armed conflict. The ledger represents a synthesis of some of the leading research on explaining and forecasting state instability. As such, the selection of factors accounted for in the ledger's underlying forecasting models was based on identifying variables for which agreement was strong among researchers about their relative importance. The complete ledger appears at the end of the chapter. We encourage readers to consult it regularly while proceeding through this overview.

The Peace and Conflict Instability Ledger

Figure 2.1 shows how the countries in the analysis were classified according to their estimated risk scores. A quick review of the map offers a broad overview of what the geographic landscape looks like from the perspective of the risks of instability. Undoubtedly, Africa remains the most serious concern. More than half the countries on the continent qualify for the high or highest risk categories. Of all the countries worldwide that qualify in those categories, African countries make up more than 75 percent of the states (28 of the 36 total). A similar concentration of states qualifying at high or highest risk exists in South Asia, a grouping that contains crucial states like Pakistan

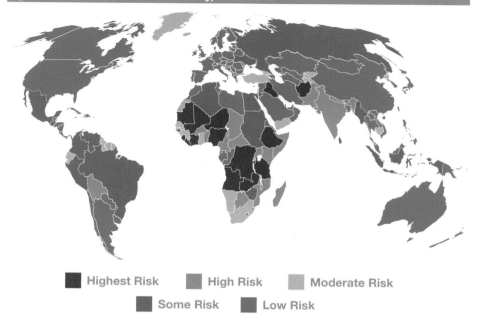

Figure 2.1 Risk of Future Instability, 2008-2010

■ Highest Risk ■ High Risk ■ Moderate Risk
■ Some Risk ■ Low Risk

(newly classified as high-risk) and Afghanistan, which are pivotal because their fates have direct repercussions for global trends in terrorism.

The ledger's conceptualization of political instability relies on the definition developed by the Political Instability Task Force (PITF).[1] That definition, which has guided the task force's comprehensive compilation of state failure events covering the period 1955–2006, encompasses a wide variety of event types. These include revolutionary wars, ethnic wars, adverse regime changes, and genocides or politicides. The onset of any of these types of episodes for a state marks the beginning of an instability event. While this set of events is quite heterogeneous, they all share a fundamental similarity— the onset of any one of these events signals the arrival of a period in which government's capacity to deliver core services and to exercise meaningful authority has been disrupted, threatening its overall stability.

Empirical studies using 60 years of historical data show that instability can emerge from a combination of five factors in four domains of government and society.[2] The key factor in the political domain is the institutional consistency of a country's governmental institutions. In the economic domain, it is openness to international trade: the more

---

1 The initial compilation of state failure events for the Task Force was done at CIDCM in 1994–1995 under the direction of Ted Robert Gurr. The roster of genocides and politicides was provided by Barbara Harff. The PITF presents full definitions for revolutionary wars, ethnic wars, adverse regime changes, genocide, and politicide in Esty et al. (1999).

2 Readers interested in some of the more significant recent contributions to this literature should consult Collier et al. (2003); Collier and Hoeffler (2004); Esty et al. (1999); Fearon and Laitin (2003); Goldstone et al. (2005); Hegre and Sambanis (2006); Hegre et al. (2001); King and Zeng (2001); Sambanis (2002, 2004); and the United States Agency for International Development (2005).

interdependent a country's economy with others, the less likely a country will experience instability in the near future. In the societal domain, the infant mortality rate is a crucial indicator of socioeconomic well-being. And in the security domain there are two factors: one is the extent to which a country is militarized, the other is whether neighboring countries have armed conflict. Box 2.1 provides a brief overview of the theoretical relationship between

Box 2.1 Factors Influencing the Risk of Instability

Factor	Domain	Description
Institutional Consistency	Political	The ledger accounts for the impact of institutional consistency. This refers to the extent to which the institutions comprising a country's political system are uniformly and consistently autocratic or democratic. Political institutions with a mix of democratic and autocratic features are inconsistent, a common attribute of polities in the midst of a democratic transition. Based on a series of findings reported in the academic literature, we expect regimes with inconsistent institutions to be more likely to experience political instability (Gurr 1974; Gates et al. 2006; Hegre et al. 2001).
Economic Openness	Economic	The ledger accounts for the impact of economic openness, which is the extent to which a country's economy is integrated with the global economy. Countries that are more tightly connected to global markets have been found to experience less instability (Hegre et al. 2003; Goldstone et al. 2000).
Infant Mortality Rates	Economic and Social	The ledger examines the impact of infant mortality rates, an indicator that serves as a proxy for a country's overall economic development, its level of advancement in social welfare policy, and its capacity to deliver core services to the population. In this respect, this indicator taps into both the economic and social domains of a country. Research findings reported by the PITF have been especially notable for the strong relationship found between high infant mortality rates and the likelihood of future instability (Esty et al. 1999; Goldstone et al. 2005).
Militarization	Security	To account for the security domain, the ledger focuses on a country's level of militarization. Instability is most likely in countries where the opportunities for armed conflict are greatest. In societies where the infrastructure and capital for organized armed conflict are more plentiful and accessible, the likelihood for civil conflict increases (Collier and Hoeffler 2004). Extensive militarization in a country typically implies that a large portion of the society's population has military skill and training, weapons stocks are more widely available, and other pieces of military equipment are more diffused throughout the country. The likelihood of instability is greater in this setting because increased access to and availability of these resources multiplies the opportunities for organizing and mobilizing.
Neighborhood Security	Security	The likelihood of political instability in a state increases substantially when a neighboring state is currently experiencing armed conflict. This risk is especially acute when ethnic or other communal groups span across borders. A number of studies have shown that neighborhood conflict is a significant predictor of political instability (Sambanis 2001; Hegre and Sambanis 2006; Goldstone et al. 2005).

each of these factors and risks of instability. A fuller discussion is given in *Peace and Conflict 2008* (Hewitt 2008).

Leveraging the strong, historical relationships that exist among the five factors and the risk of future instability, the ledger uses a statistical model to obtain risk scores for all countries having a population of at least 500,000 in 2007 (162 countries total). The data collection that serves as the foundation for this analysis contains an annual observation for each country for every year that data exist for the five factors. Each annual observation in the data collection records whether the country experienced an onset of a new instability event in any of the three years following the year of the observation. In this fashion, the data can be analyzed to assess the empirical relationship that the five factors have with the risk of future instability. To maintain comparability with the results presented in the previous volume of *Peace and Conflict*, we continue to estimate the model using data from 1950–2003. The logistic regression procedure for estimating the model on this data (sometimes called "training data") produces weights for each factor that reflect the relative influence that each has on explaining future instability. The previous ledger results (Hewitt 2008), which used 2004 data to produce forecasts for the period 2005–2007, were based on the same 1950–2003 training data. For the updated ledger, we now use 2007 data (the last year for which complete data are available for all five factors) to produce a three-year forecast indicating the risk of instability at any time during the period 2008–2010. It should be noted that in the absence of significant change to any of the five factors, risks change only gradually from year to year. Therefore, a high-risk country that experiences no major structural change to its regime, socioeconomic status, or security situation in the period 2008–2010 will likely remain at high risk beyond this forecast period.

The full listing of all 162 countries is presented at the end of the chapter. The table includes an indication of how each country is performing on each of the risk factors, which enables a quick assessment of how the ultimate risk estimate relates to each indicator. In this fashion, the full ledger table serves as a diagnostic tool, offering comprehensive information about all countries so that comparisons can be drawn about how the levels of each factor influence risk.

Over the past two years, the risks of instability and conflict have increased significantly in the regions of the world where these dangers were already very high.

To ease interpretation of the results, the ledger presents each country's likelihood of future instability as a *risk ratio*. The risk ratio gives the relative risk of instability in a country compared to the average estimated likelihood of instability for 28 members of the Organization for Economic Cooperation and Development (OECD). The OECD serves as a useful baseline because its membership is widely viewed to contain the most stable countries in the world. The estimated probability of the average OECD country's experiencing an instability event in the period 2008–2010 is 0.007. To illustrate, Nicaragua's estimated probability of experiencing instability in the next three years is 0.029, which yields a risk ratio of approximately 4.1. Presented in this way, the analysis indicates that Nicaragua's risk of instability is about four times greater than an average OECD country—a more useful characterization of its risk than the simple probability 0.029 by itself.

The risk ratios appearing in the ledger are statistical estimates and, accordingly, are accompanied by varying levels of confidence, depending on the particular attributes of a given country. An under-appreciated characteristic of statistical inferences is that they are always associated with some level of uncertainty. For instance, in the model used to create the ledger, infant mortality rates were found to be positively related to the onset of instability. The level of uncertainty for that estimate was sufficiently small to rule out the possibility that the model was pointing erroneously to a positive relationship when the "true" relationship was actually negative (or nonexistent). However, uncertainty around the estimate remains. The uncertainty exists because many countries with high infant mortality rates have not experienced instability (e.g., Malawi, Saudi Arabia, or Bolivia) and some with a low rate do (e.g., Israel). These outlier states create "noise" in the estimated relationship between instability and infant mortality rates. Each of the variables in the model is accompanied by this kind of uncertainty or noise.

Information extracted from the statistical model for instability can be used to compute the total amount of uncertainty surrounding an individual country's estimate for instability risk. The ledger reports this level of uncertainty. For each country, the ledger reports a single best estimate of the overall risk of instability. Additionally, the ledger reports a range of values within which the best estimate lies. Statistically speaking, the "true" risk of instability lies within this range with a 95 percent probability. The graphical display of the confidence range shows how it extends across risk categories. For some countries, the confidence range is confined largely within one category. For others, large segments may extend across multiple categories, which suggests that assessments about the country's status should be drawn with more caution.

The updated ledger presented in this volume features an innovation that leverages information from the confidence intervals to inform the classification of countries into separate risk categories. In the previous ledger, the three-category classification scheme (high risk, moderate risk, and low risk) was based simply on the percentile ranking of states. We improve on this method by incorporating greater gradation into the set of risk categories and informing the classification of states based on statistical confidence. A brief comment is warranted about the new classification procedure to better appreciate its advantages.

With the list of 162 countries sorted from highest score to lowest, the country with the highest risk score (Afghanistan) establishes a new grouping of states. Moving down the list, any country whose upper bound on its confidence range is higher than Afghanistan's risk score is assigned to the same group as Afghanistan (Niger, Burundi, DRC, and Djibouti). For each of these countries, the extensive overlap across their respective confidence ranges indicates little qualitative difference in their respective risk scores. The first country with an upper bound less than Afghanistan's score begins a new grouping. In this case, that would be Ethiopia. Moving further down the list, any country with an upper bound value greater than Ethiopia's risk score of 26.8 would be grouped with Ethiopia. These two groups are combined to form the "highest risk" category.

Moving down the list in a similar manner, the third grouping of states (beginning with Kenya) will be assigned to the "high risk" category. Proceeding in the same fashion, the next grouping makes up the "moderate risk" category, followed in turn by the next grouping that makes up the "some risk" category. All remaining groups below the "some risk" grouping are combined into the "low risk" category.

The new procedure establishes risk categories that have qualitative meaning. Within each grouping, a solid empirical basis exists that indicates that the identified states are quite comparable in terms of risk. Moreover, we can be more confident that states assigned to different groupings are qualitatively distinct. Since the groupings were created by using information from the confidence ranges, it is unlikely that states in lower groupings have a true estimated risk that is higher than countries assigned to higher risk categories. In sum, by moving away from arbitrary categories of risk, the new classification procedure provides better guidance for making more accurate country assessments.

Overview of Results

Table 2.1 lists the 25 countries with the highest risk scores. With the exception of three states (Afghanistan, Iraq, and Nepal), all of them are African. Indeed, the concentration of African states among the grouping of states with the highest estimated risk is even higher than the previous findings reported in 2008, when 19 of the 25 states were from Africa. Higher estimated risk scores in the Democratic Republic of the Congo, Guinea-Bissau, and Mauritania have led these countries into the top 25, supplanting Bangladesh, Lebanon, and Haiti. No doubt, a quick review of the top 25 list reveals that problems in Africa remain acute and, as the discussion below suggests, they are likely getting worse.

Overall, the mean instability scores across countries formerly classified at moderate or high risk have increased significantly since the last report. Among countries classified at high risk in the previous analyses, the average risk score was 14.1. For the same set of countries, the average is now 17.3, a difference that is statistically significant. For the countries previously classified at moderate risk, the previous average was 5.3. It is now 7.4 for those countries, a difference that is also statistically significant. Among countries classified previously at low risk, the average score did increase somewhat

Table 2.1	Highest Estimated Risk for Instability, 2008–2010	
Rank	Country	Risk Score
1	Afghanistan	38.9
2	Niger	33.1
3	Burundi	30.3
4	Congo, Democratic Republic*	29.1
5	Djibouti	28.2
6	Ethiopia	26.8
7	Mali	25.9
8	Nigeria	25.6
9	Tanzania	24.5
10	Zambia	24.2
11	Sierra Leone	23.3
12	Liberia	22.7
13	Mauritania*	21.4
14	Guinea-Bissau*	20.2
15	Angola	20.0
16	Iraq	19.7
17	Côte d'Ivoire	19.5
18	Kenya	18.0
19	Central African Republic	17.6
20	Somalia	16.9
21	Chad	16.6
22	Benin	16.0
23	Mozambique	15.8
24	Malawi	15.5
25	Nepal	15.2

*New to the top 25 in the most recent rankings.

(from 1.5 to 1.6), but that difference is not statistically meaningful. What factors explain the upward shift in risk estimates among states that are already vulnerable to instability and conflict?

The modest push of democratization and the inherent inconsistency of regime that follows is one of the key factors contributing to increased risks of instability. In the most recent data available on regime characteristics, seven countries formally classified at moderate or high-risk transitioned to partial democracies from more autocratic regime types. No countries in either of those categories of risk transitioned to consolidated democracies.[3] One country, Bangladesh, experienced a setback in its democratic transition and was reclassified as a more autocratic state in the most recent data, which contributed to a lower estimated risk. On the whole, though, the net effect of regime changes in the class of states with at least moderate risk was an exertion of more upward pressure on risk scores.

A slight increase in the number of active armed conflicts around the world has also contributed to the overall increase in the risk of instability. With more neighborhoods experiencing the volatile externalities generated by violent conflict—refugee flows, arms trafficking, threats of intervention—the risk of instability for the residents has increased.[4] All told, risk estimates for 13 countries increased because a

3 In the low-risk category, Chile and the Slovak Republic transitioned to more coherent democracies, which led to significantly lower risk scores for both countries.

4 Since the last publication of the rankings, a slight improvement has been implemented to the definition of a neighborhood conflict. As a result, several states that were originally coded as involved in active conflict are no longer coded as such. Previously, a neighbor was classified at war when it was involved in any armed conflict, even a conflict not being fought on its territory. But that definition was inconsistent with the theoretical expectation about how a neighborhood conflict relates to the risks of instability. In almost all imaginable circumstances, the spillover effects of neighborhood conflict operate only when the conflict is being fought directly on the neighbor's territory. As a result of this coding change, the only significant coding change implemented in the new analyses, the risk

new conflict erupted in a neighboring state (or an old conflict resurged). Only one state—Papua New Guinea—has a lower risk estimate because a conflict subsided in a neighboring state (the conflict in the Aceh territory in Indonesia, which subsided in 2006).

With more neighborhoods experiencing the volatile externalities generated by violent conflict—refugee flows, arms trafficking, threats of intervention—the risk of instability for the residents has increased.

Changes Since 2007

To see more clearly how democratization and neighborhood conflict can have an immediate impact on increasing the risks of instability, let us take a more detailed look at the circumstances in some countries that experienced significant change from the previous rankings.

For purposes of identifying cases in which significant change has occurred, we adopt a clear standard that utilizes information from each country's confidence interval. To identify cases in which the risk of instability has significantly increased, we require that the lower end of the new confidence range be greater than the risk estimate from the previous analysis. This standard allows us to conclude that the change in underlying risk has increased or has remained largely unchanged, but we can be nearly certain that it has not decreased. Cases of significant improvement require that the upper bound of the new confidence range be less than the risk estimate from the previous analysis. In this case, the standard permits an interpretation that the risk in a given country has likely declined or remained unchanged, but it has not increased.

Table 2.2 lists the 17 countries with the largest increase in risk scores. Of these, the change in 13 of the countries satisfies the standard for a significant worsening. For each of the countries, data are presented corresponding to the previous ledger rankings (based on the forecast period 2005–2007) alongside data used for the current forecast period (2008–2010). The net change in risk score is listed with an indication (*) of whether the change satisfies the threshold defined above. In most of these cases, the increase in risk can be traced to two separate factors: transitions to democratic governance and armed conflict in neighboring countries.

Undoubtedly, the process of democratization is a welcome development because it brings desirable qualities to governance (e.g., greater citizen participation, broader competition for leadership positions, more expansive civil liberties, etc.). For many observers, though, the heightened dangers of instability during this period are often under-appreciated.

Partial democracies are at greater risk for instability than autocracies or full democracies. Repressive tactics adopted by autocratic governments

---

scores for some states declined. Examples of such states include any state that bordered a state that had contributed troops to the multilateral efforts in Iraq or Afghanistan. This set of countries tended to have relative low risks of instability in the first place, so the impact of the definitional change was slight.

Table 2.2   Largest Increases in Risk of Instability

Forecast Period	Country	Risk Ratio	Net Change	Confidence Range	Regime Consistency	Partial Democracy	Infant Mortality	Economic Openness	Militarization	Neighborhood War
2005-07	Congo, Dem. Rep.	6.9		3.7 – 11.8	0	O	129	70%	115	●
2008-10		29.1	22.2*	18.0 – 42.5	25	●	128	65%	115	●
2005-07	Burundi	11.1		6.5 – 18.0	0	O	114	40%	1112	O
2008-10		30.3	19.2*	19.0 – 45.2	36	●	109	59%	1112	●
2005-07	Mauritania	5.1		3.1 – 7.5	36	O	78	25%	671	●
2008-10		21.4	16.3*	12.6 – 33.0	16	●	77	123%	690	●
2005-07	Nigeria	13.4		7.6 – 21.5	16	●	101	92%	124	O
2008-10		25.6	12.2*	15.9 – 37.4	16	●	98	69%	112	●
2005-07	Djibouti	17.1		8.4 – 31.3	4	●	101	133%	1412	O
2008-10		28.2	11.1	15.7 – 45.3	4	●	86	137%	1412	●
2005-07	Guinea-Bissau	9.3		4.8 – 16.6	1	O	125	87%	585	O
2008-10		20.2	10.9*	11.3 – 32.7	36	●	119	89%	547	O
2005-07	Angola	10.5		4.7 – 20.6	4	O	154	125%	762	O
2008-10		20.0	9.5	9.2 – 35.8	4	O	154	108%	664	●
2005-07	Zambia	14.8		9.1 – 23.1	25	●	101	47%	139	O
2008-10		24.2	9.4*	14.9 – 36.8	25	●	101	78%	137	●
2005-07	Pakistan	5.2		3.3 – 7.9	25	O	80	31%	606	●
2008-10		14.6	9.4*	9.2 – 22.0	4	O	77	36%	581	●
2005-07	Nepal	6.4		3.8 – 10.0	36	O	59	48%	493	●
2008-10		15.2	8.8*	10.6 – 21.1	36	●	46	41%	474	●
2005-07	Uganda	4.9		2.8 – 8.1	16	O	80	41%	198	●
2008-10		12.9	8.0*	8.0 – 19.8	1	O	77	45%	198	●
2005-07	Burkina Faso	8.3		5.0 – 12.9	0	O	97	32%	80	O
2008-10		14.1	5.8*	8.8 – 21.4	0	O	122	38%	80	O
2005-07	Cameroon	6.8		4.2 – 10.5	16	O	87	39%	143	O
2008-10		12.5	5.7*	7.3 – 19.7	16	O	86	43%	143	●
2005-07	Tanzania	18.9		12.3 – 27.9	4	●	78	46%	74	●
2008-10		24.5	5.6	16.2 – 35.5	1	●	74	50%	74	●
2005-07	Chad	11.2		5.4 – 20.7	4	O	117	100%	360	●
2008-10		16.6	5.4	8.8 – 27.7	4	O	124	83%	360	●
2005-07	Kyrgyz Republic	3.5		1.7 – 6.2	9	O	59	96%	333	●
2008-10		8.8	5.3*	4.7 – 14.6	9	●	36	116%	404	O
2005-07	Bolivia	7.6		4.5 – 12.1	64	●	54	58%	759	O
2008-10		12.8	5.2*	7.8 – 19.3	64	●	49	66%	887	●

NOTE: An asterisk (*) indicates a net change that qualifies as significant according to the definition offered above. The numbers in the infant mortality column are the total infant deaths per 1,000 live births. The percentage in the economic openness column refers to the percentage of a country's GDP accounted for by the value of its imports plus exports. The number in the militarization column refers to the number of active military personnel per 100,000 people. Finally, the symbol ● means "yes" and the symbol O means "no."

often smother the potential for political instability. Coherent and mature democracies possess the capacity to address group grievances and manage the competition between groups that vie for political power and other resources, thereby reducing the risks of instability. Partial democracies typically possess neither of the qualities of full autocracies nor those of democracies, leaving them more vulnerable to the drivers of instability and conflict (Pate 2008). Indeed, the historical data over the past half-century shows a strong empirical relationship between partial democracy and the future onset of instability or conflict.

The bout of instability that raged in Kenya after its December 2007 presidential election serves as a recent illustration. In the ledger published in *Peace and Conflict 2008*, data from 2004 were used to produce Kenya's risk estimate for the period 2005–2007. At the time, Kenya was classified as a partial democracy, according to the Polity project, because the competitiveness of political participation was still seen as in transition from competition that had been largely suppressed by the regime. Its risk score, 12.9, reflected the potential for instability associated with these regime characteristics, placing it squarely among other high-risk states in Africa, despite a record of relative stability compared to neighbors like Ethiopia, Somalia, and Sudan. Those institutions would prove to lack the resilience to withstand forces that developed in the months preceding the close presidential election, as well as the pressures that were released in its aftermath. After months of campaigning with appeals to rectifying injustices based on advantages accorded to ethnic Kikuyus, opposition candidate Raila Odinga appeared to be positioned to win the election based on pre-election polling. When reports indicated that he had lost by a slim margin, amid widespread reports of election fraud, the forces driving the potential for instability were catalyzed. In the weeks following the election, approximately 1,000 people were killed in ethnically based violence throughout the country.

The experience of Kenya in late 2007 and early 2008 illustrates the vulnerabilities of partial democracies to some of the forces that can catalyze major episodes of instability. Kenya continues to be classified as a partial democracy, receiving an updated risk score of 18.0, which reflects some of the worsening conditions in the country in the aftermath of recent instability. With Kenya's experience in mind, let us briefly note some other countries that have been newly classified as partial democracies in the updated rankings, a change that has significantly increased their respective risk for future instability.

The Democratic Republic of Congo, Burundi, Mauritania, Guinea-Bissau, Nepal, and the Kyrgyz Republic all transitioned in varying extents to partial democratic rule during the 2005–2007 period. For any of these countries, much could be written about how the transition to more democratic governing arrangements influences the estimated risk for instability. Space constraints permit a focus on just one of these states. For the purposes of illustrating the impact that democratic transition can have on the estimated risk of instability, the case of the Kyrgyz Republic will be most suitable.

In the previous ledger rankings, the Kyrgyz Republic estimate for risk of instability from 2005 to 2007 was based on data from 2004. In that year, governing arrangements in the country tended toward autocracy, although constitutional provisions did allow for some competitive elections and fewer restrictions on political participation. Still, Kyrgyzstan did not qualify as a partial democracy, which contributed to an estimate of only moderate risk for instability (3.5). By late 2006, a new constitution was in place that gave more political authority to the parliament. The changes in regime characteristics were sufficient to reclassify Kyrgyzstan as a partial democracy according to the Polity project's coding rules. In subsequent months, that authority would shift back to the presidency, but Kyrgyzstan continues to be coded as partially democratic. Predictably, the tenuous step toward democratization in Kyrgyzstan led to an increase in the estimated risk of instability (8.8). What makes the case of Kyrgyzstan notable is that the estimated risk of instability increased despite significant improvement in other areas. From 2004 to 2007, the country's infant mortality rate declined from roughly 58 deaths per 1,000 live births to 36. Moreover, a low-intensity armed conflict in neighboring Uzbekistan in 2004 had subsided by 2007. Despite these changes, which exert modest downward pressure on risk estimates, the movement toward democracy had a more powerful impact on pushing the estimated risk upward.

The experience of Kenya in late 2007 and early 2008 illustrates the vulnerabilities of partial democracies to some of the forces that can catalyze major episodes of instability.

For other countries listed in Table 2.2, the heightened risk of instability is due to the onset (or recurrence) of armed conflict in a neighboring state. In Burundi, for example, the risk of instability increased substantially, due to renewed fighting in the neighboring Democratic Republic of the Congo (DRC). That same recurrence of conflict in the DRC is responsible for the heightened risk estimates in Angola. Nigeria's risk of instability increased with the recurrence of conflict in Chad in 2005 and less intense violence in Niger in 2007.

Table 2.3 presents a list of ten countries that showed the largest improvement in risk scores. Of these countries, seven made improvements that satisfied the requirements for significance outlined above. Glancing down the "Net Change" column of the table, it can be seen that the absolute level of reductions in risk is much lower than the absolute level of increases observed in Table 2.2. Given the overall global trend toward greater levels of instability, these differences should be expected.

Just as the risk of instability can increase substantially in a short period of time, it can decrease just as suddenly. For instance, the termination of a neighborhood conflict can reduce the risk of instability for a country abruptly. As mentioned previously, the lower risk score for Papua New Guinea is the result of the cessation of serious armed violence in neighboring

Table 2.3 Largest Reduction in Risk of Instability

Forecast Period	Country	Risk Ratio	Net Change	Confidence Range	Regime Consistency	Partial Democracy	Infant Mortality	Economic Openness	Militarization	Neighborhood War
2005-07	Iraq	29.9		20.0 – 43.2	0	●	101	22%	668	●
2008-10		19.7	-10.2*	12.0 – 28.8	0	●	50	62%	668	●
2005-07	Bangladesh	13.1		9.1 – 18.7	36	●	56	36%	180	●
2008-10		3.0	-10.1*	1.7 – 5.2	36	○	51	51%	137	●
2005-07	Serbia	4.5		2.4 – 8.0	36	●	13	74%	1350	●
2008-10		1.7	-2.8*	0.7 – 3.5	64	●	7	76%	324	○
2005-07	Fiji	3.6		1.9 – 6.0	36	●	16	40%	357	○
2008-10		0.8	-2.8*	0.3 – 1.7	16	○	16	128%	480	○
2005-07	Papua New Guinea	5.1		2.5 – 9.3	100	○	69	32%	52	●
2008-10		2.4	-2.7*	1.1 – 4.8	100	○	55	147%	48	○
2005-07	Honduras	6.6		3.9 – 9.3	49	●	32	85%	284	●
2008-10		4.2	-2.4	2.2 – 6.8	49	●	23	130%	287	○
2005-07	Albania	4.5		2.6 – 7.3	49	●	16	65%	691	●
2008-10		2.6	-1.9*	1.4 – 4.3	81	●	15	79%	363	○
2005-07	Nicaragua	5.9		3.4 – 9.5	64	●	31	81%	260	●
2008-10		4.1	-1.8	2.2 – 6.7	81	●	29	120%	253	○
2005-07	Guatemala	7.3		4.8 – 11.0	64	●	33	48%	390	●
2008-10		5.6	-1.7	3.5 – 8.7	64	●	31	66%	269	○
2005-07	Vietnam	2.3		0.6 – 5.8	49	○	17	140%	6772	○
2008-10		0.6	-1.7*	0.2 – 1.1	49	○	15	159%	589	○

NOTE: An asterisk (*) indicates a net change that qualifies as significant according to the definition offered above. The numbers in the infant mortality column are the total infant deaths per 1,000 live births. The percentage in the economic openness column refers to the percentage of a country's GDP accounted for by the value of its imports plus exports. The number in the militarization column refers to the number of active military personnel per 100,000 people. Finally, the symbol ● means "yes" and the symbol ○ means "no."

Indonesia in 2006—the only conflict termination since the previous publication of the ledger.

For some countries in Table 2.3, the estimated risk of instability decreased because the country experienced a setback in its transition to democracy. Both Fiji and Bangladesh were coded as partial democracies in the previous rankings. In the most recent data, governing arrangements in both countries have shifted toward greater autocracy, which produces lower estimated risk scores. In Bangladesh the lower risk estimate may be short-lived. Parliamentary elections were postponed in January 2007 due to serious concerns of potential electoral fraud and corruption. President Iajuddin Ahmed resigned from office, and a series of measures were implemented as part of a general state of emergency. The changes led to the Polity project's recoding Bangladesh's regime as essentially autocratic in 2007. Since the parliamentary elections were held in December 2008, it is conceivable that

Bangladesh may qualify as a partial democracy in a future release of Polity data, which would cause risk estimates to return to higher levels.

For many of the other countries in Table 2.3, improvements in the economic and social domains were most responsible for reductions in the underlying risk of instability. Iraq posted the largest improvement from the previous rankings for the 2005–2007 period. Large improvements in infant mortality rates and in economic openness are the main sources of the reduced risk estimate. The figures from 2004 were particularly bad, an unsurprising artifact of the vast disruption caused by the war that began in 2003. Iraq's infant mortality rate (as estimated in the CIA Factbook) was approximately 100 per 1,000 live births, the twentieth highest figure of all countries worldwide. The proportion of its GDP accounted for by trade was just 22 percent, ninth worst in the world. By 2007, those indicators had improved. Now, Iraq's infant mortality (about 50 deaths per 1,000 live births) is more comparable to that of Bangladesh. In addition, the indicator for economic openness has improved substantially to 62 percent. While the improvements are notable, Iraq's overall risk score (19.7) continues to place it in the highest risk category, a solemn reminder of how grim the circumstances remain there.

In Serbia, improvements on several dimensions contributed to substantial reductions in its risk score. Although coded as a partial democracy, Serbia's regime consistency score improved from 36 in 2004 to 64, reflecting steady movement toward greater democratic consolidation. Infant mortality rates decreased from about 12 per 1,000 births to about 7. Finally, the militarization indictor dropped significantly, reflecting a sizeable reduction in the number of active armed personnel in Serbia from 2004 to 2007. In Albania and Vietnam, combined improvements in infant mortality, economic openness, and militarization all contributed to modest, yet significant, reductions in estimated risk. The achievement in Albania is notable because it qualifies as a partial democracy, illustrating how countries in the midst of a democratic transition can mitigate the profound risks inherent in that transformation through effective governance.

Conclusion

The sudden and significant increase in the estimated risk of instability across countries that were already vulnerable should be a cause for concern for policy-makers involved with managing conflict and addressing the larger challenges to state stability. There are two distinct causes for heightened levels of risk, which means that policy-makers should be attentive to how policy responses relate to each.

As regimes transform from autocracies to partial democracies, the estimated risks of major instability events increases. Policy responses that address the specific vulnerabilities of such regimes have the potential to mitigate instability risks. For example, any government policies that reduce the extent of factional-based political competition can increase the prospects that multiple sub-national groups (ethnic or non-ethnic) see themselves as stakeholders in the current set of institutional arrangements. A greater sensitivity to the importance of transparency in electoral procedures can reduce the catalytic potential for tightly contested elections to trigger instability. And, of course, while the volatile transition to consolidated democracy occurs, it is crucial that attention be paid to policies that enhance government's ability to deliver core services to the population (as illustrated by Albania's recent experience). Doing so will enhance the likelihood that it is viewed as legitimate, mitigating the risks faced by typical partial democracies.

As regimes transform from autocracies to partial democracies, the estimated risks of major instability events increases. Policy responses that address the specific vulnerabilities of such regimes have the potential to mitigate instability risks.

At the same time, estimated risks may suddenly become elevated because of the onset or recurrence of a neighborhood conflict. In these cases, appropriate policy responses should address some of the contagion effects of conflicts. For a country with a neighbor involved in civil conflict, attention should be paid to the relationship that ethnic groups located near the border may have with warring parties in the country at war. Where there is potential for cross-border activity, appropriate responses may include heightened border monitoring and control to prevent the transfer of arms or the movement of soldiers into the warring country.

Ultimately, the key to effective policy responses to heightened risks of instability depends heavily on an ability to trace back from the estimate to the particular factors that exert the most influence on it. The Peace and Conflict Instability Ledger places an emphasis on making information about the risk estimates as accessible and interpretable as possible, so that diagnosing the foundations of these risks can be more effective. Moreover, by explicitly reporting confidence ranges associated with each country estimate, the ledger offers policy-makers enhanced leverage for making more confident assertions about the substantive importance of any year-to-year change observed in a particular country—a crucial necessity for making precise assessments about progress in at-risk countries. This chapter has offered several brief discussions of cases to be suggestive of how information from the ledger can be used to help clarify risk trends in a particular country. Employed alongside the detailed information (both qualitative and quantitative) available to country experts, the ledger can be a powerful diagnostic tool in any policy-makers' toolkit for assessing risk levels across countries.

The Peace and Conflict Instability Ledger ranks states according to the forecasted risk of future instability. See notes on pp. 25–26 for a description of the color codes for each indicator and also a detailed explanation of the confidence range (note 10).

Recent Instability	Country	Regime Consistency	Infant Mortality	Economic Openness	Militarization	Neighborhood War	Risk Category	Risk Score	Confidence Range
	Africa								
	Niger	●	●	●	●	●	●	38.9	21.3 — 47.6
	Burundi	●	●	●	●	●	●	30.3	19.0 — 45.2
■	Dem. Rep. of Congo	●	●	●	●	●	●	29.1	18.0 — 42.5
	Djibouti	●	●	●	●	●	●	28.2	15.7 — 45.3
	Ethiopia	●	●	●	●	●	●	26.8	18.2 — 38.0
	Mali	●	●	●	●	●	●	25.9	15.7 — 38.7
	Nigeria	●	●	●	●	●	●	25.6	15.9 — 37.4
	Tanzania	●	●	●	●	●	●	24.5	16.2 — 35.5
	Zambia	●	●	●	●	●	●	24.2	14.9 — 36.8
	Sierra Leone	●	●	●	●	●	●	23.3	12.4 — 37.7
	Liberia	●	●	●	●	●	●	22.7	12.3 — 38.1
	Mauritania	●	●	●	●	●	●	21.4	12.6 — 33.0
	Guinea-Bissau	●	●	●	●	●	●	20.2	11.3 — 32.7
	Angola	●	●	●	●	●	●	20.0	9.2 — 35.8
■	Côte d'Ivoire	●	●	●	●	●	●	19.5	11.7 — 30.1
	Kenya	●	●	●	●	●	●	18.0	11.6 — 26.0
■	Central African Rep.	●	●	●	●	●	●	17.6	10.6 — 28.0
■	Somalia	●	●	●	●	●	●	16.9	10.7 — 25.4
■	Chad	●	●	●	●	●	●	16.6	8.8 — 27.7
	Benin	●	●	●	●	●	●	16.0	10.5 — 22.6
	Mozambique	●	●	●	●	●	●	15.8	9.2 — 25.9
	Malawi	●	●	●	●	●	●	15.5	10.5 — 22.4
	Burkina Faso	●	●	●	●	●	●	14.1	8.8 — 21.4
■	Uganda	●	●	●	●	●	●	12.9	8.0 — 19.8
	Botswana	●	●	●	●	●	●	12.6	6.7 — 21.6
	Cameroon	●	●	●	●	●	●	12.5	7.3 — 19.7
	Madagascar	●	●	●	●	●	●	12.0	7.5 — 18.1
	Lesotho	●	●	●	●	●	●	11.9	5.6 — 20.9
	Ghana	●	●	●	●	●	●	10.3	5.9 — 16.8
	Guinea	●	●	●	●	●	●	9.9	5.7 — 15.5
	Senegal	●	●	●	●	●	●	9.6	5.8 — 15.1
	Namibia	●	●	●	●	●	●	9.5	5.6 — 15.0
	South Africa	●	●	●	●	●	●	8.1	4.7 — 12.7
	Comoros	●	●	●	●	●	●	7.9	4.8 — 12.5
	Rwanda	●	●	●	●	●	●	7.5	4.5 — 12.1
	Eritrea	●	●	●	●	●	●	7.2	4.6 — 11.1
	Togo	●	●	●	●	●	●	6.6	3.9 — 10.5
	Zimbabwe	●	●	●	●	●	●	6.2	3.5 — 10.4
■	Sudan	●	●	●	●	●	●	4.6	2.5 — 7.6
	Congo, Rep.	●	●	●	●	●	●	4.3	2.3 — 7.4
	Equitorial Guinea	●	●	●	●	●	●	3.8	2.1 — 6.6
	Gambia	●	●	●	●	●	●	2.8	1.6 — 4.8
	Gabon	●	●	●	●	●	●	2.7	1.5 — 4.6
	Swaziland	●	●	●	●	●	●	2.4	1.2 — 4.4
	Cape Verde	●	●	●	●	●	●	1.5	0.8 — 2.7
	Mauritius	●	●	●	●	●	●	0.7	0.3 — 1.3

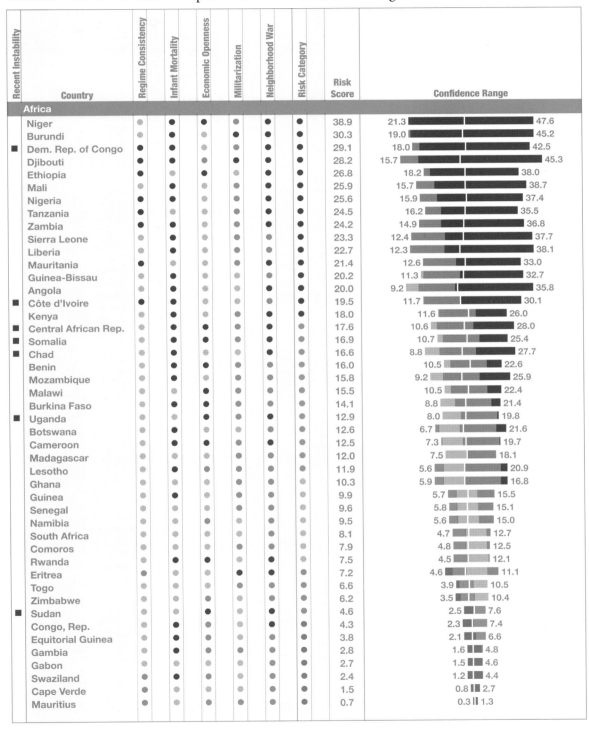

Recent Instability	Country	Regime Consistency	Infant Mortality	Economic Openness	Militarization	Neighborhood War	Risk Category	Risk Score	Confidence Range
Asia									
■	Afghanistan	●	●	●	●	●	●	38.9	23.7 ▬▬▬▬▬ 58.2
	Nepal	●	●	●	●	●	●	15.2	10.6 ▬▬ 21.1
■	Pakistan	●	●	●	●	●	●	14.6	9.2 ▬▬ 22.0
	Timor-Leste	●	●	●	●	●	●	14.3	14.3 ▬▬ 20.3
■	India	●	●	●	●	●	●	12.0	7.1 ▬▬ 18.2
	Kyrgyz Republic	●	●	●	●	●	●	8.8	4.7 ▬▬ 14.6
	Korea, Dem. Rep.	●	●	●	●	●	●	8.7	3.2 ▬▬ 17.9
	Tajikistan	●	●	●	●	●	●	8.3	4.7 ▬▬ 14.0
	Cambodia	●	●	●	●	●	●	7.8	4.1 ▬▬ 13.6
■	Myanmar	●	●	●	●	●	●	6.0	3.9 ▬ 8.9
	Indonesia	●	●	●	●	●	●	5.2	3.1 ▬ 7.9
■	Sri Lanka	●	●	●	●	●	●	4.9	2.5 ▬ 8.9
	Laos	●	●	●	●	●	●	4.3	2.4 ▬ 7.0
■	Philippines	●	●	●	●	●	●	4.3	2.5 ▬ 6.9
	Malaysia	●	●	●	●	●	●	3.7	1.5 ▬ 7.6
	Bangladesh	●	●	●	●	●	●	3.0	1.7 ▬ 5.2
	Bhutan	●	●	●	●	●	●	3.0	1.6 ▬ 4.9
	Mongolia	●	●	●	●	●	●	2.6	1.3 ▬ 4.8
	Papua New Guinea	●	●	●	●	●	●	2.4	1.1 ▬ 4.8
	Turkmenistan	●	●	●	●	●	●	1.6	0.8 ▮ 2.8
	Uzbekistan	●	●	●	●	●	●	1.6	0.9 ▮ 2.7
■	Thailand	●	●	●	●	●	●	1.6	0.6 ▮ 3.6
	Kazakhstan	●	●	●	●	●	●	1.6	0.7 ▮ 3.0
	Korea, Rep.	●	●	●	●	●	●	1.4	0.5 ▮ 3.0
	China	●	●	●	●	●	●	1.2	0.5 ▮ 2.3
	Fiji	●	●	●	●	●	●	0.8	0.3 ▮ 1.7
	Taiwan	●	●	●	●	●	●	0.7	0.3 ▮ 1.3
	Singapore	●	●	●	●	●	●	0.7	0.7 ▮ 1.7
	Vietnam	●	●	●	●	●	●	0.6	0.2 ▮ 1.1
	Japan	●	●	●	●	●	●	0.4	0.1 ▮ 1.2
	Australia	●	●	●	●	●	●	0.4	0.2 ▮ 1.0
	New Zealand	●	●	●	●	●	●	0.4	0.2 ▮ 1.0
Eastern Europe									
	Armenia	●	●	●	●	●	●	10.8	6.0 ▬▬ 17.2
	Georgia	●	●	●	●	●	●	9.0	5.5 ▬▬ 13.6
	Russia	●	●	●	●	●	●	6.7	3.4 ▬▬ 11.4
	Ukraine	●	●	●	●	●	●	5.8	3.4 ▬ 9.6
	Bosnia	●	●	●	●	●	●	4.2	1.6 ▬ 8.7
	Azerbaijan	●	●	●	●	●	●	3.9	2.3 ▬ 6.4
	Romania	●	●	●	●	●	●	3.1	1.7 ▬ 5.4
	Montenegro	●	●	●	●	●	●	2.9	1.3 ▬ 5.5
	Bulgaria	●	●	●	●	●	●	2.8	1.4 ▬ 4.9
	Moldova	●	●	●	●	●	●	2.7	1.5 ▬ 4.9
	Albania	●	●	●	●	●	●	2.6	1.4 ▬ 4.3
	Latvia	●	●	●	●	●	●	2.4	1.1 ▬ 4.6
	Estonia	●	●	●	●	●	●	1.9	0.6 ▬ 4.3
	Serbia	●	●	●	●	●	●	1.7	0.7 ▮ 3.5
	Croatia	●	●	●	●	●	●	1.1	0.4 ▮ 2.4
	Belarus	●	●	●	●	●	●	0.9	0.4 ▮ 1.8
	Czech Republic	●	●	●	●	●	●	0.7	0.2 ▮ 1.7

Recent Instability	Country	Regime Consistency	Infant Mortality	Economic Openness	Militarization	Neighborhood War	Risk Category	Risk Score	Confidence Range
	Eastern Europe (continued)								
	Lithuania	●	●	●	●	●	●	0.7	0.3 ‖ 1.3
	Poland	●	●	●	●	●	●	0.6	0.3 ‖ 1.2
	Slovakia	●	●	●	●	●	●	0.4	0.2 ‖ 0.9
	Hungary	●	●	●	●	●	●	0.4	0.2 ‖ 0.8
	Slovenia	●	●	●	●	●	●	0.2	0.1 ‖ 0.5
	Latin America and the Caribbean								
	Haiti	●	●	●	●	●	●	13.1	8.3 ▩ 19.1
	Bolivia	●	●	●	●	●	●	12.8	7.8 ▩ 19.3
	Ecuador	●	●	●	●	●	●	7.8	4.5 ▩ 12.7
	Guyana	●	●	●	●	●	●	7.7	4.0 ▩ 13.6
	Mexico	●	●	●	●	●	●	7.3	4.6 ▩ 11.1
	Venezuela	●	●	●	●	●	●	7.2	4.0 ▩ 11.7
■	Colombia	●	●	●	●	●	●	6.6	4.1 ▩ 10.8
	Brazil	●	●	●	●	●	●	6.6	4.0 ▩ 10.3
	Peru	●	●	●	●	●	●	5.9	3.6 ▩ 9.0
	Guatemala	●	●	●	●	●	●	5.6	3.5 ▩ 8.7
	Dominican Republic	●	●	●	●	●	●	4.9	3.0 ▩ 7.7
	El Salvador	●	●	●	●	●	●	4.8	2.8 ▩ 7.8
	Honduras	●	●	●	●	●	●	4.2	2.2 ▩ 6.8
	Nicaragua	●	●	●	●	●	●	4.1	2.2 ▩ 6.7
	Jamaica	●	●	●	●	●	●	3.6	1.9 ▩ 6.1
	Paraguay	●	●	●	●	●	●	3.4	2.0 ▩ 5.6
	Argentina	●	●	●	●	●	●	3.3	1.7 ▩ 5.6
	Trinidad and Tobago	●	●	●	●	●	●	1.8	0.8 ‖ 3.2
	Panama	●	●	●	●	●	●	1.7	0.8 ‖ 3.0
	Uruguay	●	●	●	●	●	●	0.9	0.5 ‖ 1.6
	Chile	●	●	●	●	●	●	0.9	0.4 ‖ 1.6
	Costa Rica	●	●	●	●	●	●	0.7	0.3 ‖ 1.3
	Cuba	●	●	●	●	●	●	0.5	0.1 ‖ 1.5
	Middle East and North Africa								
■	Iraq	●	●	●	●	●	●	19.7	12.0 ▩ 28.8
■	Yemen	●	●	●	●	●	●	11.6	7.7 ▩ 16.5
	Lebanon	●	●	●	●	●	●	10.5	6.4 ▩ 16.4
■	Turkey	●	●	●	●	●	●	8.3	5.3 ▩ 12.3
	Egypt	●	●	●	●	●	●	6.0	3.4 ▩ 9.9
	Algeria	●	●	●	●	●	●	5.0	2.8 ▩ 8.1
	Jordan	●	●	●	●	●	●	4.7	2.3 ▩ 8.1
	Tunisia	●	●	●	●	●	●	3.2	1.6 ▩ 5.6
	Morocco	●	●	●	●	●	●	2.2	1.2 ‖ 3.9
	Iran	●	●	●	●	●	●	2.1	1.1 ‖ 3.7
	Libya	●	●	●	●	●	●	1.2	0.5 ‖ 2.3
	Syria	●	●	●	●	●	●	1.1	0.5 ‖ 2.2
	Saudi Arabia	●	●	●	●	●	●	0.8	0.4 ‖ 1.5
	Kuwait	●	●	●	●	●	●	0.7	0.2 ‖ 1.6
	Bahrain	●	●	●	●	●	●	0.6	0.2 ‖ 1.3
	Qatar	●	●	●	●	●	●	0.6	0.3 ‖ 1.1
■	Israel	●	●	●	●	●	●	0.6	0.2 ‖ 1.1
	Oman	●	●	●	●	●	●	0.5	0.2 ‖ 1.0
	UAE	●	●	●	●	●	●	0.3	0.1 ‖ 0.8

Recent Instability	Country	Regime Consistency	Infant Mortality	Economic Openness	Militarization	Neighborhood War	Risk Category	Risk Score	Confidence Range
North Atlantic									
	Macedonia							2.5	1.3 ▮▮ 4.3
	United States							0.9	0.4 ▮ 1.9
	Belgium							0.8	0.2 ▮ 1.8
	Greece							0.6	0.2 ▮ 1.4
	Cyprus							0.6	0.2 ▮ 1.3
	Canada							0.5	0.2 ▮ 1.1
	United Kingdom							0.4	0.2 ▮ 0.9
	France							0.4	0.1 ▮ 0.9
	Norway							0.4	0.1 ▮ 0.8
	Finland							0.4	0.1 ▮ 0.8
	Italy							0.4	0.1 ▮ 0.8
	Spain							0.3	0.1 ▮ 0.8
	Switzerland							0.3	0.1 ▮ 0.7
	Portugal							0.3	0.1 ▮ 0.7
	Denmark							0.3	0.1 ▮ 0.7
	Netherlands							0.3	0.1 ▮ 0.7
	Austria							0.3	0.1 ▮ 0.7
	Germany							0.3	0.1 ▮ 0.6
	Ireland							0.3	0.1 ▮ 0.6
	Sweden							0.2	0.1 ▮ 0.5

The ledger is based on a model that estimates the statistical relationship between the future likelihood of instability and each of the five factors in the chapter. We estimated the model based on data for the period 1950–2003 and found that each of the five factors were strongly related to the future risk of instability. Using the model estimates for the causal weight assigned to each factor, we used data from 2007, the last year for which complete data are available for all five of our factors, to produce a three-year forecast indicating the risk of instability in the period 2008–2010. The color codes used in the ledger to present a country's standing on each of the five factors are based on the values in 2007. The notes below explain the various color codings.

(1) Recent Instability This column indicates (with a red square) whether the country has been coded by the Political Instability Task Force (PITF) as being involved in an instability event as of the end of 2006. The country's risk score (see column 9) provides an assessment of the likelihood of the country's experiencing future instability. One might interpret the risk score for countries currently experiencing instability as the risk of continued instability, but we caution readers that the causal factors that drive the continuation of instability are likely not the same as the factors that drive the onset of instability.

(2) Country The ledger examines only those countries with populations greater than 500,000 in 2007.

(3) Regime Consistency The risk of future instability is strongly related to the extent to which the institutions comprising a country's political system are uniformly and consistently autocratic or democratic. Political institutions with a mix of democratic and autocratic features are deemed inconsistent, a common attribute of polities in the midst of a democratic transition (or a reversal from democratic rule to more autocratic governance). We expect regimes with inconsistent institutions to be more likely to experience political instability. In the ledger, highly consistent democracies (Polity score greater than or equal to 6) and autocracies (Polity score less than or equal to -6) receive a green marker. A red marker has been assigned to regimes with inconsistent characteristics that also qualify as partial democracies according to PITF. Regimes with these characteristics have been found to have the highest risk for instability. We assign a yellow marker to partial autocracies because the propensity for instability in these regimes is somewhat less than in partial democracies.

(4) Infant Mortality Infant mortality rates serve as a proxy for overall governmental effectiveness in executing policies and delivering services that improve social welfare in a country. High infant mortality rates are associated with an increased likelihood of future instability. The states with the best records are indicated with a green marker (scoring in the bottom 25th percentile of global infant mortality rates). States with the worst record (scoring in the highest 25th percentile)

are indicated with a red marker. States in the middle 50th percentile are indicated with a yellow marker.

(5) Economic Openness Closer integration with global markets reduces the likelihood of armed civil conflict and political instability. Policies that integrate global and domestic markets can produce higher growth rates and sometimes reduce inequality. To that extent, economic openness can remove or weaken common drivers for civil unrest related to economic grievances. We focus on the proportion of a country's GDP accounted for by the value of all trade (exports plus imports) as a measure for economic openness. The countries with the lowest score for economic openness are considered to be at the highest risk for instability. We designate these states with a red marker. The highest 25th percentile of states receive a green marker in the ledger. The middle 50th percentile receives a yellow marker.

(6) Militarization Instability is most likely in countries where the opportunities for armed conflict are greatest. In societies where the infrastructure and capital for organized armed conflict are more plentiful and accessible, the likelihood for civil conflict increases. The ledger measures militarization as the number of individuals in a country's active armed forces as a percentage of the country's total population. Countries with militarization scores in the bottom 25th percentile are indicated with a green marker. Countries in the top 25th percentile are presented with a red marker. The middle 50th percentile is indicated with a yellow marker.

(7) Neighborhood War The presence of an armed conflict in a neighboring state (internal or interstate) increases the risk of state instability. The contagion effects of regional armed conflict can heighten the risk of state instability, especially when ethnic or other communal groups span across borders. We use the most recent data release from the Uppsala Conflict Data Project at the International Peace Research Institute to determine the conflict status of states in 2007 (see Gleditsch et al. 2002, for more information). For a neighbor to be considered involved in armed conflict, we further require that the conflict produces 25 or more battle-related fatalities per year. A red marker indicates when at least one neighbor is involved in armed conflict. A green marker indicates the absence of armed conflict in all neighboring states.

(8) Risk Category States have been placed in one of five categories corresponding to their risk score. The chapter text discusses the procedure for assigning states to the highest risk category (red), the high risk category (orange), the moderate risk category (yellow), the some risk category (green), or the low risk category (blue).

(9) Risk Score The risk score gives a three-year forecast of the relative risk (compared to an average member of the OECD) of experiencing instability. The score is computed based on the results of estimating a statistical model using global data from the period 1950–2003. Then, using the model estimates, data from 2007 were used to obtain the three-year forecasts for each country for the period 2008–2010.

(10) Confidence Range The confidence range provides information about the degree of uncertainty corresponding to a country's estimated risk score. Statistically speaking, the "true" risk of instability lies within this range with a 95 percent probability. The width of the confidence range is drawn to scale. The widest confidence range observed in the data has been set to the width of the full column with all other confidence ranges drawn accordingly. When the bar is one color, the confidence range is confined to a single risk category. In cases where the confidence range spans multiple risk categories, the different colors of the bar reflect the extent of the overlap with those categories. Using a sample country (Liberia), the key below (Figure 2.2) illustrates how to read the information contained in the graphic for each country's confidence range. The color blue indicates the low risk range, green indicates the some risk range, yellow indicates the moderate risk range, orange indicates the high risk range, and red indicates the highest risk range.

Figure 2.2 Understanding Information Contained in the Confidence Range

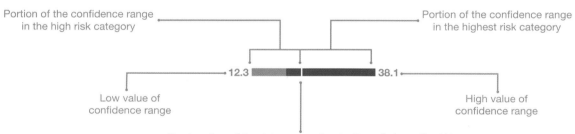

Portion of the confidence range in the high risk category

Portion of the confidence range in the highest risk category

12.3 ▬▬▬ 38.1

Low value of confidence range

High value of confidence range

The location of the risk score estimate (from Column 9) within the confidence range is depicted with a vertical white line. In this example, the estimate is approximately 22.0. Note, the location of the risk score estimate does not necessarily fall in the midpoint of the confidence range.

3. TRENDS IN GLOBAL CONFLICT, 1946–2007

J. Joseph Hewitt

At the beginning of 2008 there were 26 active armed conflicts worldwide, raging in some places and smoldering in others.[1] All of them were civil conflicts between the government of a state, on one hand, and at least one internal group on the other. All of them were fairly long-standing contests that had begun in the years previous to 2007. That is, none of the conflicts that were active in 2007 actually began in 2007. Renewed fighting returned to one conflict that had been largely dormant since 1999—the 30-year-old conflict involving the Shining Path in Peru. The return of significant violence in Peru is an example of the growing problem of conflict recurrence, a primary focus of this chapter.

The return of significant violence to a conflict that had previously subsided will be termed a "conflict recurrence" in this chapter. Analyses presented in this chapter will show that the risks of conflict recurrence in countries that have recently emerged from active conflict pose one of the most serious threats to the downward trend in worldwide conflict that began when the Cold War ended. When reviewing conflict trends through the end of 2005, the 2008 edition of *Peace and Conflict* noted that the dramatic increase in the number of active conflicts in 2005—the largest annual increase since the end of the Cold War—was largely the result of formerly terminated conflicts' reoccurring (Hewitt 2008). This chapter will expand on that observation.

Figure 3.1 presents a graph showing the number of active conflicts in each year during the period 1946–2007. The data used to produce this graph come from the most recent release from UCDP/PRIO Armed Conflict Dataset (see Gleditsch et al. 2002, for more information), which has been compiled and maintained by the Uppsala Conflict Data Program and the International Peace Research Institute. The graph shows trends for internal conflicts, for interstate conflicts, and for total conflict (the sum of the first two categories). Definitions for the types of conflict tracked in the UCDP/PRIO Armed Conflict Dataset can be found in Box 3.1. For any given year, the graph includes only those conflicts that satisfy two conditions: the conflict must have accumulated at least 1,000 battle-related fatalities over the entire course of the conflict, and the conflict must have produced at least 25 battle-related fatalities in the given year. These two conditions limit the analyses of conflict trends to armed violence that has established a track record of significant severity and has been active in the most recent past.

The graph shows a trend that has become familiar to most observers. After the number of active conflicts increased steadily throughout the Cold War, the number began to decline after 1991. The high point for active

---

[1] The Appendix provides a descriptive overview of all active conflicts, including updated material regarding the most recent developments in each one.

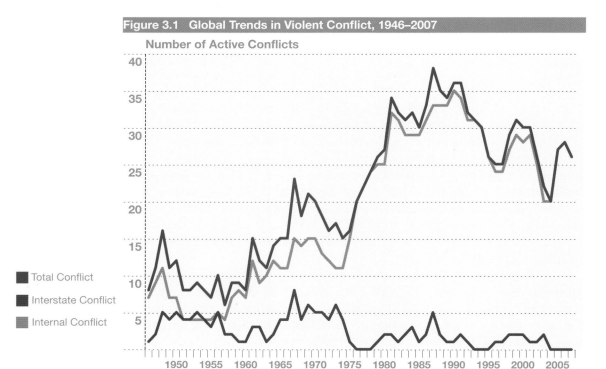

Figure 3.1 Global Trends in Violent Conflict, 1946–2007

Number of Active Conflicts

Total Conflict

Interstate Conflict

Internal Conflict

conflict was 1987, when 38 armed contests raged in various parts of the world. With the end of the Cold War, that number slowly declined to a low of 25 in 1997. In the following two years, the number of active conflicts shot up dramatically to 31 where the level hovered until 2002 when the number dropped again to 26. By 2004, the number fell to 20, the smallest number of active conflicts in the last 30 years. Since 2004, the number of active conflicts has risen significantly. In 2005, the number of active conflicts worldwide increased by seven—one of the largest annual jumps in conflict since the end of World War II. Since then, the number has remained largely unchanged, with 26 active conflicts at the end of 2007 (down from 28 in 2006).

Breaking Down the Data:
New Onsets, Recurrences, and Terminations

To assess why the downward trend has stalled, it will be helpful to disaggregate the data in Figure 3.1 and look more carefully at trends in new conflict onsets, conflict recurrences, and terminations.[2] Breaking the data down in this fashion will help to identify whether the current pattern in active global

---

2 For the purposes of this chapter, a conflict is considered terminated when it produces fewer than 25 battle-related fatalities in a given year. Often, as we will see, such terminations are temporary. By focusing exclusively on the decline in overt violence, the definition does not necessarily capture whether a formal cease-fire or any other agreement has been implemented. However, the definition has the advantage of clearly defining a period in any conflict in which visible hostilities with lethal consequences have diminished significantly, presumably creating an opportunity for the antagonists to implement a more durable peace.

Box 3.1　Definition of Armed Conflict

The UCDP/PRIO Armed Conflict Dataset defines conflict as "a contested incompatibility that concerns government and/or territory where the use of armed force between two parties, of which at least one is the government of a state, results in at least 25 battle-related deaths" (from the UCDP/PRIO Armed Conflict Dataset Codebook, page 4). Although UCDP/PRIO tracks conflicts with low-level intensity, we limit our focus to conflicts that have exceeded 1,000 battle-related deaths. Specifically, to be counted as an active conflict in any given year, the battle-deaths in the conflict must have a cumulative total greater than 1,000 since the conflict's inception and must have recorded 25 or more battle-related deaths in that year. The UCDP/PRIO dataset identifies four types of armed conflict: extrasystemic armed conflict, interstate armed conflict, internal armed conflict, and internationalized internal armed conflict.

Interstate Conflict	
Extrasystemic Armed Conflict	Extrasystemic armed conflict involves a state against a non-state actor outside the territory of the state. An example includes the armed conflict between France and the forces of the Viet Minh from 1946–1954. There have been no extrasystemic armed conflicts since the mid-1970s.
Interstate Armed Conflict	Interstate armed conflict involves two or more independent states (e.g., Iran and Iraq, 1980–1988).
Internal Conflict	
Internal Armed Conflict	Internal armed conflict involves the government of a state against one or more internal actors (e.g., domestic opposition groups, guerrilla forces, etc.). India's longstanding conflict with Kashmir insurgents is an example.
Internationalized Internal Armed Conflict	Internationalized internal armed conflict involves the government of a state against one or more internal actors with outside intervention by at least one other state in support of either the government or the internal opposition groups. The five-year civil war (1996–2001) in the Democratic Republic of the Congo is an example, as is the current civil war in Iraq.

conflict is the result of lower numbers of terminations or higher numbers of new onsets or recurrences.

The top graph in Figure 3.2 shows an annual breakdown of the number of combined conflict onsets and recurrences with the number of terminations. In any year when the blue line for terminations lies above the red line, there is a net reduction in active conflict. The graph helps to show that net reductions in active conflicts are the result of relatively quick bursts of conflict terminations confined to short periods of time. For instance, looking at the early years of the post–Cold War period, the number of terminations remains higher than the combined number of onsets and recurrences for only the period 1990–1997. It is worth noting that during that period many new and recurring conflicts continue to occur. Indeed, the rate of new onsets and recurrences has been slightly *higher* in the post–Cold War than during the last 20 years of the Cold War. The average rate of new and recurring conflict per year in the 20-year period 1970–1989 was 3.6. For the subsequent 18-year period 1990–2007, the rate was 4.5.

The second graph disaggregates the red line in the first graph, showing the separate trend lines for new onsets and recurrences. There is some positive news to be gleaned here. In the last ten years, the number of new conflicts has been quite low, never exceeding three in a given year. Since 2000, there have already been five years with no new conflicts at all. No decade since the end of World War II has witnessed so many years in

Figure 3.2   New, Recurring, and Terminated Conflicts

Number of Terminated versus New or Recurring Conflicts

■ New onsets and
recurring conflict

■ Terminated
conflicts

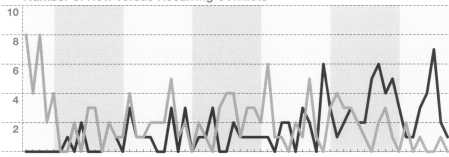

Number of New versus Recurring Conflicts

■ Recurring conflict

■ New conflict onset

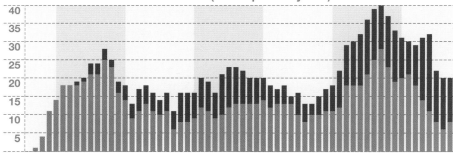

Number of Terminated Conflicts (within past 10 years)

■ Conflicts with
history of
recurrence

■ Conflicts with no
history of
recurrence

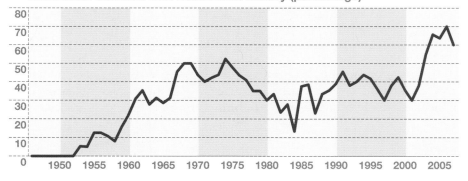

Terminated Conflicts with Recurrence History (percentage)

which no newly triggered conflicts have been added to the roster of active conflicts. Still, the second graph contains some sobering news, too. The number of conflict recurrences has surged to unprecedented levels. Since the mid-1990s, recurrences outnumber new onsets by significant margins. Undoubtedly, this new development helps to explain why the overall trend in global conflict has been relatively stagnant for the last ten years.

> *The number of conflict recurrences has surged to unprecedented levels. Since the mid-1990s, recurrences outnumber new onsets by significant margins.*

The year 2005 is a striking example of how conflict recurrences can affect overall global trends. The jump in total active conflict in 2005—up to 27 active conflicts from the previous year's total of 20—is the sole result of recurrences in seven conflicts that had been terminated for at least one year. These included renewed fighting in Sri Lanka involving the Liberation Tigers of Tamil Eelam (dormant since 2003), in Azerbaijan over the disputed region of Nagorno-Karabakh (dormant since 1994), in India involving rebel groups in Nagaland (dormant since 2000), as well as resurgent internal violence in Chad, Iran, and two separate conflicts in Myanmar.

The third graph depicts annual data for the number of recently terminated conflicts. For each year, the bar reflects the number of conflicts that terminated in the previous 10 years and remain terminated in the given year. It is helpful to think of the height of each bar as the depth of a pool of recently terminated conflicts that have some unobserved risk of recurring. Terminated conflicts are removed from this pool after ten years on the assumption that a decade with no recurrence is sufficient for a durable peace. The graph shows how the conflict termination pool increases substantially in the wake of the large number of conflict terminations in the early 1990s. The red portion of each bar indicates the number of terminated conflicts with a history of recurrence. That is, any conflict that had been terminated, subsequently restarted, and then terminated again is treated as a conflict with recurrence history. The striking feature of the third graph is that the portion of terminated conflicts with a history of recurrence has increased steadily in recent years. The average percentage of such conflicts in the period 1950–1990 was 26 percent. Since 1990, that percentage has nearly doubled, rising to 45 percent.

For clarity, the bottom graph shows the annual percentage of terminated conflicts with recurrence history. Over the past twenty years, there has been a steady increase in a troubling pattern whereby armed violence returns in societies after a promising period in which it had subsided. Taken together, the four graphs in Figure 3.2 underscore an important feature of the global landscape as it relates to active armed conflict. The numbers of recurring conflicts are increasing. And, moreover, the high number of recently terminated conflicts with a demonstrated history of recurrence is higher now than at any other time. Thus, there is clear potential for significant numbers of conflict recurrences in the future.

Conclusion

The analyses presented in this chapter indicate that a downward trend in the number of armed conflicts worldwide has leveled off. A brief burst of conflict terminations in the early 1990s and 2000s can be credited with lowering the numbers of active conflicts. To sustain a longer trend, there would have to be clear evidence that the rate of conflict terminations continues to be higher than onsets and recurrences. Or, the data should demonstrate that onsets and recurrences are dwindling in numbers. While there is some preliminary evidence that the number of new onsets is declining, the increased number of recurrences is sufficiently high to prevent a sustained downward trend.

The high number of recently terminated conflicts with a demonstrated history of recurrence is higher now than at any other time. Thus, there is clear potential for significant numbers of conflict recurrences in the future.

If the recent rate of conflict recurrences continues into the future with no significant change in the rate of terminations, the overall trends in conflict will likely fluctuate with no clear downward or upward trend. An important factor in avoiding this dire conclusion is to mitigate the likelihood of recurrence subsequent to the termination of an armed conflict. The key, in other words, resides in a better understanding of post-conflict transitions, an understanding that will support more informed policy responses to help usher countries through challenging periods of reconciliation, reconstruction, and stabilization.

The shifting dynamics of conflict documented in this chapter provided the impetus for this volume's focus on post-conflict transitions. While there are myriad challenges that must be confronted when a country emerges from conflict, we have selected a small sampling of topics that touch upon some of the most central concerns. First, in the wake of devastating violence, societies must rebuild their economies and recover from the enormous costs of warfare (see Hoeffler, Chapter 7). Second, democratization should proceed such that major stakeholders in society perceive newly constructed governmental institutions as both legitimate and effective (see Hegre and Fjelde, Chapter 8). The role of women in post-conflict contexts must be accounted for to better understand the prospects for recovery (see Caprioli et al., Chapter 9). And, finally, the potential impact of transitional justice (war crimes tribunals or truth and reconciliation commissions) should be weighed to properly assess the impact they might have on post-conflict recovery (Meernik et al., Chapter 10). Each of these issues is taken up in considerable depth in later chapters in this book.

4. TRENDS IN DEMOCRATIZATION: A FOCUS ON MINORITY RIGHTS

Amy Pate

In 1950, the world was almost equally divided between autocracies, anocracies (or hybrid regimes), and democracies. In the following two decades, the departure of colonial powers from Africa and Asia resulted in an explosion in the number of independent countries. By 1977, the year in which the number of autocratic regimes peaked, there were 89 autocracies, 16 hybrid regimes, and 35 democracies. Then, beginning in the late 1970s and accelerating through the 1980s, a wave of democratization took place. By the end of the Cold War in 1991, there were more democracies (66) than either anocracies (47) or autocracies (44). The spread of democracy continued throughout the 1990s, and by 2008 there were 86 democratic countries, 45 anocracies, and only 28 autocracies in the world (see Box 4.1 for definitions of each regime type).[1] While democracy continues to be the dominant form of governance in the world, a downward trend starting in 2006 is emerging, with the steepest decline in the number of democracies in the post–World War II era. Although the number of democracies has declined in single years since World War II, the number generally quickly rebounded. The last time span in which there were consecutive years of decreases in the number of democracies was 1968–1971.

Countries that have experienced democratic declines since 2006 include Armenia, Bangladesh, Ecuador, Guinea, Mauritania, and Russia, among others. Two causes emerge as the most common for democratic retrenchment: military coups and manipulation of electoral systems by parties in power. Bangladesh, Guinea, and Mauritania are examples of countries that have experienced military coups or other interference in the political system by military actors. Democratic reversals in Armenia, Ecuador, and Russia were all due to the activities of ruling parties to limit political competition and/or popular participation in politics.

There are, however, some bright spots in terms of countries that experienced movement towards democracy. Bangladesh, to a degree, re-democratized in 2008 after military rule was imposed in 2007. In 2008, Bhutan re-engineered itself as a constitutional monarchy after decades of existence as an absolute monarchy. Pakistan also has made positive moves towards re-democratization with the re-establishment of an elected, civilian

---

1 Polity scores are publicly available through 2007 (see the Polity Project Web site at *http://www. systemicpeace.org/polity/polity4.html*). Estimated scores for 2008 were generated using a conversion factor based on the Freedom House political liberties indicator. (Freedom House data are available through 2008 online at *http://www.freedomhouse.org/template.cfm?page=439.*) The Polity score from 2008 was carried from 2007 for those countries that did not show a change in the Freedom House score. If a country's Freedom House rating changed, the conversion factor was applied. For more information on the development of the conversion factor and how it was applied, refer to the Peace and Conflict 2010 companion Web site or contact the author.

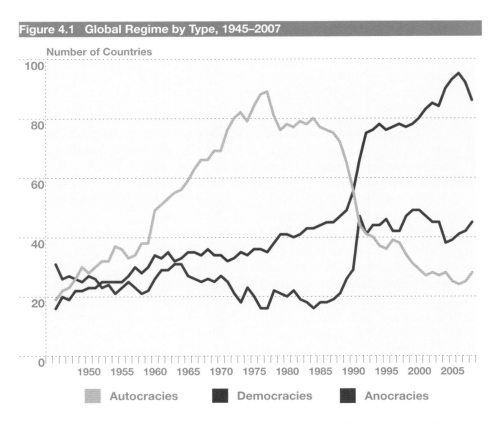

Figure 4.1 Global Regime by Type, 1945–2007

Number of Countries

Autocracies   Democracies   Anocracies

government in 2008. Sierra Leone has also transitioned from a hybrid regime to a democracy in the last two years.

Democratization and Respect for Minority Rights

When the "third wave" of democratization started to sweep through the developing world in the late 1970s and into the 1980s, there were few discussions on the role ethnic diversity played, either in terms of how diversity affected the likelihood of a successful transition or in terms of how democratization affected ethnic relations within the state. However, with the collapse of the multiethnic Soviet Union and Yugoslavia, as well as democratization in such states as South Africa, ethnic relations became more of a focal point in the democratization literature. Many scholars focused on the behavior of ethnic groups under democratization (see, e.g., the discussion in Chapter 5). However, the focus in this section will be on how different types of regimes differ in their respect for minority rights and on how that treatment has changed over time.

The Minorities at Risk (MAR) project collects annual information on the political status and activities of ethnic groups globally. Currently MAR tracks 385 ethnic groups that are mobilized politically around group identity and/or that face discrimination vis-à-vis other ethnic groups in the country. Among the data the project collects is information on political discrimination. Political discrimination is coded on a five-point scale. As

The Polity Project scores all independent countries of the world with a population of at least 500,000 on autocratic and democratic features, resulting in a 21-point scale going from -10 to 10 to measure regime type. Polity categorizes all regimes as autocracies, anocracies, or democracies, based on Polity scores.

Autocracies are those regimes scored between -10 and -6 on the Polity scale. Autocracies are characterized by closed political recruitment, lack of restraints on executive political power, and limitations on political competition. Autocracies in 2008 include hereditary monarchies, such as Saudi Arabia; one-party states, such as China; and countries ruled by military juntas, such as Burma (Myanmar).

Anocracies are hybrid regimes, with both authoritarian and democratic institutional features. Countries with Polity scores ranging from -5 to 5 are classified as anocracies. Some anocracies are competitive authoritarian regimes, in which elections are contested but not freely nor fairly, such as Chad and Kyrgyzstan. Other anocracies are weakly institutionalized electoral democracies, such as Niger and Cambodia.

Democracies are characterized by open political recruitment, restraints on executive power, and political competition. Countries with Polity scores ranging from 6 to 10 are classified as democracies. Democracies include both parliamentary regimes, such as the United Kingdom and India; and presidential systems, such as the United States, South Africa, and Argentina.

of 2006, the year for which the most recent data are available, 34 percent of minorities at risk did not face political discrimination. Approximately 17 percent still suffered from political discrimination, but the government had implemented remedial policies to alleviate its effects. Remedial policies vary from guaranteed seats in national legislatures to cabinet positions to devolution of authority to allow some degree of minority self-governance. Minorities in this category in 2006 include the Bodos of India, who reached a deal to form a self-governing council in 2003; Afars in Djibouti, who are guaranteed cabinet seats as part of a 2001 peace agreement; and the Roma in Hungary, where local governance councils have been created for Roma communities and a Roma Affairs Office created with a Roma named as its head. Eleven percent of groups suffered from the consequences of historical neglect. While these groups live on the edges of political society, they are not actively discriminated against, either by their government or the larger society. However, there are also no policies in place to encourage or guarantee their political participation. Groups in this category include the Kirdi or Montagnards of Cameroon, who live in the north of the country and are not politically active; and Bakhtiari, a tribal group in Iran. Active discrimination by members of more dominant ethnic groups left members of 21 percent of minorities at risk on the political sidelines. These include many indigenous and Afro-descended groups in Latin America, as well as many Roma groups in Europe. Governments of 17 percent of minorities had formal policies in place that limited political participation of the group. These include Haitian blacks in the Dominican Republic, the Black Muslims of Darfur in Sudan, Baha'is in Iran, Kurds in Syria, and Tibetans in China.

The percentage of governments that actively discriminate against ethnic minorities has been declining steadily since 1990, a trend noted in earlier work (Asal and Pate 2005). Societal discrimination has also decreased, although not as steeply as public policy exclusion. Over the same time

Table 4.1 Percentage of Ethnic Groups Experiencing Political Discrimination

Type of Discrimination	1990	2006
No Discrimination	22	34
Remedial Policies	13	17
Historical Neglect	11	11
Societal Discrimination	26	21
Public Policy Exclusion	27	17

period, the number of ethnic groups benefiting from remedial policies has also increased. The greatest change has been in the percentage of ethnic minorities that experience no political discrimination. Table 4.1 shows the change from 1990 to 2006 in the percentage of minorities in each category of political discrimination.

Levels of discrimination faced by minority groups vary considerably among democracies, hybrid regimes, and autocracies. Figures 4.2 through 4.4 show the percentage of minorities at risk that face political discrimination in democracies, hybrid regimes, and autocracies each year from 1990 through 2006.

Most minorities living under democratic regimes, not surprisingly, either do not suffer from any political discrimination or are beneficiaries of policies designed to offset the effects of discrimination. Also not surprisingly, minorities suffer greater levels of formal political exclusion under autocratic regimes. It is important to note that to be coded as suffering formal political exclusion, the government in question must implement policies that target the ethnic group in question. Lack of political participation due to the autocratic nature of the regime (since it applies to all members of the society) is not sufficient to code formal political exclusion for the minority group. Therefore, many members of minority groups in autocracies suffer political exclusion above and beyond that experienced by other members of the society. Also noteworthy are recent declines in the percentage of ethnic groups benefiting from remedial policies under both democratic and autocratic regimes. However, coinciding with those decreases is an increase in the percentage of ethnic minorities targeted with remedial policies under anocratic regimes. This increase in remedial policies under hybrid regimes has also occurred simultaneously with decreases in levels of formal exclusion. In recent years, there has been a movement of hybrid regimes from policies that exclude ethnic minorities to policies that encourage their inclusion. The shift towards remedial policies seems to be driven by two distinct dynamics. The first is the implementation of remedial policies as part of peace settlements, a trend most noticeable in sub-Saharan Africa. Groups in Ethiopia, Djibouti, Angola, and Mali are examples of this dynamic at work. The second is the implementation of remedial policies due to external pressures. This has been especially relevant in the post-communist states of Eastern Europe, many of which began to implement remedial policies because of aspirations to join the European Union. This is encouraging news, both for the minorities benefiting as well as for the sustainability of democratization efforts. However, on a cautionary note, there has also been an increase in the percentage of groups that face societal exclusion.

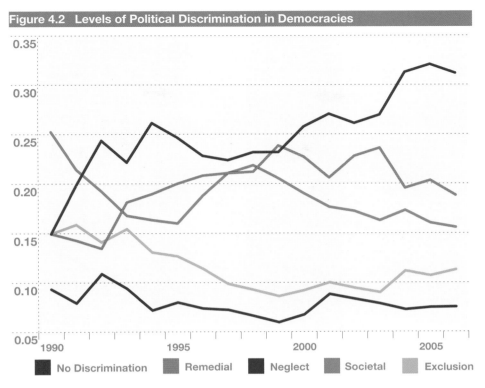

Figure 4.2 Levels of Political Discrimination in Democracies

Legend: No Discrimination · Remedial · Neglect · Societal · Exclusion

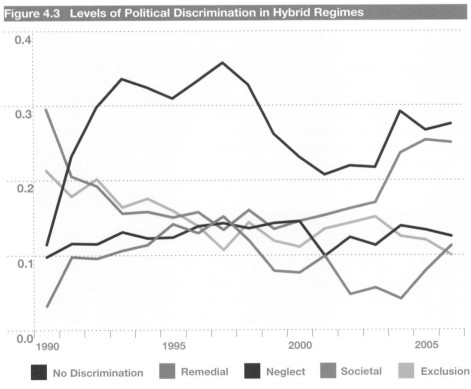

Figure 4.3 Levels of Political Discrimination in Hybrid Regimes

Legend: No Discrimination · Remedial · Neglect · Societal · Exclusion

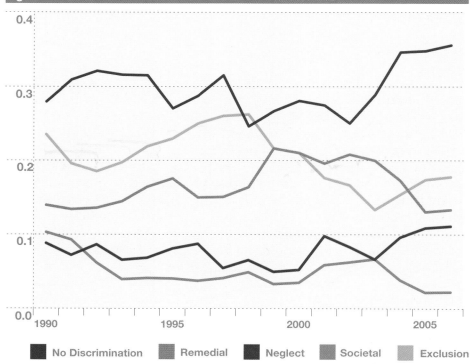

Figure 4.4 Levels of Political Discrimination in Autocracies

No Discrimination   Remedial   Neglect   Societal   Exclusion

The overall trend is one of increasing political inclusion of ethnic minorities. In 1990, only 35 percent of minorities either did not experience political discrimination or were beneficiaries of policies meant to alleviate the effects of discrimination. By 2006, the majority of minorities (51 percent) fit into one of those two categories. Participation in the national political life of their countries reflects the improved political conditions of ethnic minorities. In 2006, 68 percent of groups in hybrid regimes and 62 percent of groups in democracies were represented in the national legislatures of their home states. Furthermore, in hybrid regimes, a majority (57 percent) were also represented in the executive branch at the level of deputy minister or higher. In democracies, minority participation at the executive level lags somewhat at 35 percent but still suggests significant representation at the highest levels of political decisionmaking.

Conclusion

Democracy, despite the possibility of majoritarian domination, has resulted in political gains for minorities at risk. Both democracies and hybrid regimes show greater inclusion of ethnic minorities, as compared to authoritarian regimes. However, there is still much room for improvement in both democracies and hybrid regimes, as 27 percent of groups in democracies and 26 percent in anocracies suffer from either widespread societal discrimination or formal exclusion. Nonetheless, democratization seems to hold the most promise for minorities at risk.

5. SELF-DETERMINATION MOVEMENTS AND THEIR OUTCOMES

Monica Duffy Toft and Stephen M. Saideman

Self-determination conflicts remain an important source of violence in the new century. As a consequence of the conflict in Darfur, approximately 2.4 million people have fled across the borders into neighboring states or have been displaced internally,[1] while hundreds of thousands have been wounded or killed in the fighting. The violence in Darfur has the potential to undermine the Sudanese government's capacity to implement the Comprehensive Peace Agreement, which ended its war with the secessionist South in 2005; further, it threatens to bring civil war to Chad. In Gaza, rocket attacks, counterstrikes, and failed ceasefires have led to a full-scale air and ground battle as Israelis and Palestinians once again engage each other. Both groups are seen, and see themselves, as minorities at risk.

As of late 2008, nine armed self-determination conflicts were ongoing, involving Kashmiri Muslims in India; Chechens in Russia; Moros in the Philippines; Karens and Shan in Burma; Tamils in Sri Lanka; Kurds in Turkey; Badme in Eritrea; and black African tribes in Sudan. This demonstrates the continuation of an ongoing trend since 1991, in which the number of self-determination conflicts worldwide is decreasing steadily. Additionally, these conflicts are resolved increasingly through negotiated settlements or stalemates/ceasefires rather than by military victory of one side over the other. The conflict in South Ossetia, for instance, flared again in the summer of 2008 but was quickly contained within a matter of weeks by a ceasefire.[2] An exception, however, might be the most recent offensive by the Sri Lankan government designed to defeat the Tamil Tigers once and for all.

Because the last update (Quinn 2008) covered the period until the end of 2006 and the latest data show similar trends, we take a different turn and highlight some of the factors that have been shown to be associated with self-determination movements; additionally, we compare separatist wars with non-separatist ones since 1940 to highlight patterns of interest through time and conclude with some implications about the difficulty in resolving self-determination conflicts.

Although self-determination conflicts tend to be localized, such crises nevertheless demonstrate that they are connected intimately to regional and global dynamics (Weiner 1971, Olzak 2006). In addition to the role of Chad

---

1 "Darfur 2007: Chaos by Design." *Human Rights Watch*. September 19, 2007. Available online at: *http://www.hrw.org/en/reports/2007/09/19/darfur-2007-chaos-design-0*

2 An Appendix includes an update of all ongoing, contained, and settled self-determination conflicts from 1940 to the end of 2008. It is available on *Peace and Conflict's* companion Web site (*http://www.cidcm.umd.edu/pc*)

in the Sudanese Darfur conflict, and of regional and international partners in the Israeli-Palestinian conflict, another highly visible case is that of Kosovo. This conflict started as an internal political struggle in the former Yugoslavia over the political status of the region and the rights of Albanians living in the republic. Russia served as the patron of Serbia, while the West, notably the United States and its NATO allies, backed Kosovo. After years of increasing hostilities between the populations, nonviolent resistance by the Muslim Albanian population, then violent resistance and external intervention in the form of air power by NATO in the spring of 1999, followed by nine years of a UN/NATO protectorate, Kosovo Albanians declared independence from Serbia in January 2008.[3] Russia was an historical ally of Serbia, and was itself mired in its own self-determination struggles (e.g., Chechnya), with a large role in Georgia's breakaway regions of South Ossetia and Abkhazia and Moldova's Transdniestra; it thus called Kosovo's independence a "terrible precedent" and threatened action.[4] Indeed, the following summer, violence erupted again in South Ossetia after the region declared the right to self-determination; Russia insisted on its right to help keep the peace and protect its citizens and troops; and Georgia asserted its right to territorial integrity and sovereignty. With the interplay of international politics and domestic politics—the power of precedent and the status quo bias of the international community versus the right of national and ethnic minorities to self determination—these conflicts and their accompanying violence remain a key feature of global politics (Mueller 2008). The point here should be that although self-determination movements tend to be defensive, territorially confined, and limited in scope, the dynamics of bargaining and the nature of stakes compel patron states and outside actors to get involved.[5] Consequently, national self-determination is often an international problem.

The number of self-determination conflicts worldwide is decreasing steadily. Additionally, these conflicts are resolved increasingly through negotiated settlements or stalemates/ceasefires rather than by military victory of one side over the other.

In essence, the right of self-determination for ethnonational groups continues to clash with the right of the territorial integrity for states. In the old days, it was empires that were threatened; today, it is multiethnic states. From an analytic perspective, we need to ask how multiethnic states differ from these empires (Roeder 2007). Both are territorially bound political units, comprising a number of peoples or nations and often ruled by a single government with supreme authority. It is no wonder then that just as the

---

3 "Kosovo." *CIA World Factbook*. Accessed March 4, 2009. Available online at: *https://www.cia.gov/ library/publications/the-world-factbook/geos/kv.html*.

4 "Kosovo 'Blows Up' International Order, Sets 'Terrible Precedent', [Vladimir] Putin" Channel One TV, February 22, 2008a.

5 There has been much work of late on countries getting involved in the ethnic conflicts of their kin (Carment et al. 2006; Regan 2000; Saideman 2001; Saideman and Ayres 2008) and on the effects of outsiders on the ethnic conflict (Brubaker 1996, Cetinyan 2002, and Jenne 2007).

empires of old faced challenges, so too do today's multiethnic states, and even more so, as more states participate in the waves of democratization that promise, but often fail to deliver, basic political and economic rights. Moreover, because these rights often apply not to individuals, but to groups, it is not surprising that groups mobilize. Even in established democracies that have guarantees in place, conflicts over national minority issues continue to plague politics. In 2008, Belgium's political system was frozen by the conflict between Flemish and Walloons, raising real questions about the future of the federation.

In some cases, it is a majority population (as in Algeria with the indigènes against France in the 1950s, in pre-1970 Pakistan with the Bengalis, or in South Africa with the Blacks) opposing what it sees as a foreign, occupying force, or a minority group seeking to overthrow the reign of a perceived or real hostile and repressive state (e.g., the Kachins, Karens and Shan in Burma/Myanmar, or Tamils in Sri Lanka). The point here is that the motives for the fight have remained the same. If you were to ask a Croat in the 1990s why she felt it necessary to separate from former Yugoslavia, she would likely make the case that being a fully realized Croat entails having a Croat state. If you were to ask a politician in Serbia why his country needed to keep Croatian territory as part of Yugoslavia, he would argue that the territorial integrity of the state is supreme (Toft 2003). Similarly, the British and the French understood all too well that once one piece of the empire was spun off, then others would follow suit. For the French, the collapse of empire began with a group of nationalists on the small island of Madagascar in 1947 and ended with the loss of Algeria in 1962. What took 400 years to create collapsed in only 15. The British empire faced a similar fate, but its growth and demise were a bit more protracted, with the first challenge coming from the Declaration of Independence of the American colonies in 1776 and a series of deals (and expansion, of course) with other colonies (e.g., Canada was granted Commonwealth status in the mid-nineteenth century) before the handover of the last remnant, Hong Kong, to China in 1997.

In the sections below, we first identify some of the key characteristics of groups that seek self-determination, comparing them to ethnic groups that may be mobilized but do not want more autonomy or independence. Then, we consider separatist civil wars in comparison to those focused on the central government to ascertain the patterns of the most violent efforts to gain self-determination. We conclude by considering the implications of these characteristics and patterns.

Characteristics of Self-Determination Movements[6]

Groups seeking to invoke their right to self-determination may vary in their grievances, but they share a few common properties that distinguish

[6] This section relies on a draft version of the latest update of the Minorities at Risk Dataset, with the figures focusing on 2006. In the tables in this section, Self-Determination refers to those groups seeking greater autonomy, independence, or changes in international boundaries to bring them into another state (irredentism). Protests refer to demonstrations (Prot > 2); Severe Rebellion refers to violence ranging from small-scale guerilla activity to civil war (Reb > 3).

Table 5.1 Self-Determination and Protest			
	Seeking Self-Determination?		
Protests	No	Yes	Total
No	139	64	203
Yes	31	68	99
Total	170	132	302

Table 5.2 Self-Determination and Violence			
	Seeking Self-Determination?		
Severe Rebellion	No	Yes	Total
No	164	113	277
Yes	6	18	24
Total	170	131	301

Table 5.3 Self-Determination and Group Concentration			
	Seeking Self-Determination?		
Regional Base	No	Yes	Total
No	83	24	107
Yes	78	93	171
Total	161	117	278

them from other mobilized ethnic groups. First, and most importantly, groups seeking to become independent or join another country are more likely to engage in dissent and the more intense forms of violence than groups with other aims. More than half of all groups seeking self-determination, or 68 of 132 (see Table 5.1), engaged in some sort of protest in 2006; this included Kurds in Turkey and Kashmiris in India engaging in demonstrations with at least 10,000 protestors. Exactly 75 percent of all groups engaging in violence in 2006, or 18 of 24 (see Table 5.2), were seeking self-determination, with the Chechens, Kashmiris, Kurds in Turkey, Tamils in Sri Lanka, and Karens and Shans in Burma topping the scale.

Second, while ethnic groups have a variety of griev-ances, and while they react to them differently, self-determination groups largely share a single complaint—that they have lost some form of autonomy. Two-thirds of all groups seeking self-determination lost some form of autonomy in the past, including several of the groups already mentioned (Kashmiris, Shans, Chechens) as well as some less violent ones such as Tibetans.[7] Other grievances do not seem to have a significant impact on the choice to engage in separatism.[8] Political and economic discrimination, cultural grievances, and the like do not have the same consistent impact on self-determination. They may be associated with groups seeking autonomy, but not with more extreme claims of independence or union.

A key structural feature, on the other hand, does: group concentration.[9] Groups that are concentrated in one region of a state, especially if that region is seen as its historic homeland (Toft, 2003), are more likely to seek self-determination, such as all of those listed thus far. As Table 5.3

---

7 The autlost variable is a composite, including the group's status before autonomy was lost, the magnitude of the change and how recently- it was lost.

8 Some of the grievances are associated with the broadest definition of self-determination, but are not if we focus on separatism: secession or irredentism. These findings for 2006 are similar to those in earlier studies of Gurr and Moore 1998, (Saideman and Ayres 2000, and Toft 2003).

9 Group concentration here refers to whether a group has a regional base (gc2). Using the traditional groupcon variable provides similar results. This is a consistent finding over the years (Gurr 1993, 2000; Jenne et al. 2007; Saideman and Ayres 2000; Toft 2003).

shows, of the 117 groups that sought self-determination in 2006, 93 (almost 80 percent) had a regional base. Group concentration matters for several reasons: political organization is easier over a compact territory; it facilitates defensive and offensive military operations; and it defines the territory over which claims can be made (Toft 2003).

Finally, international politics matters a great deal. Groups seeking self-determination are more likely to have support from external states than are groups having other goals. Of the 121 groups enjoying external state support in 2006, 69 (or 57 percent) were seeking self-determination (see Table 5.4).[10] The same phenomenon holds true for groups with a strong diaspora: as Table 5.5 shows, of the 48 groups that received external kin support in 2006, 34 (or 70 percent) were seeking self-determination.[11] Among those groups with diaspora and external state sponsorship are the Palestinians, Tibetans, Chechens, Tamils, and Kashmiris. The relationship can work in both directions—that groups seeking self-determination may receive more support than other groups (Saideman 2002), or it may be the case that groups are encouraged by outside support and then radicalize their claims (Jenne 2007). Regarding the former, states may choose to support an ethnic group seeking self-determination for a variety of reasons, including destabilizing a neighbor, retaliating for support of domestic groups by the offending outsider, providing for the oppressed, or due to domestic political purposes. Thus far, most of the evidence suggests that decisions to support self-determination movements are driven by coalition politics at home rather than the plight of the group, particularly when ethnic ties come into play (Saideman 2001; Saideman and Ayres 2008).

Interestingly, while states discriminate among conflicts and are somewhat more likely to give support to those groups seeking self-determination than to those involved in other conflicts (contrary to the literature on precedents and norms), relatives of groups are more likely than states to discriminate in favor of those kin seeking autonomy, independence, or union (such as the Tamils, the various Kurds, Tibetans, and Kashmiris). Almost 75 percent of groups receiving support from kin in 2006 were seeking

Table 5.4 Self-Determination and State Support

External State Support	Seeking Self-Determination?		
	No	Yes	Total
No	116	62	178
Yes	52	69	121
Total	168	131	299

Table 5.5 Self-Determination and Kin Support

Kin Support	Seeking Self-Determination?		
	No	Yes	Total
No	156	95	251
Yes	14	34	48
Total	170	129	299

10 State support, or state sponsorship, refers to whether a group gets at least some political or military support from at least one state.

11 Kin state support refers to whether a group gets at least some political or military support from kin outside the country.

self-determination. We should not be surprised that diasporas might matter in international relations (Shain 2007), but it is still an open question why diasporas would favor groups seeking self-determination over others.

Trends in Self-Determination and Separation in Relation to Civil War

A common thread among self-determination movements is the desire to have control over territory. This explains why lost autonomy and regional concentration have been found to be significant indicators of rebellion and separatism. Moreover, this sentiment is also shared by the states with whom they compete for control. Just as these competing visions for who will control the state and its territory result in protest and rebellion, sometimes they result in large conflagrations in the form of civil war. In fact, almost half of all civil wars since 1940 involved groups vying with the state over territory and issues of self-determination and separation.

Since 1940, there have been 136 civil wars.[12] Of these, 62 were "separatist," whereby an identity group sought greater autonomy or self-determination over a portion of a state's territory. The key to these conflicts is that they featured a fight for greater control over or the cutting off of a portion of a state's territory, not capture and control of the entire territory of the state. The case of Sudan stands out here with two episodes of war between the north and south. Following independence, northerners—predominantly Arab and Muslim—dominated the government. The South contained a relatively more economically backward Christian and animist Black population that came to resent what it viewed as a patronizing northern government that sought to extend Islam to the south. During the first Sudanese civil war (1955–1972), the South sought only greater autonomy, not secession or capture of the government. This war ended in a negotiated settlement, the Addis Ababa agreement. However, after the government abrogated key elements of the treaty, the South expanded its aims and sought independence from the North (1983), resulting in new episodes of violence that ended in 2005 with the signing of another peace treaty that contains provisions for the South to vote on independence in 2011.[13]

The remaining 74 civil wars were "centralist" in the sense that the combatants fought for control over the state and government offices in order to control and govern the entire territory of the state. Historically, these struggles have tended not to involve ethnicity but have an ideological and class component (n=47); such was the case in El Salvador, a civil war that pitted the leftist FMLN and its allies against the entrenched landed class.

---

12 For purposes of the analysis, a civil war is here defined as large-scale violence within the borders of an internationally recognized state, involving at least two groups of organized combatants, with the state being one of those combatants, resulting in at least 1,000 deaths on average per year of the war, with the stronger side suffering at least 5 percent of those deaths. This section relies on data from Toft (forthcoming). The data are available from the author.

13 "Sudan." *CIA World Factbook*. Accessed March 4, 2009. Available online at: *https://www.cia.gov/library/publications/the-world-factbook/geos/su.html*.

Nevertheless, when ethnic majorities and minorities have fought for control over the state, there have been cases in which the core issues were identity and dominance. The multiple wars in Burundi and Rwanda between the Hutu and the Tutsi are key examples here, as was the fight in South Africa to end Apartheid. Although these do constitute self-determination struggles in which representatives of ethnic groups vied for control over these states in order to safeguard rights against repressive regimes (i.e., the ultimate aim is self-governance), these are considered centralist conflicts in the analysis that follows.[14]

This analysis provides a quick overview of where separatist conflicts have broken out, when, and how these wars have ended.

Where?

If we consider where the different types of conflicts have broken out, it is clear that different regions of the world have been plagued by different types of conflicts. As Figure 5.1 shows, Latin America has faced no separatist challenges by ethnic populations. Europe is the opposite, with 13 of 15 wars involving secessionists. This is not the case in Africa, which has faced a mix of centralist (n=25) and separatist (n=21) fights. Asia, too, has had a balance of the different types of civil wars (centralist, n=18/separatist, n=23). The Middle East has suffered through 14 centralist wars and six separatist wars.

When Started?

In terms of trends in onsets, there has not been a precipitous increase in the number of wars or types of civil war through the decades.[15] As Figure 5.2 shows, between 1940 and 2008, the proportion of centralist and separatist civil wars remained relatively constant, and the number of wars initiated has decreased gradually since the early 1990s. The exceptions to this rule include the post–World War II period, the 1970s, and to some extent the post–Cold War period. Nevertheless, the end of the Cold War did not usher in a shift in the type or frequency, but rather a culmination of those wars across the decades that remained unsettled through the preceding decades. This is captured by the ongoing wars trend line.

The proportion of separatist wars that started in each decade varied only between 13–21% of the total, while centralist wars that were started per decade varied only between 11–19%. Furthermore, a comparison of separatist and centralist wars over the decades does not reveal a shift in the proportions, with new or ongoing centralist wars representing 21–61% of all conflicts and separatist wars representing 37–78%.

---

14 Of the 74 centralist wars, 27 had an identity component. For a listing of the 136 civil wars, see Appendix 2.

15 Please note that the final period listed in all figures, 2005–2008, is only four years; thus, it is not comparable to the other, five-year, periods listed. Additionally, please note that there is a certain amount of speculation involved in listing the more recently terminated civil wars.

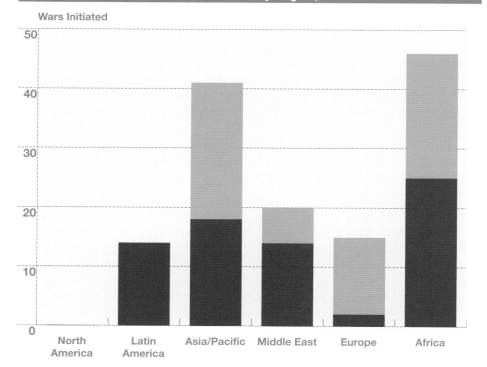

Figure 5.1   Number of Civil Wars Initiated by Region, 1940–2008

Wars Initiated

Separatist
Centralist

North America   Latin America   Asia/Pacific   Middle East   Europe   Africa

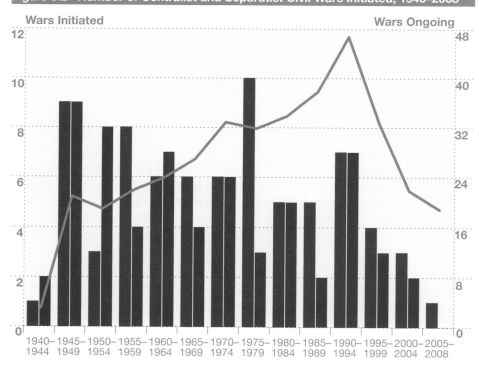

Figure 5.2   Number of Centralist and Separatist Civil Wars Initiated, 1940–2008

Wars Initiated   Wars Ongoing

Centralist Wars
Separatist Wars
— All Ongoing Wars

1940–1944 1945–1949 1950–1954 1955–1959 1960–1964 1965–1969 1970–1974 1975–1979 1980–1984 1985–1989 1990–1994 1995–1999 2000–2004 2005–2008

Figure 5.3 Number of Centralist and Separatist Civil Wars Terminated

Figure 5.3 Number of Centralist and Separatist Civil Wars Terminated

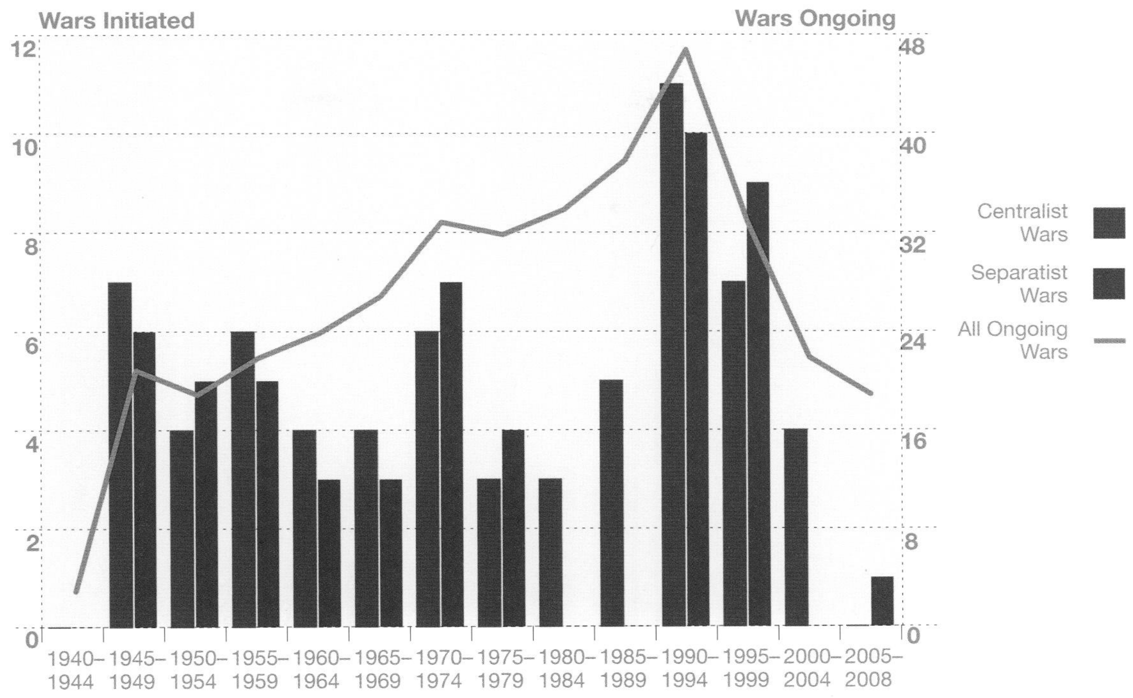

When Ended?

In terms of when and how civil wars ended, we see a significant change in the post–Cold War era. As Figure 5.3 shows, the 1990s saw a disproportionate increase in the number and proportion of terminations. Of the 47 civil wars initiated or ongoing in 1990, 37 (79 percent) were terminated in that decade. Moreover, the ways in which these civil wars ended also changed.

How Civil Wars End?

Civil war termination involves a number of possible outcomes: a military victory for the government, a military victory for the opposition or rebels (sometimes resulting in partition and independence), a negotiated settlement in which the parties formally agree to lay down their arms and form a shared government, or a stalemate that entails only laying down one's arms and agreeing to a ceasefire.

Prior to the 1990s, most civil wars ended by military victory. Between 1940 and 1990, two-thirds to all of the civil wars in those decades ended in victory for one side. Only a handful ended in negotiated settlements or stalemates. As Figure 5.4 shows, for the Cold War period, 85 percent of separatist wars ended in victory, followed by percent in negotiated settlement and percent in stalemates (n=33). Similarly, 84 percent of centralist wars ended in victory and another 11 percent in negotiated settlement and 5 percent in stalemates/ceasefires.

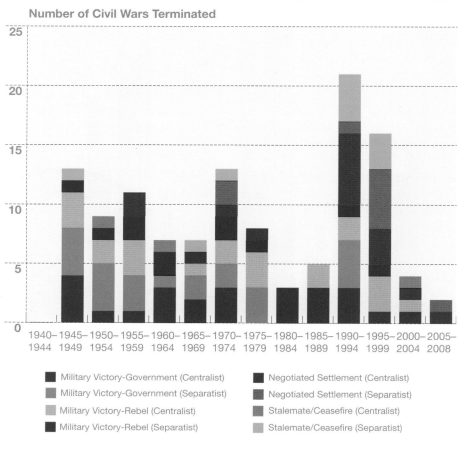

Figure 5.4 Trends in Civil War Termination by Type

Number of Civil Wars Terminated

Legend:
- Military Victory-Government (Centralist)
- Military Victory-Government (Separatist)
- Military Victory-Rebel (Centralist)
- Military Victory-Rebel (Separatist)
- Negotiated Settlement (Centralist)
- Negotiated Settlement (Separatist)
- Stalemate/Ceasefire (Centralist)
- Stalemate/Ceasefire (Separatist)

However, for the post–Cold War period, 30 percent of separatist conflicts ended in victory, 35 percent in negotiated settlement, and 35 percent in stalemates. In contrast, 48 percent of centralist conflicts resulted in victory, 48 percent in negotiated settlement, and only 4 percent in stalemates. In all, fights over separatism today are likely to be contained rather than terminated by victory. Centralist conflicts likewise have shifted toward termination by negotiated settlement, but not by stalemate or ceasefire. Fights over separation today are less likely to be permanently settled by victory, but contained by means of stalemates/ceasefires or negotiated settlements. The case of Sudan is representative here, as are the conflicts in Georgia with Abkhazia and South Ossetia. Kosovo is exceptional.

A Note on Recurrence

Finally, in terms of recurrence, it turns out that most wars do not recur. Of the 117 wars that ended before 2004, only 19 wars recurred (17 percent): Sudan is the exception rather than the rule. Additionally, there appears to be no difference among the types of wars in their likelihood of recurrence: 11 of 65 (17 percent) centralist wars recurred compared with 8 of 52 (15 percent) separatist. This finding holds even if we exclude the colonial wars, or wars of independence against colonial powers (n=12). In this narrower set, 8 of 40 (17 percent) separatist wars recurred, the same proportion of centralist wars that recurred. Thus, we cannot make the case that there is anything statistically remarkable here.[16]

Conclusion

On balance, self-determination conflicts appear likely to stay. They present a number of difficult problems for the states that contain them as well as for the international community.

At the domestic level, granting greater levels of autonomy to these movements may work to help squelch violence. Dawn Brancati (2006), for example, argues that political decentralization holds the potential to decrease violent ethnic conflict and secessionism. The same potential to lessen conflict also holds true in many cases when governments grant autonomy to ethnic groups seeking self-determination. In Indonesia, for example, a peace agreement between the government and the Free Aceh Movement (GAM) stipulated that non-local forces would be withdrawn from the region and that GAM would disarm; additionally, the government agreed to accord more autonomy to Aceh than to any other province.[17] Likewise, in India, the creation of the state of Mizoram and the transition of the primary rebel force into a political party settled the government's conflict with the Mizos and fulfilled that group's demands for self-determination. A year after the establishment of Mizoram in 1986, the former rebels won the state elections.[18] Finally, in Nicaragua, the conflict between the government and indigenous peoples and Creoles was settled in 1988, when autonomy was granted to two coastal regions populated primarily by these ethnic groups. Since then, the ongoing threat of renewed violence has been assuaged, and the indigenous peoples have successfully pressed the government for compensation for being forcibly displaced, as well as for additional titles to ancestral lands.[19] Nevertheless, these same arrangements that grant greater autonomy and decrease the likelihood of violence in the short- and medium-term may

---

[16] We caution the reader not to view these points as contradictory to what Hewitt offers in Chapter 3. Compared to that analysis, the totals above are based on stronger criteria for what qualifies as a civil war (an average of 1,000 fatalities per year) and for how a civil war can be deemed terminated (a cessation of at least five years). We suspect that fewer of these terminated conflicts experience a recurrence because they represent cases in which more of the preconditions for durable peace hold. Also, the figures here refer to the aggregate recurrence rate for the past 60 years without showing how that rate has changed more recently (as Chapter 3 does).

[17] See Lucy Williamson. "Indonesian MPs Back Aceh Autonomy." BBC News, 11 July 2006. Available online at: *http://news.bbc.co.uk/2/hi/asia-pacific/5168718.stm*. See also "Briefing on the Study of Durable Political Violence and Policy Recommendations." SSRC-NUPI, 2006. p. 13. Available online at: *http://programs.ssrc.org/gsc/publications/SSRC-NUPI.pdf*.

[18] Minorities at Risk Project, Assessment for Mizos in India, 31 December 2000. Online. UNHCR Refworld. Available online at: *http://www.unhcr.org/refworld/docid/469f3a911f.html*.

[19] Sandra Brunnegger. "From Conflict to Autonomy in Nicaragua: Lessons Learnt." Minority Rights Group International, April 2007. Available online at: *http://www2.ohchr.org/english/bodies/cescr/docs/info-ngos/mrginicaragua39wg.pdf*.

undermine stability in the longer term by providing these movements with greater resources and mobilization capacity (Brancati 2006, Roeder 2007).

In terms of outside actors, self-determination movements present a related but different set of issues, especially once violence emerges. Self-determination conflicts, like most conflicts in the developing world, are facilitated by fairly low-technology military equipment: small arms are sufficient in most places to wreak enormous destruction. The rebels in Chechnya, for instance, relied largely on small bands of guerrilla fighters who wreaked havoc on police and military facilities with small arms and explosives (similar types of violence have now spread to neighboring North Ossetia). This matters because there is no practical way to remove the technology itself, so solutions to the intensity of violence must be sought elsewhere. Yet self-determination conflicts are precisely the sort of conflict where bribes or threats tend to be least effective. This leaves military intervention as a next logical step, which leads to at least four distinct difficulties.

The "nation building" steps that work best tend to look a lot like colonialism to those in whose interest the reconstruction is being forwarded.

Military intervention by an external power often seems the only reliable solution to a self-determination conflict. Yet as a lasting solution, military intervention exhibits four problems. First, publics in the states that possess the forces capable of halting the violence have, since WWII, shown themselves to be impatient (three to five years at most are granted), and these interventions take a minimum of seven to ten years to succeed. Second, at this time, the militaries of many countries are stretched by current and recent efforts in Afghanistan, Iraq, the Congo, and elsewhere, so any new effort would face a significant challenge—where to find the troops? Third, force is only the first of a set of impositions needed to cause lasting peace. Yet the "nation building" steps that work best tend to look a lot like colonialism to those in whose interest the reconstruction is being forwarded. Fourth, intervention works best when there is an international consensus about whom to support. Frequently, two or more combatants receive outside support, which can perpetuate the conflict. Thus, interventions are apt to fail, leading back to violence.

This is not to say successful intervention to stop self-determination violence is hopeless, but rather to bracket the difficulties that emerge from empirical survey of past conflicts. The keys to success are (1) educate public support before engaging a threat, so as to lengthen the amount of time and forgiveness an operation will be granted in order to succeed; (2) use minimal, not maximum, armed force and in addition, see to it that these armed forces are specifically trained and equipped for an intervention mission; (3) make sure there is consensus among the outside actors; and (4) once initial violence has been stopped, work tirelessly to evaluate and address local grievances with targeted economic support and political reform, preferably as part of a multilateral effort.

6. TRENDS IN GLOBAL TERRORISM, 1970–2007

Gary LaFree, Laura Dugan, and R. Kim Cragin

One of the most notable advances in the study of terrorism and political violence in recent years has been the construction of large and increasingly comprehensive databases that document characteristics of terrorist attacks over time. Beginning in the late 1960s, a growing number of governmental and private entities began collecting open-source data on terrorist attacks. In general, all of these databases rely on the collection and analysis of information based on a combination of unclassified print and electronic media. The most serious limitation of these event databases is that they emphasize transnational events—those involving a national or a group of nationals from one country crossing international borders and attacking targets in another country. This limitation is serious; studies that have compared domestic and transnational terrorist attacks (LaFree et al., 2009; Schmid 2004) have concluded that the former outnumber the latter by as much as seven to one. Consider the fact that many of the most noteworthy terrorist attacks of recent years—for example, the March 1995 nerve gas attack on the Tokyo subway and the April 1995 bombing of the federal office building in Oklahoma City—lack any known foreign involvement and hence were pure acts of domestic terrorism.

This chapter reports new results from a recently compiled database that includes both international and domestic terrorist attacks from 1970 until 2007. It was created by combining the Global Terrorism Database (GTD) maintained by the National Consortium for the Study of Terrorism and Responses to Terrorism (START; LaFree and Dugan 2007) for the years 1970 to 1997 with the RAND-St. Andrews Terrorism Chronology data on international terrorism from 1970 to 1997 (Hoffman and Hoffman 1998) and the RAND-MIPT Terrorism Incident Data Base from 1998 to 2007 (Dugan et al., 2008). The resulting merged dataset includes more than 77,000 known domestic and international terrorist attacks from around the world, making it the most comprehensive unclassified event database yet assembled.

In this chapter we present worldwide trends in terrorist attacks and fatalities from the GTD-RAND merged database. We have developed the following operational definition of terrorism: *the threatened or actual use of illegal force, directed against civilian targets, by non-state actors, in order to attain a political goal, through fear, coercion, or intimidation.* Thus, the data presented exclude state terrorism and genocide, topics that are important and complex enough to warrant their own separate reviews. We provide baseline information on terrorist targets, primary tactics, weapons, and the regional distribution of terrorist attacks since 1970. To do this, we begin each section by summarizing the conventional wisdom on the topic and then consider how well these views are supported by the empirical evidence.

Global Terrorism Trends

The tragic events of September 11, 2001, had an immediate and dramatic impact on levels of public concern about terrorism in the United States and well beyond. Similarly, more recent attacks such as those in Madrid on March 11, 2004, in London on July 7, 2005, and in Mumbai on November 26–29, 2008, also raised concerns about terrorism among citizens, not only in the countries attacked but from observers around the world. Accordingly, many might assume that terrorist attacks and fatalities were up sharply in the years leading up to the twenty-first century. But Figure 6.1 shows that trends in terrorism since 1970 have actually been more complex.[1]

According to Figure 6.1, terrorist attacks reached their twentieth-century peak in 1992 (with over 3,500 attacks worldwide) but had substantially declined in the years leading up to the 9/11 attacks. In fact, total attacks in 2000 (1,151) were at about the same level as total attacks in 1977 and 1978 (1,067 and 1,285, respectively). Looking more broadly at overall trends, Figure 6.1 shows that worldwide terrorist attacks through the mid-1970s were relatively infrequent, with fewer than 1,000 incidents each year. But from 1978 to 1979 the frequency of events nearly doubled. The number of terrorist attacks continued to increase until the 1992 peak, with smaller peaks in 1984, at almost 2,500 incidents, and 1989, with almost 3,000 events. After the first major peak in 1992, the number of terrorist attacks declined until the end of the twentieth century, before rising steeply to a series high in 2006—three years after the start of the Iraq war. Total attacks in 2006 were 82 percent higher than total attacks for the 1992 peak. The series ends in 2007 with just under 3,500 attacks.

Fatal attacks also declined in the year prior to the 9/11 attacks. In fact, total fatal attacks in 2000 (235) were at about the same level as they had been more than two decades earlier, in 1978 (246). In general, the number of fatal attacks clearly followed the pattern of total attacks (r = 0.96), but at a substantially lower magnitude (averaging 798 fatal attacks per year compared to 2,094 total attacks per year worldwide). Fatal attacks rose above 1,000 per year for the first time in 1988. After hovering close to 1,000 attacks annually for most of the 1980s, they more than doubled between 1985 and 1992. Like total attacks, fatal attacks declined somewhat after 1992, bottoming out in 1999 with 180 attacks and then rising again to a global peak of more than 3,500 fatalities in 2006. The peak in 2006 was 160 percent higher than the 1992 peak.

One of the greatest challenges in collecting open source data on terrorism is distinguishing terrorist attacks from other types of violence, especially civilian casualties that occur during uprisings, insurgencies, and armed conflicts. This distinction has proven to be a particular challenge with regard to Iraq, following the U.S.-led invasion in 2003. The RAND-

---

1 Most of the 1993 data in the GTD were lost by the original collectors, and we have never been able to recover them (LaFree and Dugan 2007). For Figure 6.1 and the other trend analyses, we estimate 1993 rates by taking the average value for 1992 and 1994. For the non-trend figures, we include 1993 data from RAND-MIPT.

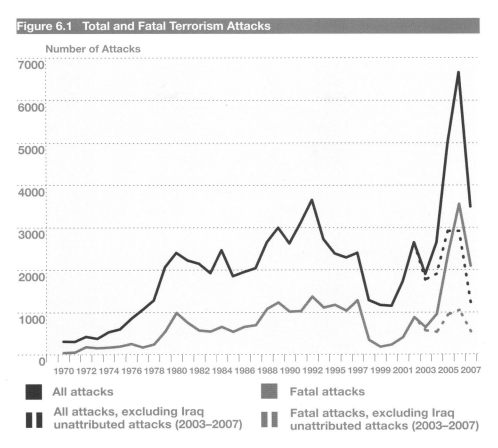

Figure 6.1 Total and Fatal Terrorism Attacks

Number of Attacks

All attacks

Fatal attacks

All attacks, excluding Iraq unattributed attacks (2003–2007)

Fatal attacks, excluding Iraq unattributed attacks (2003–2007)

MIPT data, like the GTD data, are designed to exclude cases involving open combat between opposing armed forces, even if these are non-state actors. But if civilians are targeted specifically as part of a wider campaign, even if this occurs amid the kind of instability and violence that characterized Iraq after the invasion in 2003, both the RAND-MIPT and the GTD seek to include them. For example, the merged data include attacks on barbershops in Iraq that have been associated with the belief by some Islamic extremist groups that men should not cut their hair. The data also include attacks against police stations, particularly recruitment centers, because police are considered civilian targets unless they fall under the jurisdiction of the military. However, the merged data exclude purely military attacks, such as improvised explosive devices placed along roadways to disrupt U.S. military convoys. Despite these efforts, we acknowledge that during wartime it is often difficult to distinguish between acts of terror and acts of sectarian or criminal violence and other violent acts resulting from warfare.

One method to distinguish further valid cases of terrorism from ambiguous cases is to examine only the proportion of attacks in post-2003 Iraq that can be attributed to specific terrorist organizations. We classify an attack as attributed to a specific group if the media source from which it is obtained contained information indicating that a specific terrorist group claimed the incident or if there was sufficient information to allow authorities to assign responsibility to a specific terrorist group. In the many cases where the terrorist groups publicly claimed their attacks, this information was compared with media reports to provide the most accurate information on the responsible terrorist group. Generally, 45 percent of the attacks in the merged database were attributed to specific groups. This pattern makes sense, as it is relatively common for terrorist groups to claim their attacks publicly. However, some terrorist groups do not claim their attacks or claim attacks under a false name or front organization. In the case of Iraq, after the beginning of 2003, only 699 (8 percent) of the 8,958 attacks could be attributed to specific organizations. Based on this information, we re-estimated attack and fatality trends in Figure 6.1 by dropping all post-2003 Iraq cases that were not attributed to a specific terrorist group.

The data strongly suggest that terrorism today is in large part a by-product of the war in Iraq, differing greatly from terrorism in the last quarter of the twentieth century.

According to Figure 6.1, the impact of dropping unattributed cases on total and fatal attacks is substantial. Without these cases, total attacks in 2007 (1,236) are less than half as large as they were at the pre-war 2002 level (2,648) and fatal attacks fall to 547, compared to the pre-war 2002 level of 883. Sorting out the boundaries between insurgency, terrorism, secular violence, and warfare is beyond the scope of the current study and worthy of research in its own right. We would disagree with the position of those (e.g., Human Security Report Project 2008) who claim that no civilian deaths in post-2003 Iraq are terrorism, but at the same time, we acknowledge that distinguishing terrorism from other forms of violence in a war-torn country poses a continuing challenge for open source databases. After acknowledging these challenges, the merged GTD-RAND data strongly suggest that terrorism today is in large part a by-product of the war in Iraq, differing greatly from terrorism in the last quarter of the twentieth century.

Distribution of Terrorism Targets

Defining terrorism has long been a challenging enterprise; in their influential review of terrorism research, Schmid and Jongman (1988: 5) identified 109 different definitions. One aspect of terrorism that receives nearly universal agreement is that it is directed against civilian targets, yet, what it actually means to be a civilian target is itself a complex issue. The most obvious challenge is deciding when to count military personnel as "civilian" targets. In general, the merged GTD-RAND database excludes attacks on military personnel. However, we include attacks on international peacekeeping forces if the peacekeeping mission was recognized by the United Nations. We also include attacks against military forces on leave away from their area of operation or attacks against military forces in their place of residence, such as the 1983 Beirut bombing against U.S. and French military forces.

Apart from decisions about what to count as civilian attacks, there are a wide variety of types of civilian targets. That is, instead of targeting specific persons, many terrorist attacks are aimed at specific institutions (e.g., government or religious buildings) or infrastructure (e.g., transportation, utilities) and the civilians attacked are randomly selected. The merged database provides considerable detail about these differences in targeting patterns.

Section A of Table 6.1 presents the targets of global terrorist strikes for all attacks in the merged data. There is considerable variation in target types, with the top three targets ranking as private citizens and property, government agents or facilities, and businesses. Together, these three targets account for just over 50 percent of the total. Following the top three target types, in order, are police, transportation, diplomats, utilities, religious institutions, the military, journalists and the media, and educational institutions. While we excluded many attacks against police and the military as being non-civilian and therefore not included under the definition of terrorism given above, police and military targets still jointly account for about 13 percent of total attacks—which puts them in fourth place behind private citizens, government officials, and businesses. The "other" category here encompasses a diverse range of targets, including airports and airlines, other terrorists or former terrorists, and non-governmental organizations. While our definition of terrorism emphasizes civilian targets, these results suggest that purely civilian targets—"private citizens and property" without a specific institutional or organizational affiliation—account for less than one-fifth of all the attacks.

> *The top three targets of terrorism are private citizens and property, government agents or facilities, and businesses, accounting for just over 50 percent of the total.*

If the unattributed post-2003 Iraqi cases are removed, as was done for Figure 6.1, the most frequently attacked target remains private citizens (now at 21 percent), with businesses ranking second at 18 percent, government third at 17 percent, and transportation surpassing police at 6 percent. This suggests that compared to the non-Iraqi cases, a larger portion of the unattributed post-2003 Iraqi attacks targeted government and police. This makes sense because attacks on police in Iraq have been designed to discourage cooperation with U.S. and coalition forces. Indeed, nearly 38 percent of the unattributed Iraqi attacks targeted police and 16 percent targeted government. Only 11 percent targeted private citizens or property.

Tactics Used by Terrorists

Definitions of terrorism generally ignore the specific tactics used by terrorists, yet the range of tactical strategies is relatively limited. In the merged database, terrorist tactics are divided into seven categories: bombings, armed attacks, assassinations, kidnappings, barricade/hostage taking, arson,

Table 6.1 Targets, Tactics, and Weapons of Terrorism

(A) Distribution of Terrorism Targets

Private Citizens and Property	19.82%
Government	16.98%
Business	15.93%
Other	9.95%
Police	9.62%
Transportation	5.56%
Diplomatic	4.60%
Utilities	4.39%
Religious Figures/Institutions	3.15%
Military	2.62%
Unknown	2.59%
Journalists and Media	2.47%
Educational Institutions	2.30%

(B) Primary Tactic of Terrorist Attacks

Bombing	51.35%
Armed Attack	25.50%
Assassination	15.49%
Kidnapping	3.09%
Barricade/Hostage	1.80%
Arson	1.43%
Unknown	0.61%
Hijacking	0.36%
Other	0.24%
Unconventional Attacks	0.14%

(C) Weapons Used in Terrorist Attacks

Explosives	47.06%
Firearms	32.38%
Unknown	8.01%
Fire or Firebomb	7.84%
Knives and Other Sharp Objects	1.79%
Remote-Detonated Explosive	1.72%
Other	1.03%
Chemical Agent	0.14%
Biological Agent	0.02%

and hijackings (for definitions, see the *Peace and Conflict* companion Web site). We classify bombings as attacks that use explosive devices or multiple explosive devices, including bombs detonated manually or by remote timer and suicide bombings. By contrast, armed attacks include assaults on persons or facilities that differ from non-specific or specific bombings. For example, the November 2008 attacks in Mumbai would be identified as an armed attack. Assassinations are attacks that involve a specific, targeted killing of a high-profile or prominent figure. Assassinations may or may not use explosive devices, but if explosive devices are used in an assassination, we identify the case as an assassination and not a bombing. Kidnappings are the abduction of a person or group of people in which ransom is not the primary objective (which would make it a criminal rather than a terrorist incident). Barricade/hostage attacks are those in which the perpetrators take hostages and/or take control over a specific building and prohibit access. Arsons are attacks in which perpetrators intentionally set fire to buildings or property. Hijackings are attacks that involve the forcible takeover of vehicles, including airplanes and ships. We include as unconventional attacks those that rely on the use of chemical, biological, radiological, or nuclear materials.

Our impressions of the tactics used by terrorists are no doubt driven in large part by the more sensational cases that receive the most media attention. Thus, aerial hijackings with hostages are likely to receive a good deal more attention than bombings of buildings where no one is killed.

Section B in Table 6.1 shows the percentage of total attacks for each of the eight tactics, including a small percentage of attacks where the primary tactic is unreported or differs from the other eight. Bombings are the most commonly used tactic accounting for more than half of the total attacks. Armed attacks are next most common, used in more than 25 percent of the attacks. Terrorists relied on assassinations in more than 15 percent of the total attacks, kidnappings, and hostage taking in nearly 5 percent, and hijackings in less than one half of 1 percent. Note that unconventional attacks are rarely used, accounting for just over one-tenth of one percent of the total attacks.

The distribution of terrorist tactics remained substantially the same when we reanalyzed the data without the unattributed post-2003 Iraqi cases. This suggests that while the target selection in Iraq varies significantly from other areas afflicted with terrorist violence, the tactics remain similar. Of course, this pattern fails to account for the numerous improvised explosive devices used against coalition forces in Iraq or even rocket attacks against coalition bases in that country because these cases were not defined as terrorism.

Terrorist Weapons

Again, because of high profile cases like 9/11 and also the ubiquitous treatment of terrorism by the film and media industry, there is a tendency to think that most terrorist strikes are complex, carefully orchestrated, and rely highly on sophisticated weaponry. In Table 6.1C we use the merged database to examine the actual range of weapons used by terrorists.

> *Because of high profile cases like 9/11 and also the ubiquitous treatment of terrorism by the film and media industry, there is a tendency to think that most terrorist strikes are complex, carefully orchestrated, and rely highly on sophisticated weaponry. However, contrary to the view of terrorism commonly offered by the media, the vast majority of terrorist attacks rely on readily accessible weapons.*

Contrary to the view of terrorism commonly offered by the media, the vast majority of terrorist attacks rely on readily accessible weapons. According to section C of Table 6.1, the most common weapons in the GTD-RAND database were explosives and firearms. These two categories account for nearly 80 percent of all attacks. For the most part, the explosives used were readily available, especially dynamite, grenades, mortars, and improvised devices placed inside vehicles ("car bombs"). Similarly, the most common firearms were also widely available, including especially automatic weapons, shotguns, and pistols. After explosives and firearms, fire or firebombs account for about 8 percent of the incidents; knives and other sharp objects each account for fewer than 2 percent of the attacks. Weapons included in the "other" category were diverse, including items such as stones and bricks.

Among the more sophisticated weapon types were 1,333 attacks using remote-detonated devices, 112 attacks using chemical agents, and 13 cases involving biological agents. Note that chemical agents were responsible for less than one-fifth of 1 percent of all incidents and biological agents were present in less than two-one hundredths of 1 percent of all attacks.

The remote-detonated devices were usually left on the roadside or attached to vehicles. Sometimes, they were planted in packages and detonated at strategic locations. Chemical agents range from letters containing rat poison to tainted water supplies. Ten of the 13 biological weapons cases were the U.S. anthrax attacks of 2001—in which seven people died.

When the post-2003 unattributed Iraqi cases are excluded, the weapons results remained very similar. That is, patterns of weapons use against civilian targets in Iraq follow terrorist violence elsewhere, but again this does not account for military attacks.

Regional Differences in Terrorist Activity

We next divide the countries of the world into nine regions: Africa, East and Central Asia, Eastern Europe, Latin America, the Middle East/Persian Gulf, North America, South Asia, Southeast Asia and Oceana, and Western Europe (for countries in each region, see Appendix B on the *Peace and Conflict* companion Web site). Given the high profile of terrorist activities originating in the Middle East in recent years, it is easy to forget about the contributions to terrorism made in other parts of the world. Figure 6.2 shows total attacks and total fatalities by region from 1970 to 2007.[2]

Perhaps the most striking feature of Figure 6.2 is the importance of Latin America: a higher proportion of total attacks (26 percent) occurred in Latin American countries than in any other world region. Latin America has been the home of a large number of highly active terrorist groups that have operated for prolonged periods during the past 30 years, including the Shining Path (Sendero Luminoso), the Farabundo Marti National Liberation Front (FMLN), and the Revolutionary Armed Forces of Colombia (FARC). Over the period spanned by our data, militant groups in the Middle East/Persian Gulf region are nearly as active as those in Latin America, accounting for just under 24 percent of total attacks. Taken together, Latin American and the Middle East account for more than half of the terrorist attacks in the merged database (51 percent). Following these two regions in terms of total attacks are Western Europe (19 percent) and South Asia (13 percent); they jointly account for another 32 percent of all terrorist attacks. None of the remaining regions accounts for more than 10 percent of the total attacks and North America and East and Central Asia each account for only 1 percent of the total.

Excluding the post-2003 unattributed Iraqi cases from the analysis has a substantial impact on the rankings for the Middle East/Persian Gulf cases. The Middle East region drops to 16 percent of total attacks—falling behind Western Europe, which now accounts for 20 percent of all attacks. Without post-2003 Iraqi cases, Latin America accounts for nearly 30 percent of all attacks. After the beginning of the Iraq war in 2003, the Middle East/Persian Gulf region rises to the lead in terrorist attacks, peaking with 4,540

---

2 We exclude two attacks that occurred in international territory and three attacks in which the country data were missing.

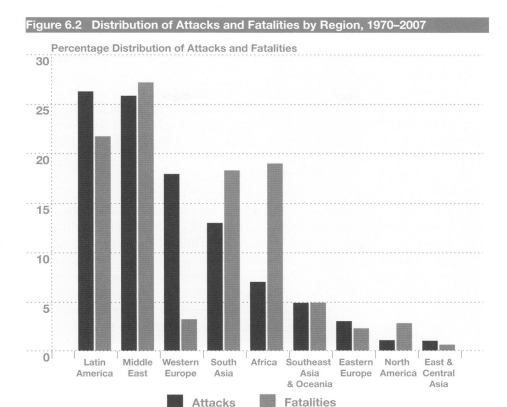

Figure 6.2 Distribution of Attacks and Fatalities by Region, 1970–2007

Percentage Distribution of Attacks and Fatalities

Attacks   Fatalities

attacks in 2006—more than three times higher than the Latin American peak of 1,448 in 1984.

Figure 6.2 shows substantially different regional patterns for total fatalities than for attacks. While Latin America and the Middle East remain the leaders in fatalities as well as in the proportion of total attacks, Africa and South Asia have the next highest percentage of fatalities, accounting for 19 and 18 percent of all terrorism-related fatalities, respectively. Figure 6.2 also shows that while Western Europe is third in the proportion of attacks, it suffers relatively few fatalities as a result of these attacks, averaging about one death for every three attacks. This rate is especially low compared to that for Africa, which averages nearly five deaths for every terrorist attack. Thus, while the African continent accounts for a relatively small proportion of total terrorist attacks during this period, when there were attacks in Africa, they were on average deadlier.

The reasons for these differences remain to be explained, although part of the explanation may simply be selective media coverage and proximate access to medical care across regions. A closer examination of the fatality rates for Africa reveals that four countries averaged 10 or more fatalities per attack: Rwanda (22.6), Chad (15.4), Burundi (13.9), and Mozambique (10.1). Much of the terrorist violence in Rwanda and Burundi was driven by the conflict between the Tutsis and the Hutus. The Lord's Resistance

Army in Uganda also staged a series of terrorist attacks with large numbers of fatalities during this period. By contrast, groups like the IRA and ETA operating in Western Europe staged large numbers of attacks resulting in relatively few fatalities.

Again, fatalities for the Middle East/Persian Gulf region are being driven especially by the war in Iraq. Without the unattributed cases for post-2003 Iraq, the Middle East/Persian Gulf region drops from the first to the fourth most lethal region (behind Latin America, Africa, and South Asia).

Regional Trends in Terrorist Activity

Based on the major impact of the war in Iraq on the ranking of the Middle East for the end of the series, it seems likely that the relative contributions to terrorist activity of global regions might also have changed considerably over time. In fact, in the last volume of *Peace and Conflict*, LaFree et al. (2008) found that from 1970 to 1978, terrorism was in large part a West European problem. But after the late 1970s, West European attacks began to decline and attacks originating in Latin America substantially increased. Increases in the 1980s and early 1990s were driven in large part by growing activity in Asia and Africa. In Figure 6.3, we extend this earlier analysis to 2007.

The most obvious difference between the new analysis and the earlier analysis is the tremendous impact of attacks from the Middle East/Persian Gulf after 2003.

The most obvious difference between the new analysis and the earlier analysis is the tremendous impact of attacks from the Middle East/Persian Gulf after 2003. If we include the unattributed post-2003 Iraqi cases, the Middle East/Persian Gulf region rises to the lead in terrorist attacks. Also striking are the attack patterns for Latin America. From 1980 to 1992 Latin America is the most frequently attacked region. But between 1994 and 2003, other regions, especially Africa, Asia (primarily South Asia), and Europe (primarily Western Europe) compete for this distinction. As in our earlier analysis (LaFree et al., 2008), during the 1970s, the most attacks targeted countries in Western Europe. However, after peaking at just over 750 incidents in 1979, West European attacks drop to an average of 371 incidents a year. By contrast, Latin American attacks continue to increase after 1979 peaking in 1991 with 1,215 incidents. After 1991, Latin America continues to average about 320 attacks a year with large fluctuations. Figure 6.3 also suggests that the increases in global terrorism attacks in the 1980s and early 1990s were driven in large part by increased activity in Asia (primarily the South Asian region) and Africa. Finally, Figure 6.3 shows that compared to other regions, the North American region has experienced a relatively small proportion of terrorist attacks during the entire period. This is true of East and Central Asia, as well, but the graph does not report these regions separately.

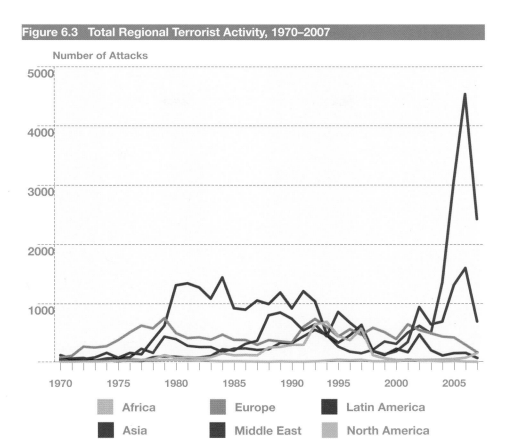

Figure 6.3 Total Regional Terrorist Activity, 1970–2007

Number of Attacks

Africa   Europe   Latin America
Asia   Middle East   North America

Based on the substantial differences in total events by region, it is unsurprising that countries vary greatly in terms of total attacks. Because of the natural transition in the series between 1997 (primarily GTD data) to 1998 (exclusively RAND), we ranked the 25 most attacked countries and territories before and after this transition for comparison (see Table 6.2). We also distinguished new countries/territories in the top 25 after 1997. High conflict territories, such as Corsica, Northern Ireland, and the West Bank and Gaza Strip are listed separately from their administering country in order to provide the most transparent ranking of activity.[3] The importance of Latin America as a regional source for terrorist incidents prior to 1998 is underscored by the fact that the three countries with the highest number of attacks are all Latin American: Peru, Colombia, and El Salvador. In addition, four other Latin American countries make the top 25: Chile, Guatemala, Nicaragua, and Argentina. Western Europe contains eight countries or territories that are in the top 25: Spain, Northern Ireland, Italy, Germany (East and West), France (excluding Corsica), Greece, Corsica, and Great Britain. Five South Asian or Southeast Asian countries are in the top 25:

---

3 The RAND data also separates Kashmir and Chechnya from their administering units, but because the GTD combines them with India and Russia, respectively, we followed the same coding scheme here.

Table 6.2 Top 25 Most Attacked Countries and Territories

	1970 to 1997		1998 to 2007	
Rank	Country	Percent of all Attacks	Country	Pecent of all Attacks
1	Peru	8.21	Iraq**	35.01
2	Colombia	7.49	West Bank/ Gaza Strip**	7.24
3	El Salvador	6.35	India	7.09
4	India	4.12	Colombia	5.39
5	Spain	4.04	Thailand**	4.32
6	Northern Ireland	4.01	Afghanistan**	3.88
7	Chile	3.77	Spain	3.86
8	Turkey	3.48	Turkey	3.42
9	Guatemala	3.25	Pakistan	3.33
10	Israel	3.16	Israel	3.24
11	Lebanon	3.10	Russia**	3.08
12	Pakistan	2.82	Northern Ireland	2.50
13	South Africa	2.71	France	2.38
14	Italy	2.67	Nepal**	1.64
15	Germany*	2.53	Greece	1.26
16	France	2.44	Sri Lanka	1.03
17	Philippines	2.43	Philippines	0.99
18	Sri Lanka	2.31	Indonesia**	0.81
19	Algeria	1.92	Algeria	0.77
20	Nicaragua	1.82	Italy	0.63
21	Argentina	1.51	Bangladesh**	0.53
22	Greece	1.46	Kosovo**	0.47
23	United States	1.30	United States	0.42
24	Corsica	1.28	Somalia**	0.40
25	Great Britain	1.02	Venezuela**	0.38

* Prior to 1991, this figure combines attacks from both East and West Germany.

** In the top 25 only after 1998.

India, Pakistan, Sri Lanka, Philippines, and Bangladesh. Only three Middle Eastern or Persian Gulf countries are in the top 25 prior to 1998: Turkey, Israel, and Lebanon. South Africa and Algeria are the sole countries from Africa in the top 25 most frequently targeted countries. The United States finishes as twenty-third among the top 25 countries.

After 1998, eleven new countries or territories have joined the top 25 terrorist attack rankings. Not surprisingly, Iraq ranks first, accounting for 35 percent of all attacks during this period. Nearly all (98 percent) of the Iraqi attacks during this period occurred after the U.S.-led invasion in 2003.

However, only a little over 1 percent of the attacks actually targeted U.S. nationals—a likely consequence of the fact that most attacks on American military personnel are counted not as terrorism but as warfare. The only other Middle East/Persian Gulf territory that entered the ranking after 1997 was the West Bank and Gaza Strip. Lebanon drops out in the late 1980s—perhaps because Hizballah began targeting civilians less and the military more during this period. This period also corresponds with the second Intifada. With just over 7 percent of all post-1997 attacks, the West Bank and Gaza Strip, combined with Iraq, made the Middle East the most frequently attacked region of the world. Israel's ranking remains the same, accounting for only slightly more attacks after 1998 than before.[4] New countries and territories in South Asia and Southeast Asia also entered the rankings after 1997. In particular, violent conflicts in Thailand and Afghanistan drew the world's attention to these regions. Russia also entered the top 25 after 1997, with a large number of attacks due to the conflict in Chechnya. Other newcomers to the top 25 include Nepal, Indonesia, Bangladesh, Kosovo, Somalia, and Venezuela.

Even after excluding post-2003 Iraqi cases where no specific group can be identified, total terrorist attacks nearly tripled between 2000 and 2006.

As before, the post-1997 country rankings were re-estimated by excluding the post-2003 unattributed Iraqi attacks. This drops Iraq from number one to number 11, accounting for about 4 percent of all attacks since the beginning of 1998. Without post-2003 unattributed Iraqi cases, the West Bank and Gaza Strip rise to the top ranking, accounting for nearly 11 percent of all attacks and India becomes second with more than 10 percent of all attacks since 1998.

Conclusion

In this chapter we examined a newly available terrorism open source database that was created by merging the GTD with the RAND-MIPT data. Our review suggests that both total terrorist attacks and lethal attacks increased dramatically from 1970 to the early 1990s, declined up until the beginning of the twenty-first century, and then increased again during the past decade. Increases are markedly higher if we include all post-2003 cases of terrorism in Iraq from the merged data. However, even after excluding post-2003 Iraqi cases where no specific group can be identified, total terrorist attacks nearly tripled between 2000 and 2006.

As in our earlier review (LaFree et al., 2008), we found that bombings and facility attacks were the most common terrorist tactics, followed by assassinations and kidnappings. Aerial hijackings were rare. The targets of these attacks were most often government, business, or police.

---

4 Note that attacks on Jewish settlements inside the West Bank and Gaza Strip are counted here as attacks on the Palestinian territories rather than on Israel.

The vast majority of attacks involved explosives or firearms. The Middle East/Persian Gulf and Latin America lead all other regions both in terms of total attacks and fatalities. And over time, the Middle East/Persian Gulf region has replaced Latin America as the most active terrorist region in the world. While sub-Saharan Africa and South Asia have higher fatalities per attack, attacks in Western Europe are less likely to be lethal compared to other regions. Prior to 1998, the top 25 countries in terms of terrorism were dominated by Western Europe (8 countries and territories) and Latin American (7 countries). But in the last decade, the distribution has included more countries from other regions, including six South Asian countries and four Middle East/Persian Gulf countries and territories. Interestingly, the United States remains the number twenty-third most attacked country, both before and after 1997.

7. STATE FAILURE AND CONFLICT RECURRENCE

Anke Hoeffler

About one billion people live in failing states, and their lives are plagued by insecurity and poverty. Failing states are marginalized and if current trends continue they will lag even further behind in the future, trapped in a vicious cycle of underdevelopment and violent conflict. Thus, the definition of state failure focuses on two main conditions: failure to provide security and failure to provide economic opportunities. State failure is costly in human and economic terms, not only to the citizens of their own state, but even more so to other states in the region. Turning around failed states is an enormous challenge. Ultimately, the change has to come from within the country, but this chapter also discusses what the international community can do to assist with the transition.

Definition of State Failure

Most international development agencies, such as the U.S. Agency for International Development or the British equivalent, Department of International Development (DFID), have specific development programs for *fragile* states. Other agencies refer to *Difficult Partnerships* (The Development Assistance Committee of the OECD) or to *Low-Income Countries under Stress* (World Bank). Their main concern is that these countries are failing to provide an adequate environment for poverty reduction. On the other hand, security agencies more often refer to *collapsed* or *failed* states and are primarily concerned with these states' inability to provide security for their own citizens, as well as their potential to cause regional and global destabilization. For the purpose of this discussion, the descriptions "weak," "failing," "fragile," and "collapsed" are treated as synonymous.

This chapter is based on the assumption that states can fail in two distinct senses: they can fail to provide economic development opportunities, or they can fail to provide security. The most basic role of the state is to provide physical security to its citizens through maintaining a monopoly of organized force within the society. Where the government fails to do this and rival organizations of violence emerge, the state descends into civil war. However, in the modern world the demands legitimately placed upon the state extend beyond this basic function of security. Governments in all modern societies also play some role as regulators of private economic activity, and as suppliers of public goods such as transportation infrastructure, health, and education. The quality of these regulation and supply functions is important for the capacity of each citizen to earn a living and thus avoid poverty. Increasingly, as globalization facilitates economic activity between countries, the quality of government matters in a relative rather than an absolute sense: governments that provide fewer public goods are likely to

Table 7.1 Listing of Failing States (German Ministry of Development, 2007)

Africa		East Asia	
Angola	Guinea	Cambodia	Papua New Guinea
Burundi	Guinea-Bissau	Lao PDR	East Timor
Cameroon	Liberia	Myanmar	Solomon Islands
Central African Rep.	Niger		
Chad	Nigeria	**South Asia**	
Comoros	Rwanda	Bangladesh	Pakistan
Congo, Dem. Rep. of	Sao Tome and Principe	Nepal	Sri Lanka
Congo	Sierra Leone		
Côte d'Ivoire	Somalia	**Latin America**	
Djibouti	Sudan	Colombia	Paraguay
Equatorial Guinea	Togo	Ecuador	Venezuela
Eritrea	Uganda	Haiti	
Ethiopia	Zimbabwe		
		Other	
Middle East and North Africa		Afghanistan	Tajikistan
Iran	Syria	Azerbaijan	Tonga
Iraq	West Bank and Gaza	Belarus	Turkmenistan
Libya	Yemen	Kiribati	Uzbekistan
		Kyrgyz Republic	Vanuatu

lose economic activities, with a resulting detrimental effect on their citizens. Hence, a state can fail merely because the quality of regulation and public goods its government provides is markedly inferior to that provided by other governments.

Although it is relatively easy to provide a basic definition of state failure, most international development and security agencies do not produce publicly available lists of states they consider to be failing. This is probably owing to a number of reasons: they do not want to appear politically biased, and they wish to avoid lengthy debates as to why they include certain countries but not others. A label of "state failure" can also lead to a change in the behavior of citizens, investors, NGOs, and international agencies, thus making an already bad situation worse—a situation for which no international agency wants to be responsible. A rare example of a published list of failing states is provided by the German Ministry of Development (BMZ 2007). It offers a relatively wide definition of failing states and lists 56 countries (see Table 7.1). It includes poor countries, many at war or having just recently ended civil wars, such as Afghanistan, Liberia, and East Timor. However, the list also includes countries with ineffective governance that are neither war-torn nor poor. Examples include countries like Belarus, Syria, and Venezuela. According to this classification, about 1.2 billion people live in failing states. As Figure 7.1 shows, almost half of all failing states are located in sub-Saharan Africa.

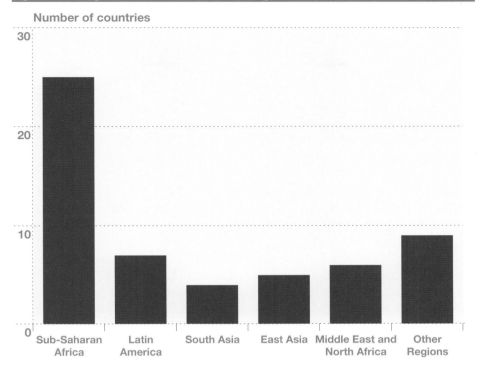

Figure 7.1 Regional Distribution of 56 Failing States (BMZ 2007)

Number of countries

Sub-Saharan Africa | Latin America | South Asia | East Asia | Middle East and North Africa | Other Regions

Other lists of failing states are provided by the Political Instability Task Force[1] and by the Fund for Peace (in collaboration with *Foreign Policy* magazine[2]). The Political Instability Task Force definition of state failure centers on security aspects: a state is failing if the country suffers a revolutionary or ethnic war, adverse regime changes, or genocides and politicides. The definition of state failure used by the Fund for Peace is more broadly based; it uses 12 social, economic, political, and military indicators to rank 177 states in order of their vulnerability to violent internal conflict and societal deterioration. In 2008 Somalia is ranked as the country most at risk of state failure, but as the report acknowledges, Somalia has failed already. This demonstrates one of the problems with using such a ranking. In the absence of a clearly defined threshold, users must decide for themselves whether states have failed or are at risk of failure. In Chapter 2, Hewitt presents the Peace and Conflict Instability Ledger, which ranks states based on their future risk of state failure.

Cost of State Failure

The consequences of state failure are dramatic for its citizens. Table 7.2 lists some economic, health, and education statistics for the 56 failing states from the BMZ list. Failing states score worse in every aspect. Comparing failing states (column 1) with non-failing states (column 3) confirms that failing

1 *http://globalpolicy.gmu.edu/pitf/*

2 *http://www.foreignpolicy.com/story/cms.php?story_id=4350*

Table 7.2 Economic, Health, and Education Indicators

Indicator	Failing States	Failing States in Sub-Saharan Africa	Non-Failing, Non-OECD States
GDP per capita (in 2000 const. US$)	963	645	4180
Aid (% of GDP)	13	18	6
Life expectancy (years)	60	48	69
Infant mortality (per 1,000 births)	71	104	30
Literacy (% of total population >15yrs)	70	56	78
Literacy female (% of females >15yrs)	63	48	74

Note: Averages calculated for 2003–2005, source: World Development Indicators (2008).

states are much poorer: their income per capita is about one-quarter of the income in non-failing states. The situation is even more desperate for failing states in sub-Saharan Africa: average per capita income is about $650, only 15 percent of the income in non-failing states. Failing states are also much more dependent on foreign aid: about 13 percent of their national income is provided through foreign assistance. This figure is higher in Africa, where aid contributes about 18 percent to national income. These poor economic outcomes are also reflected in life expectancy: in failing states people die on average ten years before people in other developing states. Infant mortality is also much higher in failing states: about 7 percent of parents will see their child die within the first year, compared with only about 3 percent of parents in other developing states. General and female literacy rates are also lower in failing states—particularly in sub-Saharan Africa. Fewer than half of African women are literate, whereas about three-fourths of women in non-failing states can read and write.

As the above discussion illustrates, state failure imposes enormous costs on people: they are poor, they die younger, and their children are less likely to survive infancy. But how large are these costs in the aggregate? To gain some idea of the magnitude of the problem, it is useful to estimate the economic cost of state failure. Chauvet et al. (2006) estimate the global combined cost of state failure at $270 billion. State failure can have three distinct consequences: (1) it fails to provide an environment in which poverty reduction is feasible, (2) it results in a failure to provide basic security for citizens, and (3) it hurts citizens in neighboring countries. In addition, there are global costs, such as illegal drug production in failing states. Because no attempt has been made to estimate the global costs, the Chavet et al. estimate of $270 billion is likely to be an underestimate. The relative size of the different cost components is depicted in Figure 7.2, and the remainder of this section discusses the individual cost components.

Cost of Poverty

Good economic policies and governance provide economic opportunities for all citizens and enable people to live a life free of poverty. Chauvet et al. (2006) confine their analysis to failing states with low income and find that

Figure 7.2   Cost of State Failure

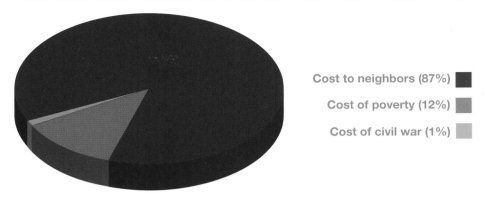

Cost to neighbors (87%)

Cost of poverty (12%)

Cost of civil war (1%)

between 1990–2001 low-income failing states experienced no economic growth, while other developing countries grew at 2.8 percent per year. One result is that a large proportion of the world's poor, defined as surviving on less than one dollar a day, live in failing states. Although the total population of this country sample makes up about only 7 percent of the world's population, 15 percent of the world's poor live in these countries. If this current trend continues, nearly 30 percent of the world's poor will live in failing states in 2015. The value of these missed opportunities for economic growth in all these failing states is estimated at $32 billion per year.

Cost of Civil War

Some countries experience state collapse, and large-scale internal violence is enormously costly to their citizens. Wars kill, but even after the fighting stops the risks to human life and health are considerable. Wars divert precious resources into fighting; during a civil war, military expenditures increase and do not return to normal levels after the fighting stops. On average, civil wars last for about seven years (Collier et al. 2004), during which economic growth is reduced considerably. Even though post-conflict countries experience a peace dividend in the form of increased growth, it takes the country about 21 years to return to its pre-war income level (Collier and Hoeffler 2004a). The total cost of civil war is calculated at slightly less than $3 billion per year. By comparison to the total economic cost of state failure, this number may seem relatively small, but this is due to the fact that civil war is a rare event, even in low-income countries.

Costs to Neighbors

The negative effects of economic stagnation and civil war spill over to neighboring countries. Neighbors' growth rates are significantly reduced by economic and security troubles. Chauvet et al. (2006) estimate this growth loss at about 0.6 percent per annum per neighbor. The average failing state has 3.5 neighbors, and these growth losses add up to lost income of about $237 billion per year.

Post-Conflict Challenges

Due to their inability to generate economic growth and opportunities for their citizens, failing states are at higher risk of experiencing large-scale violent conflict. Once they have experienced a war, they are at a much higher risk of experiencing a recurrence of violence. It is thus of particular interest to discuss the challenges posed by post-conflict.

The pattern of aid disbursements should probably gradually rise during the first four years, and gradually taper back to normal levels by the end of the first post-conflict decade. Has actual aid practice followed this pattern? The historical evidence suggests the opposite: aid tapers off just when it should be ramping up.

Because the global prevalence of civil war has been decreasing over the past 15 years, there are now more post-conflict countries (see Chapter 3). This declining trend in the number of major armed conflicts is of course very welcome news. Many countries, for example, Angola, Liberia, and Sierra Leone, are now at peace after long, devastating wars. However, these post-conflict countries face two distinct challenges: economic recovery and risk reduction. Post-conflict peace is typically fragile: about 40 percent of all civil wars are post-conflict relapses within a decade (Collier et al. 2008). The two objectives of economic recovery and risk reduction are likely to be complementary: economic recovery reduces risks, and risk reduction speeds recovery.

Economic Recovery

The following discussion addresses two questions: (1) do post-conflict societies experience a peace dividend in terms of increased economic growth after the end of the conflict? and (2) can this economic recovery process be supported by aid and policy reform? Research suggests that post-conflict economies experience additional growth during the middle of the post-conflict decade. This peace dividend can be increased through international development assistance and domestic policy reforms. However, historically, aid donors have provided a lot of aid at the end of the conflict and scaled assistance down just when they should have scaled it up. Governments of post-conflict countries do not seem to have sequenced policy reforms, although there is some evidence to suggest that policies of social inclusion are particularly growth enhancing after the war and should thus become a priority.

These conclusions are based on the study by Collier and Hoeffler (2004c). They offer evidence for a peace dividend: during the post-conflict decade, countries experience an extra one percentage point growth per year. Further investigation shows that this additional growth occurs during the fourth to the seventh year of peace. Such a pattern of recovery is not a priori surprising. The immediate aftermath of conflict holds many uncertainties, and basic functions of government have yet to be reestablished. If peace is maintained, there is then a phase of catch-up, but this peters out, and the economy reverts to its long-term growth rate. Can this peace dividend be supported by international development aid? Evidence suggests that the end of a civil war creates a temporary phase during which aid is particularly effective in the growth process. During the fourth to seventh year of peace, the absorptive capacity for aid is approximately double its normal level. Thus, the pattern of aid disbursements should probably gradually rise during the first four years, and gradually taper back to normal levels by the end of the first post-conflict decade. Has actual aid practice followed this pattern? The historical evidence suggests the opposite: aid tapers off just when it should be ramping up.

> *Social policy reforms have the largest positive impact on growth, followed by structural policies (such as trade policies and property rights) and macroeconomic policies (such as fiscal policy and debt management). These findings suggest that a sequencing of reforms is most likely to aid economic recovery. Historically, during the first decade of peace, policymakers have tried to improve all of these policies in tandem.*

As in normal circumstances, the absorptive capacity for aid depends upon domestic policy. In general, economic policies tend to be worse in post-conflict societies than in other societies. Do the poor policies and weak governance offset the benefits from aid? Collier and Hoeffler (2004c) find no evidence for this. They investigated whether the contribution of policy to growth is systematically different in post-conflict countries, and in particular, whether particular components of policy are differentially important. Growth seems more sensitive to policy in post-conflict societies. Thus, to be effective, aid should become a priority to policy reformers. This leads to the question as to which policy reforms are most likely to increase the peace dividend. The authors find some evidence that social policy reforms have the largest positive impact on growth, followed by structural policies (such as trade policies and property rights) and macroeconomic policies (such as fiscal policy and debt management). These findings suggest that a sequencing of reforms is most likely to aid economic recovery. Historically, during the first decade of peace, policymakers have tried to improve all of these policies in tandem.

Post-Conflict Risks

The path to economic recovery depends crucially on maintaining the peace. Collier et al. (2008) estimate the risk of the peace breaking down through conflict recurrence as substantial: 40 percent of all post-conflict societies revert to conflict within the decade. The authors use a wide definition of conflict recurrence. If a civil war breaks out during the post-conflict decade, this is classified as "conflict recurrence," although the protagonists and the issues of this recurring conflict may not be the same. The authors study which of the economic, political, and military variables are most important in maintaining the peace. Their analysis suggests that economic development does substantially reduce risks. If a post-conflict country achieves a growth rate of 10 percent, the decade risk falls to 27 percent. This risk reduction is due to higher growth, as well as to the cumulatively higher income. One implication of this result is that the international community should concentrate the post-conflict assistance disproportionately in the poorest countries, with a heavy focus on economic recovery.

Does increased military expenditure stabilize the peace? During a civil war, military spending is naturally high—typically around 5.2 percent of GDP, as opposed to 3.3 percent in societies at peace. After a civil war, military expenditure remains high at about 4.7 percent. Does this higher military expenditure reduce the risk of conflict recurrence? One could argue that the most obvious effect of high military spending is deterrence through reduced prospects of military success for rebel groups. However, in their empirical study Collier and Hoeffler (2006) find that high post-conflict military spending in fact significantly increases the risk of renewed conflict. This adverse effect of military spending is distinctive to post-conflict societies: it is not general across societies. What could account for this empirical pattern? Many civil wars end in negotiated settlements. Walter (1997) argues that, in contrast to international wars, the parties to a civil war usually lack effective means of binding themselves to respect the terms of such settlements. The critical and distinctive difficulty in restoring peace during civil wars is the lack of credible commitment technologies: neither party can trust the terms of a proposed settlement, even though it might be mutually advantageous. In the absence of credible commitment and trust, the parties have to interpret actions as signs of true intentions. Military expenditure may act as a signal of government intentions: high military spending signals that the government intends to renege on the terms of the peace settlement and so increases the risk of renewed rebellion. The empirical evidence is consistent with this signalling interpretation.

Domestic military expenditure does not deter renewed conflict, but perhaps international military assistance has a different effect on stabilizing the peace? There are insufficient data to examine the impact of all international (peacekeeping) operations. For example, no data are available for most interventions by the so called coalitions of the willing. Thus, Collier et al. (2008) concentrate on the question whether UN peacekeeping operations stabilize fragile post-conflict situations. Empirical examination suggests that UN peacekeeping expenditures significantly reduce the risk of renewed war. The effect is large: doubling expenditure reduces the risk from the benchmark 40 percent to 31 percent. Interestingly, this effect is strongest when peacekeeping expenditure is measured in absolute terms and not relative to the country's population or size of the economy, suggesting that UN peacekeeping operations do act as a deterrent. Since all rebel armies necessarily begin small—even if they subsequently grow to a formidable size—they can perhaps be effectively deterred in the inception phase by a peacekeeping force of a sufficient size.

Collier et al. (2008) also examine the impact of democracy on the duration of peace. The most interesting result is that elections do not appear to exert any systematic influence on the reduction of war risk. Elections shift the risk between years, rather than either raising or lowering it. Specifically, an election reduces risk in the year of the election, but increases it in the year following the election. Presumably, in the election year antagonists divert their efforts from violence to political contest, whereas once the election is concluded the losers have a stronger incentive to return to violence. Therefore, post-conflict elections should be promoted as intrinsically desirable rather than as mechanisms for increasing the durability of the post-conflict peace. Perhaps second post-conflict elections contribute more strongly to peace building; however, the sample of post-conflict societies with two post-conflict elections is too small for statistical analysis.

Figure 7.3 summarizes the impact of economic development, peacekeeping, and democracy on the risk of conflict recurrence. Based on these results, peace appears to depend upon an external UN military presence sustaining a gradual economic recovery, with political design playing a somewhat subsidiary role. There is strong evidence that the poorer the country is and the longer economic recovery takes the higher is the

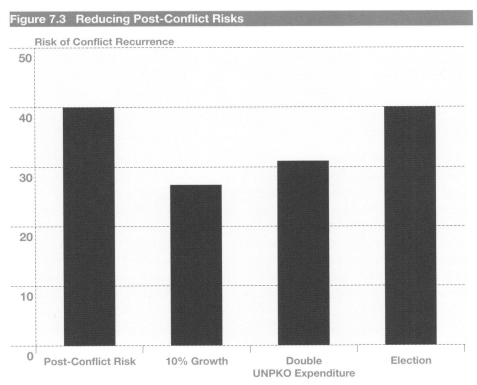

Figure 7.3 Reducing Post-Conflict Risks

Risk of Conflict Recurrence

(Bar chart with y-axis "Risk of Conflict Recurrence" from 0 to 50, and x-axis categories: Post-Conflict Risk, 10% Growth, Double UNPKO Expenditure, Election)

risk to revert to civil war. The simple and statistically strong relationship between the severity of post-conflict risks and the level of income at the end of the conflict provides a clear and simple principle for resource allocation: resources per capita should be approximately inversely proportional to the level of income in the post-conflict country. To date, economic and military resources have not been allocated on this simple principle.

What Can Be Done About State Failure?

Before turning to policy recommendations it may be useful to recall why state failure should receive international attention. First, there is a global consensus to prevent or end human suffering. In September 2005 the UN unanimously endorsed the Responsibility to Protect, which creates the right to intervene if a government relinquishes its responsibility to protect, whether by lack of will or lack of capacity.[3] "Responsibility to protect" is defined as protection of citizens from large-scale violent conflict that the government is either unwilling to prevent or incapable of preventing, but which international intervention could feasibly curtail.

Second, poverty reduction is not seen as an exclusively national responsibility. The Monterrey Consensus of 2002 formally recognizes the responsibilities of international aid donors as well as recipients.[4] The UN norm is that governments of OECD countries should contribute 0.7 percent of their national income as aid, with a counterpart responsibility of the governments of recipient countries to manage their affairs in such a way as to be conducive to poverty reduction. However, the threshold of policies and governance necessary for poverty reduction is currently less well defined than that for aid.

In an interconnected world, social and economic catastrophe in one country spills over onto neighbors. The cost to neighbors is by far the largest component. About 87 percent of the cost of state failure is borne by neighboring countries.

Third, in an interconnected world, social and economic catastrophe in one country spills over onto neighbors. In the estimate by Chauvet et al. (2006), the cost to neighbors is by far the largest component. About 87 percent of the cost of state failure is borne by neighboring countries. This estimate of regional costs does not include global costs: no attempt was made to calculate the cost of terrorism, the illegal drug trade, and human trafficking—to name a few consequences of state failure. These high regional costs may provide reasons to intervene in failing states and thus reduce the cost to neighboring nations. Whether it be humanitarian concerns regarding

---

3 The full text of UN Resolution A/RES/60/1 can be found at: *http://daccessdds.un.org/doc/UNDOC/GEN/N05/487/60/PDF/N0548760.pdf? OpenElement.* The responsibility to protect populations from genocide, war crimes, ethnic cleansing, and crimes against humanity is set out in paragraphs 138 and 139.

4 Full text at *http://www.un.org/esa/ffd/monterrey/MonterreyConsensus.pdf.*

security or poverty or the cost imposed on other countries, any intervention raises the difficult issue of the right to limit another nation's sovereignty.

What can be done to help failing states? The current debate is dominated by the discussion of development assistance. However, aid is likely to have a limited impact on state failure, and aid alone will not rescue failing states (Collier 2007). Ultimately, reform has to come from within the failing states, but international efforts can assist these internal reforms. The discussion turns to how internal reforms can turn around state failure before external efforts are debated.

> *Peace appears to depend upon an external UN military presence sustaining a gradual economic recovery, with political design playing a somewhat subsidiary role. There is strong evidence that the poorer the country is and the longer economic recovery takes the higher is the risk to revert to civil war.*

Internal Reforms: Achieving Accountability

Failing states do not provide sufficient public services to their citizens; a particular concern is public service delivery to the poor. Investment in health and education enables individuals to lead economically productive lives and to lift themselves out of poverty. There are many reasons why service delivery does not happen. Often there is insufficient public expenditure. In many cases corruption reduces the amount actually spent on public services. One important step to stamp out corruption is to improve accountability. In a democratic system where information on public expenditure is available and scrutinized, it is much more difficult to embezzle public money. One mechanism for ensuring that public money provides services to poor people is through public expenditure tracking surveys. These surveys show how much of the centrally allocated budget reaches the local service providers. Reinikka and Svensson (2004) pioneered these surveys in Uganda. They found that approximately 87 percent of the budget for primary education did not reach schools. They then staged a local campaign, informing teachers, parents, and pupils of how much money their school should receive. Using this information, local stakeholders demanded to know why they were receiving so little of the allocated funds. When these schools were visited two years later they received almost 90 percent of the allocated funds. There was still corruption, but improved transparency allowed local stakeholders to demand accountability and hence reduced the opportunity for corruption.

External Reforms

Collier (2007) lists a number of external initiatives that could help to turn around failed states. He focuses on trade and finance reforms and on the management of revenues from natural resources.

A reform of trade policies would provide new income-generating opportunities for poor countries. An obvious candidate for reform is the abolition of agricultural subsidies in rich countries. These subsidies for food and non-food items (e.g., cotton) in the United States and Europe are making it impossible for poorer countries to compete. But poor countries themselves have also generated trade distortions; their high import tariffs have generated industries in which profitability depends on lobbying rather than effective production.

Reform of the international financial system could make corruption more difficult. A large proportion of hot money leaves failing states and is invested in rich countries. For example, Baker (2005) estimates that about $25 billion of illegal funds leaves sub-Saharan Africa every year and is laundered outside the region. This is roughly equivalent to the amount of development aid the region receives. A higher degree of transparency would make it more difficult for international banks and funds to invest illegally acquired wealth, and tighter regulation of unaccountable offshore financial organizations would reduce the opportunities to send and launder money abroad.

The combined total cost of state failure ($270 billion) is much larger than the total amount of global development aid (about $80 billion). Currently, only a very few donors provide aid according to the UN target of 0.7 percent of national income. But even if all donor countries raised aid to the UN target, it would only amount to about $130 billion (i.e., to about half of the cost incurred due to state failure).

Many failed states are rich in natural resources, for example Angola, Chad, and Turkmenistan. In many cases, natural resources distort the economic and political system. The presence of natural resources also makes countries more conflict prone (Collier and Hoeffler 2004b; Collier et al. 2009). Typically, these economies remain undiversified, and their tax collection efforts are low. This hampers economic development and political accountability of governments to their citizens. Poor governance in countries rich in natural resources results in poverty, corruption, and war. A reform of trade in natural resources would not only increase income flows from international extraction companies to governments of poor countries but would also increase accountability and transparency. Some natural resource initiatives have already been started. The Extractive Industries Transparency Initiative supports improved governance in resource-rich countries through the verification and full publication of company payments and government revenues from oil, gas, and mining.[5] A further initiative is the Kimberly Process, a certification scheme that imposes extensive requirements on its members to certify shipments of rough diamonds as "conflict-free."[6] This results in reduced financing opportunities of rebel movements and thus lessens the risk of large-scale violent conflict.

---

[5] More information at *http://eitransparency.org/*.

[6] More information at *http://www.kimberleyprocess.com/*.

External Assistance

State failure was defined above in two ways: (1) the inability of the government to reduce poverty and (2) the inability of the government to provide security. Thus, the obvious possible remedies provided by third parties are aid and peacekeeping.

Economic Assistance

The combined total cost of state failure ($270 billion) is much larger than the total amount of global development aid (about $80 billion). Currently, only a very few donors provide aid according to the UN target of 0.7 percent of national income. But even if all donor countries raised aid to the UN target, it would only amount to about $130 billion (i.e., to about half of the cost incurred due to state failure). Thus, the total global aid effort is substantially less than what would be contributed by turning around failing states. Failing states and donors have to find ways to spend aid more effectively and to find new solutions to turning around poor governance. Often, aid tends to be dismissed as not being up to the task of bringing about change, or even as being part of the problem. This sentiment reflects the now widely held belief that donor conditionality, where donor countries provided aid conditional upon changes in governance, has failed. Moreover, research on aid also indicates that aid is only effective in good policy environments (Burnside and Dollar 2000). This would suggest that failing states cannot be turned around with external development assistance. However, Chauvet and Collier (2009) find that targeted aid can help failing states to achieve sustained turnarounds. First, they confirm the commonly held beliefs about aid. They present some evidence that external finance prior to reform, either additional rents on resource exports or aid, significantly retards reform. On the other hand, more targeted forms of aid can be effective in promoting policy turnarounds. Technical assistance significantly and substantially promotes reform, as does aid for the expansion of secondary education.

Military Assistance

States that have failed due to poor governance and economic policies are much more likely to experience large-scale violence. Unfortunately, these countries can then become stuck in a conflict trap: once they had a war, they are even more likely to experience another war. Cross-national studies suggest that increased domestic military expenditure does not deter renewed conflict, while UN peacekeeping does stabilize the peace. While there is international agreement that civilian security must be guaranteed, this agreement is currently not matched by an international willingness to organize, finance, and deploy military force. In 2005 the United Nations committed themselves to protect populations from genocide, war crimes, ethnic cleansing, and crimes against humanity. Although this Responsibility to Protect was endorsed unanimously, it has not led to a de facto change of United Nations' policies. A recent empirical study (Collier et al. 2008) suggests that doubling UN peacekeeping expenditure would significantly reduce the risk of renewed conflict. Doubling UN peacekeeping expenditure may seem fanciful; however, at its current level of roughly $7 billion, the UN peacekeeping budget is dwarfed by global military expenditure of about $1,300 billion (SIPRI Yearbook 2008). Thus, UN peacekeeping is less than half of a percent of total global military expenditure, and it should be feasible to significantly increase UN peacekeeping expenditure. An international rapid-reaction force could also help to prevent conflict recurrence. For example, the British military intervention in Sierra Leone was decisive in ending the civil war in 1999. Currently, only a very small number of troops are deployed, but there is a guarantee by the British government to send more troops on short notice if the security situation deteriorates. These "over the horizon guarantees" should make it possible to withdraw large numbers of troops and maintain a light footprint, once the security situation is stabilized. Currently, there is no international rapid-reaction force that could be deployed on short notice, as in the Sierra Leone example, although the European Commission is working towards creating such a force.

Conclusion

State failure means human misery in terms of poverty and insecurity for about 1 billion people worldwide. The international community faces the twin challenges of security and development. Ultimately, reforms have to come from within failed states. But as outlined above, reforms of international markets, a more effective use of development assistance, as well as increased UN peacekeeping can help to turn around failed states. To help reduce poverty and prevent failing states from becoming stuck in a conflict trap, comprehensive assistance strategies that consist of military assistance (peacekeeping) as well as targeted, longer-term development aid are needed.

8. DEMOCRATIZATION AND POST-CONFLICT TRANSITIONS

Håvard Hegre and Hanne Fjelde

Democratization is often suggested as a means to prevent post-conflict societies from reverting back to war. This chapter will review the empirical literature that evaluates the accuracy of this claim. One certain conclusion is that an increasing number of countries are post-conflict democracies. As Hewitt (Chapter 3) discusses, a large number of internal armed conflicts have ended over the last 15 years, and encouragingly few new conflicts have started.[1] The second graph in Figure 3.2 in Chapter 3 shows the trends in the number of new onsets, as well as recurrences, over the 1960–2007 period. It is clear that in the most recent years, a majority of conflict eruptions have been recurrences of old conflicts.

A country with a legacy of armed conflict is at a far higher risk to experience a new conflict than are countries with no such previous experience. At the same time, the surge of terminations after the Cold War left behind a large number of post-conflict societies. These recent trends have made the management of post-conflict transitions much more important than before. Policy interventions that succeed in preventing recurrences have become the key elements in avoiding future armed conflict.

Can democracy break this "conflict trap?"[2] Democratic institutions are designed to allow individuals and social groups to sort out their differences in a regulated and nonviolent manner. UN peacekeeping operations, possibly the main reason for the decline in the incidence of conflict over the past 15 years, are frequently coupled with provisions to strengthen democratic institutions. Indeed, influential voices within the international community hold the establishment of political parties and the holding of elections as the main vehicles to promote societal reconciliation and peace in polarized and conflict-ridden societies. For example, the war-to-democracy transitions in Namibia, Kosovo, Liberia, and Afghanistan all envisage this approach. Data from the Uppsala Conflict Data Program show that the most common provision in peace accords for resolving conflicts over government power is elections (Jarstad and Sisk 2008: 3). Scholars even include the retention of democratic institutions as a criterion for "peace-building success" (c.f. Doyle and Sambanis 2000).

Partly a result of the international community's efforts, an increasing proportion of post-conflict societies are governed by some form of

---

This chapter draws on research funded by the Norwegian Research Council grant no. 163115/V10. Thanks to Mimmi Söderberg Kovacs for comments and language editing.
1 For other reviews of trends in armed conflicts, see Harbom, et al. (2008) and Gleditsch et al. (2002).
2 See Collier et al. (2003) for a discussion of the conflict trap.

democratic regime.[3] These efforts have also coincided with a global trend of democratization. In Chapter 4 (Figure 4.1), Pate reports the global distribution of democracy, autocracy, and semi-democracy (termed anocracies in that chapter) for the period 1945–2007.[4] The "third wave of democratization" (Huntington 1991) is evident in the figure. In 1970, 53 percent of the countries were non-democratic. In 2007, only 16 percent lack any democratic institutions, and 58 percent are fully democratic. The exact relationship between democratization and conflict, however, is ambiguous. While the overall decline in the number of conflicts since the early 1990s coincided with an increase in the number of democratic and semi-democratic institutions, a surge in the number of armed conflicts occurred during the early phase of this wave in the 1970s, suggesting that the infusion of many new democracies at that time had no conflict-inhibiting impact.

The wave of democratization is also reflected in the political institutions of post-conflict societies, as shown in Figure 8.1. In 1970, 11 percent of the post-conflict countries were democratic. In 2007, this figure had risen to 47 percent. Even though this figure is lower than among non-conflict countries, it means that an unprecedented share of the countries that experience a post-conflict transition now has some form of democratic regime. Is the surge of post-conflict democracy likely to help manage post-conflict transitions and prevent the recurrence of armed conflicts?

Our review indicates that democratic institutions in themselves have limited impact on the risk of conflict recurrence. This is partly because democracy has an ambiguous effect on the risk of armed conflict in general, and partly because armed conflict in many cases undermines the requirements for creating stable democracy. Democracy is desirable in itself, but the role of democratization in post-conflict transitions is complex because factors necessary to stabilize democracy also are essential to avoid violent conflict, and vice versa.

Do Democratic Institutions Reduce the Risk of Post-Conflict Recurrence?

Democracy has become the standard approach to peace-building in post-conflict societies, despite the fact that democracy is not sufficient to prevent armed conflict in general. When we take into account the fact that most democracies are high-income countries, they are no less likely to experience internal conflict onsets than non-democracies (Muller and Weede 1990; Hegre et al. 2001; Fearon and Laitin 2003). Moreover, semi-democracies— regimes that are partly democratic, partly autocratic—have the highest risk of civil war onset. Democracies are not in a better position to end conflicts, either. A number of studies find no link between regime type and duration of conflict (Collier et al. 2004; Fearon 2004; de Rouen and Sobek 2004). Gleditsch et al. (2009) even find democracies to have longer conflicts than

---

3 As is the convention in the literature, we regard a country as in a post-conflict state in the first ten years after the conflict terminated (or at least ceased to be very violent).

4 The figure also includes countries that are in regime transition.

Figure 8.1 Political Systems among Post-Conflict Countries, 1960–2007

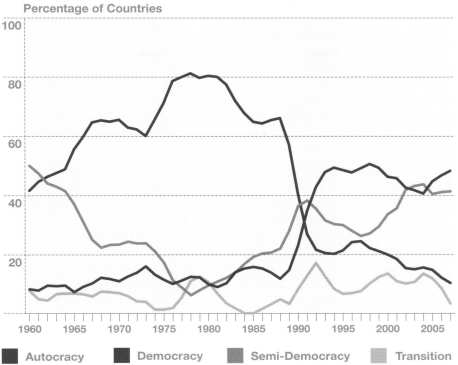

Percentage of Countries

■ Autocracy   ■ Democracy   ■ Semi-Democracy   ■ Transition

other regime types, as exemplified by the conflicts in Colombia, Sri Lanka, and Northeast India.

Why are democratic institutions unable to accommodate dissent in a nonviolent manner and avoid armed conflicts? One possible explanation is that armed conflicts and dissent are very different phenomena. Some scholars dismiss the idea that internal conflicts are fought by broad social groups that aim to redress injustice or grievances. Rather, they contend, most rebel groups are narrow "conflict entrepreneurs" that use organized violence to further private gains—they are motivated by "greed" rather than "grievance" (Collier and Hoeffler 2004). Indeed, Collier (2000) argues convincingly that the financial requirements of rebellion and the logic of collective action force actors that seek justice either to use other means of protest, or to run a serious risk of degenerating into more narrow forms of rebellion. Economic factors, such as the opportunities for financing the insurgency, are thus much more important predictors of conflict than the setup of the political system. Democratic institutions may even be better targets for such "loot-seeking" rebels, as they are constrained from using brutal but effective counter-insurgency strategies (Hegre 2003; Collier and Rohner 2008). This may be why democracies often become embroiled in very long conflicts.

Democratic institutions have a mixed record in preventing the onset of new conflicts. Do democratic institutions succeed better in preventing the *recurrence* of violent conflict in post-conflict societies? Surely, the benefits of finding institutional mechanisms for negotiating conflicting interests are particularly salient in polarized societies emerging from conflict. Ideally, inclusive democratic institutions should reduce the ability of the winner to permanently exclude former adversaries, or renege on promises on political concessions (Mukherjee, 2006a, 2006b). They provide former combatants with nonviolent channels through which they can seek government reform and representation in order to redress grievances (Walter 2004, Wallensteen 2007).

Unfortunately, in spite of the salience of establishing legitimate and responsive authority in post-conflict societies, there is no conclusive evidence that democratic institutions do better in post-conflict settings than they do in general in terms of avoiding conflict recurrence. Just as for all conflict onsets, conflicts recur most frequently among semi-democracies (7.7 percent of post-conflict country-years). They happen least frequently among democracies (3.9 percent), with non-democracies in-between (6.0 percent). There are three possible explanations for the conflict-preventing failure of semi-democracies. First, such institutions open up for popular participation and organization of opposition groups but do not allow the opposition influence consistent with their electoral strength, creating incentives for violent insurrections. Second, the very fact that they are not fully democratic signifies that a struggle is going on over the setup of the institutions, a struggle that may turn violent. Third, semi-democracies are often newly established and often located in poor and middle-income countries, making it harder for them to apply the resources necessary to maintain stability. In fact, much of the difference between regime types can be explained by differences in income levels—democracies have a low risk of conflict because they are rich, not because they are democratic. Controlling for income, the empirical evidence suggests that democracies in general, and new democracies in particular, have a higher likelihood of conflict recurrence than non-democracies (Quinn et al. 2007; Collier et al. 2008c). In fact, Flores and Nooruddin (2009: 18) suggest that transitions away from democracy are the best institutional guarantor against short-term recurrence. Collier et al. (2008) also suggest that non-autocracies have a greater risk of reverting to conflict than do full autocracies. The majority of the non-autocracies in their sample of post-conflict societies are semi-democracies, however, and such countries have a higher risk of conflict in all situations.

It is hard to dismiss the conclusion that democratization does little to reduce the risk of conflict recurrence. Figure 8.2, however, suggests that the effect of democracy may be changing. The figure shows the development over time in the annual proportion of post-conflict countries that revert to conflict (without control for income). Up to the mid 1990s, it is hard to distinguish any differences among the three regime types. From then on, however, the few remaining non-democracies appear to have the highest

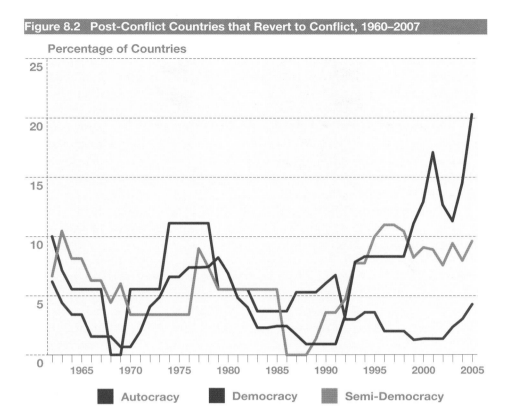

Figure 8.2 Post-Conflict Countries that Revert to Conflict, 1960–2007

Percentage of Countries

Autocracy   Democracy   Semi-Democracy

risk of conflict recurrence, and democracies have the lowest. It is too early to draw firm conclusions regarding these trends, however.

Above, we discussed the risk of conflict recurrence in post-conflict societies in general. Since the Cold War, the share of conflicts that end in some form of negotiated settlement, rather than for example military victory, is increasing (Kreutz 2010). How do democratic institutions influence the durability of peace agreements? Some scholars argue that belligerents with previous experience from democratic institutions are more likely to craft durable, negotiated settlements (Hartzell et al. 2001). However, the weight of the evidence seems to suggest otherwise, giving no support to the idea that democratic regimes have more durable peace agreements (Hartzell and Hoddie 2003; Fortna 2004; Nilsson 2006).

Does the presence of democratic provisions in peace agreements matter more than regime type for the durability of the agreements? In a majority of cases, peace-building efforts entail components that are related to democracy, without necessarily satisfying the standard definition of such institutions. Political power-sharing arrangements—e.g., joint control of the executive office or minority veto-powers—are included in post-conflict settlements to guarantee representation to all groups, to promote moderate and cooperative behavior among contending groups, and to minimize the danger that any conflict party can become dominant and threaten the security of others (Walter 1999; Roeder and Rothchild 2005; Jarstad and

Nilsson, 2008).[5] The quantitative literature does not support the notion that political power-sharing in general enhances the durability of peace, and this holds independently of whether such democratic provisions are implemented or not (Hoddie and Hartzell 2005; Jarstad and Nilsson 2008a; Mukherjee 2006a).

Why Do Democratic Institutions Perform Poorly?

Post-conflict democratization, then, does not decrease the risk of conflict recurrence and may even exacerbate the situation. What explains this lackluster performance? We identify three particular obstacles to democratic governance in post-conflict societies: the socio-economic legacy from the earlier conflict; the unconsolidated character of democratic institutions; and the limits of "warlord democracy." Moreover, we show that elections are a particular challenge to post-conflict democracies.

Post-conflict democratization, then, does not decrease the risk of conflict recurrence and may even exacerbate the situation.

First, the legacy of violent conflict undermines the ability of democratic institutions to function optimally. Conflict not only exacerbates the conditions that increase the risk of conflict, it also erodes democracy or conditions that facilitate democratization (Collier et al. 2003). Conflicts hamper economic growth and increase poverty by destroying physical infrastructure, deterring economic investment and scaring off mobile capital. This increases the economy's dependence on conflict-inducing natural resources, and worsens the fiscal balance of the state (Collier 1999; Murdoch and Sandler 2002). These effects increase both the risk of conflict and of democratic reversals. Furthermore, conflicts tend to deepen cleavages between social groups since recruitment to rebel groups tends to follow ethnic lines (Gates 2002). These changes increase the risk of conflict recurrence, giving rise to a "conflict trap." But the same factors also impede democratization, as well as endangering the survival of democracy once installed. Democratic political institutions are less stable in poor, slow-growing, and natural resource-dependent economies (Gates et al. 2006; Przeworski et al. 2000).

Second, many post–civil war democracies are new democracies. Several studies document democratization during wars. A frequently cited figure is that nearly 40 percent of all civil wars that took place between 1945 and 1993 resulted in an improvement in the level of democracy (Wantchekon 2004). Other quantitative studies also find a positive effect of civil war on the likelihood of democracy in the country (Rost and Booth 2008; Chen et al. 2008), suggesting that such cases as Indonesia, Mozambique, and

---

5 These characteristics are not fully reconcilable with the idea of democracy, as we have shown above. The spirit of democracy is competition and uncertainty in the outcome. Power-sharing arrangements are, on the other hand, explicitly designed to reduce uncertainty, generate predictable outcomes, and prevent a single social group from monopolizing state power (Gates and Ström 2009).

Bangladesh that democratized during conflict are quite common.[6] Post-conflict democracies consequently tend to share the characteristics of newly established democracies, which tend to lack formal (e.g., legislative checks) and informal (e.g., moderating influence from civil society) institutions to keep leaders accountable (Flores and Nooruddin 2009). Within these weak institutions, it is difficult for politicians to make credible commitments to limit competition to peaceful means vis-à-vis the electorate, economic investors, and conflict adversaries (Clague et al. 1996; Keefer 2007; Flores and Nooruddin 2009). Several scholars recognize the perils associated with immature democracy and the problems of committing to a peaceful post-conflict order (Paris 2004; Walter 1999). The fragility of post-war democratic institutions may contribute to the high risk of war recurrence, just as changes to formal political institutions—including democratization—increase the risk of conflict onset in general (Hegre et al. 2001; Snyder 2000).

Third, the democratic institutions implemented after civil war might be very different from democratization that follow a peaceful authoritarian breakdown. Whereas democratization after autocratic breakdown implies a shift in the balance of power in favor of more moderate elements of a democratic opposition, democratization after civil war rarely entails a democratic opposition with support from society. Instead, political compromise must be negotiated between warring factions, themselves militant, undemocratic, and sectarian (Söderberg Kovacs 2008). According to Wantchekon (2004), post-conflict democracy is essentially a tool for elite cooperation in the process of creating political order, playing down issues of accountability and representation.

In sum, post-conflict democratic institutions are severely hampered by the very same factors that make conflicts likely to recur. Internal armed conflicts are struggles over the control of government. Hence, democratic institutions are only as effective as conflict resolution mechanisms insofar as they are able to withstand the pressures that undermine their very institutions. But post-conflict stability and democratization are not incompatible goals, since democracy thrives under the same conditions as does peace.

> *Post-conflict democratic institutions are severely hampered by the very same factors that make conflicts likely to recur. But post-conflict stability and democratization are not incompatible goals, since democracy thrives under the same conditions as does peace.*

Elections, however, constitute a particular challenge to post-conflict democracies. Elections are an integral element in establishing legitimate and democratic government in post-conflict societies, and are often used as a mechanism to end the conflict-to-peace transition. There is no evidence,

6 The counterfactual in these studies, however, is not well defined. As shown above, most countries in the world have democratized. Indonesia and Mozambique might have democratized even quicker if they had not been at war. Chen et al. (2008) discern a tendency toward democratization among post-conflict countries, but they do not perform better than relevant non-conflict comparisons. Armed conflicts may have a tendency to make non-democracies more authoritarian and hinder semi-democracies from becoming fully democratic, but the patterns are not strong (Hegre et al. 2007).

however, that post-war elections reduce the risk of conflict recurrence in the short term. Election periods are associated with a heightened risk of civil war overall. This is particularly true in semi-democratic regimes where open and broad participation tends to coincide with weak executive constraints, which increases the value of holding political office (Strand 2007). In post-conflict situations, moreover, the uncertainty surrounding elections is endemic. In the words of Reilly (2008: 164) "institutions are weak or non-existent, voters are suspicious and elites' hold on power is tenuous." Elites will often hold elections aiming to legitimize their rule, but with no real intention of deferring power if they lose. For political entrepreneurs, elections provide opportunities to capitalize on popular discontent and thus exacerbate societal conflict (Paris 2004; Höglund et al. 2009). In this context, the stakes of the electoral contest are high, thus increasing incentives to contest power through violent means. Post-war elections lead to a temporal shift in the risk of conflict recurrence—reducing it the year of the elections, but increasing it the year after the elections (Collier et al. 2008). The net effect is a modestly increased risk, adding to the conflict proneness of non-autocracies in the short-term. The first and second elections seem to be the critical test. After that, the risk of violence decreases.

Should Democracy Be a Goal of Post-Conflict Reconstruction?

Democratization cannot be expected to reduce risk of conflict recurrence on its own, and may also bring in some new challenges with which non-democratic post-conflict countries do not have to deal. This, however, does not imply that democratization should be avoided in countries coming out of conflict.

First, democracy obviously has an intrinsic value beyond its effect on conflict recurrence. Even if a switch to autocratic governments could enhance the stability of post-conflict society in the short term, there are strong normative grounds to promote legitimate and democratic institutions in societies emerging from war. There are also conflict-related reasons to support democracy in the long term. We know that democratic institutions are by far the most stable and durable forms of government if democratization culminates in consistent democracy (Gates et al. 2006; Epstein et al. 2006). The main rewards of democratization, however, are harvested many years after the post-conflict transition is completed. The first hurdle is to come through the first couple of elections. After this, the stability of consolidated democracies serves to decrease the risk of further armed conflict and other forms of serious political conflict, and thereby provide growth-conducive environments that can generate a virtuous circle. The stability of democratic institutions, moreover, tends to spill over onto their neighbors. Countries located close to democratic regimes have fewer internal conflicts and regime changes than their domestic characteristics imply (Gleditsch et al. 2002; Hegre and Sambanis 2006). Democratization certainly has advantages, but they tend to lie beyond the immediate post-conflict transition.

Democracies have also been shown to have less brutal wars than other regime types (Colaresi and Carey 2008; Gleditsch et al. 2009). In the event of conflict recurrence, democratization may possibly reduce the costs of the subsequent war, even if democratic institutions may tend to increase the duration of the war.

Moreover, we cannot evaluate the counter-factual in the turbulent cases. What would unstable post-conflict societies with democratic institutions have looked like if they were not democratic? Creating a stable political order is more difficult where the societal and economic costs of protracted conflict are high, and where society is polarized along ethnic and religious lines. These might also be conditions that increase the international pressure for political power sharing and other democratic institutions.

Democratization cannot be expected to reduce risk of conflict recurrence on its own, and may also bring in some new challenges with which non-democratic post-conflict countries do not have to deal. This, however, does not imply that democratization should be avoided in countries coming out of conflict.

Figure 8.3 shows the share of democracies that are in a post-conflict phase. Figure 8.4 and Figure 8.5 show the same information for semi-democracies and non-democracies. The figures demonstrate that the surge in conflict terminations just after the Cold War left behind a large number of post-conflict countries, an increasing proportion of which have democratic regimes. This change is partly due to the general global wave of democratization and partly because the United Nations and other international actors push to establish democratic institutions as part of post-conflict peacekeeping operations. Considering whether democratization is desirable or not may be an increasingly theoretical and irrelevant exercise given this trend. Below, we make some recommendations for what can be done to assist these countries.

Conclusion

The management of post-conflict transitions has become more important over the last decades—a reality made clear by recent trends on conflict recurrence reported in this chapter and by Hewitt in Chapter 3. The international community has encouraged post-conflict democratic institutions, partly motivated by a hope that they will help societies avoid recurrence of conflicts. Our review, however, shows that democratic post-conflict countries are no better at avoiding conflict recurrence than other regime types. Semi-democracies—democracies combined with autocratic features—fare even worse. The poor record of post-conflict democracy, we find, is partly explained by the fact that internal armed conflicts undermine the very conditions that allow democracies to be stable and effective. Moreover, if reversion to armed conflict is possible, the overturning of the democratic institutions often follows suit. This is particularly true when the democratic institutions were introduced as part of a peace agreement.

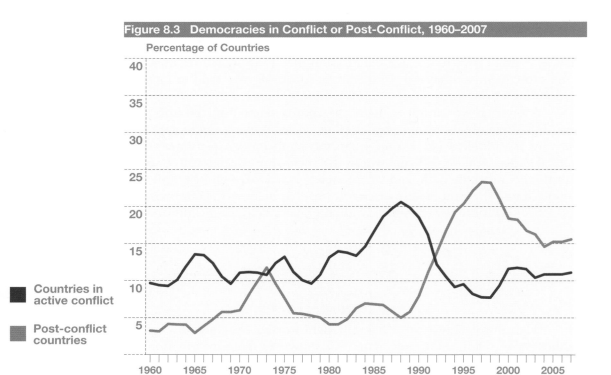

Figure 8.3 Democracies in Conflict or Post-Conflict, 1960–2007

Percentage of Countries

Countries in active conflict

Post-conflict countries

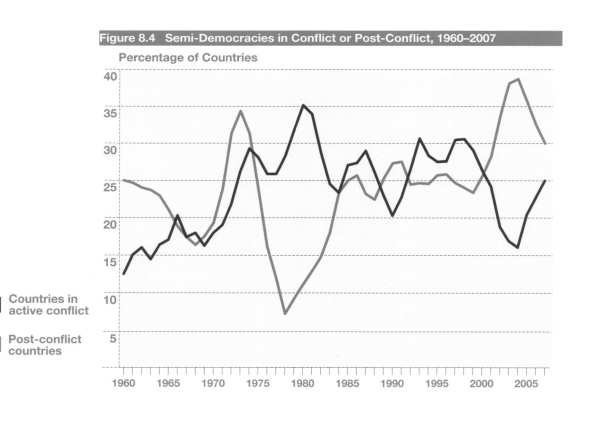

Figure 8.4 Semi-Democracies in Conflict or Post-Conflict, 1960–2007

Percentage of Countries

Countries in active conflict

Post-conflict countries

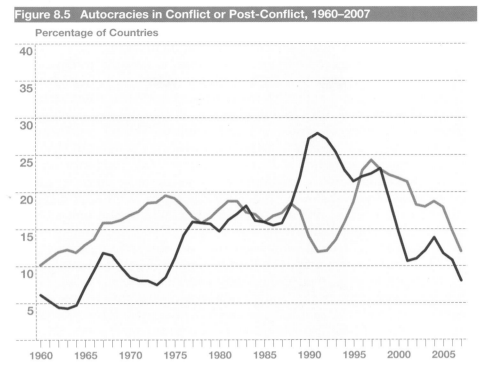

Figure 8.5 Autocracies in Conflict or Post-Conflict, 1960–2007

Percentage of Countries

Countries in active conflict

Post-conflict countries

At the same time, in recent years post-conflict countries more frequently have democratic institutions. What are the policy recommendations from our review? The first thing to note is that the same conditions that weaken the durability of post-conflict peace and security also undermine the stability of newly established democratic institutions. Accordingly, policies that have been found effective in reducing post-conflict risks, such as growth-promoting aid, also work in favor of democratic stability. We will comment briefly on three particularly important topics: rapid economic recovery, protection of elections, and decentralization of power.

Several studies show that economic growth, reduction of unemployment, and diversification of the economy (i.e., reducing natural resource dependence) are important conditions both for promoting democratic stability and avoiding conflict recurrence. Economic growth has important short-term effects, but the long-term impact is also to solidify democratic institutions through the strengthening of a middle class and a civil society with the means to monitor elected leaders.

Elections are particularly dangerous events in post-conflict democracies. Delaying elections in post-conflict societies is rarely a viable (nor desirable) option, but the effective monitoring of elections by international peacekeepers probably reduces the risk of conflict recurrence. These activities should be scaled up and extended at least to the second post-conflict election, which has been shown to be the most dangerous. It has been argued that peacekeeping operations tend to crowd out domestic processes and thereby slow down a transition to a complete and autonomous democratic regime. When the risk of renewed conflict is high, however, they are indispensable as protection of the democratic institutions that do function.

The most important lesson, we believe, is that the international community may have been overly focused on the holding of elections at the expense of accountability. Electoral regimes with few constraints on the executive are particularly civil war–prone. Without proper constraints, elections are contests for extremely lucrative offices. Hence, the incentives for using violence are necessarily larger than when the winners of elections are held properly accountable to the electorate. Any insistence on the holding of elections must be accompanied by an insistence on transparency and accountability, as well as on the active support of institutions designed to monitor the political systems such as general auditors and independent judiciaries. One should also note that some power-sharing arrangements may be detrimental to this aim when they decrease accountability. This should be taken into account by mediators in peace negotiations.

Efforts to strengthen civil society and an independent media are other policy interventions that could promote accountability by supporting the electorate's ability to monitor and check the executive. Also, promoting decentralization of power, partly through local governance, partly through strengthening other branches of government, such as the parliament, may also lessen the stakes of the electoral contest.

9. WOMEN AND POST-CONFLICT SETTINGS

Mary Caprioli, Rebecca Nielsen, and Valerie M. Hudson

War and conflict are often considered to be "male" activities. Initiating, prosecuting, and ending conflict have also been seen as the province of men. However, in recent years these unspoken gendered assumptions about war and peace have been challenged. In this chapter, we will survey what is known about the effects of including or excluding women from post-conflict decision making.

Conflict transforms society in ways we do not yet fully understand—demographics change, internal migration and emigration across borders occur, and with the breakdown of civil society during civil war, there may be very little security for the remaining population. The greatest threats in the post-conflict period include violence, disease, and famine. Women, in particular, experience reduced security in the wake of conflict, which may manifest itself in rape and domestic violence. They may become heads of household or homeless, become soldiers, or be forced into prostitution. Their burden of care for persons injured in the fighting, or for children born of rape, increases tremendously. Deniz Kandiyoti, who recently completed a project on the politics of gender and reconstruction in Afghanistan, notes that "women and men experience conflict and war differently; they may be exposed to different types of hazard and vulnerability and have different stakes in peace-building and stability" (2008: 161). Clearly, women are not peripheral to war, but at the same time, they may be "invisibilized" by war and its aftermath.

Indeed, while men may constitute a majority of deaths in battle, recent statistical analyses of total deaths resulting from war indicate a higher death rate for women than men for both interstate and intrastate war. Women certainly bear greater burdens in the post-war period, which may include a "post-war backlash against women" as societies try to return to the pre-war status quo by relegating women to traditional subordinate roles. Other research suggests that women may acquiesce in this because they prioritize the restoration of peaceful relationships with men, rather than risk further conflict pursuing rights for themselves. Furthermore, even foreigners who influence the recovery period may marginalize women; for example, one Kosovar woman stated,

> It is really amazing . . . that the international community cared only about Kosovar women when they were being raped—and then only as some sort of exciting story. We see now that they really don't give a damn about us. What we see here are men, men, men from Europe and America, and even Asia, listening to men, men, men from Kosovo. (quote in Rehn and Sirleaf 2002: 125)

Given the profound effect of war on women and those whom women care for, it may seem obvious that women should not be sidelined during negotiations to bring the conflict to an end. And yet, women are, generally speaking, notably absent from such negotiations. Indeed, the Women in Armed Conflict section of the 1995 Beijing Platform for Action specifically called for increased women's participation in conflict resolution and decision making, and the October 2000 UN Security Council Resolution 1325 calls for increased participation of women in peacemaking, peacekeeping, and peace negotiations. While women may influence outcomes through grassroots movements and with the help of NGOs, they are often in practice excluded from the formal peace process. Furthermore, several notable "truth commissions" and "war crimes tribunals" operating in post-conflict environments have specifically exempted sexual violation and other abuses predominantly experienced by women, such as sexual slavery and forced pregnancy, from their mandate, even when they regard sexual violence perpetrated upon men as torture. The International Crimes Court, however, considers such crimes under universal jurisdiction as war crimes and crimes against humanity—but not as torture or genocide. As will be discussed, this exclusion of sexual violence against women as torture may have profound consequences for a sustainable peace.

The greatest threats in the post-conflict period include violence, disease, and famine. Women, in particular, experience reduced security in the wake of conflict, which may manifest itself in rape and domestic violence. They may become heads of household or homeless, become soldiers, or be forced into prostitution.

Gender-based violence can take forms other than rape. Denial of reproductive rights or access to AIDS medication needed as a result of rape, or obstruction of a woman's ability to economically maintain herself and her loved ones in the post-conflict period because she may not be accorded the same rights as a male head of household must also be considered in this regard. There are many decisions to be made with reference to the rebuilding and restructuring of societal institutions in the post-conflict period, and when these decisions are made in gender-blind fashion, gendered harm can result.

Similarly, reconstitution of government in the post-conflict period may hold special peril for women's legal rights. In both Afghanistan and Iraq, new constitutions took away from women certain rights of personal status that had existed under previous constitutions and also enshrined Islamic law as supreme. On the other hand, such newly reconstituted states as Afghanistan have acceded to international conventions, such as Convention on the Elimination of All Forms of Discrimination Against Women (CEDAW)—indeed, in the case of Afghanistan, without reservation—which will mandate official attention to women's rights and have accepted quotas for women in national legislatures.

The Peacetime-Wartime Continuum for Women

An understanding of the dynamics of the post-conflict period must start with the realization that in terms of gender-based violence, while men may perceive a discontinuity between peacetime and wartime, women perceive a continuum. For example, Kandiyoti illustrates how during peacetime Afghani women are subject to "forced prostitution, forced labor, and practices akin to slavery (abduction and forced marriage, exchange of women to settle disputes, or marriage in exchange for debt repayment)" (2008: 165). Some studies indicate that up to 80 percent of Afghan women experience physical abuse at the hands of their husbands. Such circumstances may cause women to feel that they live in a war zone, even if it is considered peacetime by men in the society and the international community. Similarly, after a conflict, the social barriers against rape and assault may be so lowered that while the war may have ended for men, it continues for women. As a result, what "peace" means for women may be very different from what it means for men in the society; it follows then that how women would build peace might also be very different than how men would build it.

An understanding of the dynamics of the post-conflict period must start with the realization that in terms of gender-based violence, while men may perceive a discontinuity between peacetime and wartime, women perceive a continuum.

A number of studies show a linkage between the security of women and the security of states (see Hudson et al. 2009). While many have taken note of the "democratic peace," which observes that societal systems based on democracy and equality are less likely to be violent and tend to be more prosperous, not as many acknowledge that women's greater equality in the household may have been the historically necessary precursor to democracy. The anomalous loosening of patriarchy in northwestern Europe, including gradual elimination of polygamy, teen marriage for girls, and patrilocality, uniquely led to the rise of both democracy and capitalism in northwestern Europe. Thus gender equity is an integral, not peripheral, aspect of peace.

The empirical evidence for this linkage is now fairly solid. Assessing the underlying social conditions leading to domestic conflict is not new, though the examination of women's status as it relates to enduring peace is a relatively new phenomenon. Gender equality has been shown to reduce the likelihood of intrastate conflict. Gender inequality has a considerable impact on civil war—an impact directly linked to the inherent hierarchical norms of discrimination and violence of inequality. In short, the higher the level of gender inequality, the greater the likelihood that a state will experience intrastate conflict. Low GDP per capita and aggressive nationalist rhetoric incite civil war, yet women's equality increases the likelihood of an enduring peace both in that women's equality increases GDP per capita and it negates nationalist calls to violence, which are often based on gender inequality.

In sum, building a sustainable peace after conflict by necessity involves attention to the gender hierarchy that fuels conflict. Furthermore, women may be the only vestiges of civil society left after a particularly intense conflict, and gender-blind policies will undermine women in their quest to rebuild lives, families, and communities. There will be no sustainable peace for men or for states unless there is also peace for women.

Women, Negotiations, and the Post-Conflict Environment

An examination of the situation and agency of women in post-conflict situations includes both practical and strategic considerations. These two sets of concerns are certainly interrelated, but "seeing" important practical considerations may depend on prior recognition of more strategic or global aspects of the situation at hand. For example, adopting a more strategic view of women in post-conflict scenarios will naturally lead to the identification of practical policy concerns.

If women are viewed by the society at large as not having a valuable perspective that may be of use in reconstruction and negotiation, then men may be assumed capable of speaking for women. If it is assumed that men are capable of speaking for women, then women will not be included in the councils of decision making during reconstruction, or in peace negotiations.

In a society where women are presumed to be dependents of men, for example, women are placed in a tenuous position after armed conflict. That is, it may be difficult to see women as heads of households with full property rights and decision making power for the family, even though they may in fact occupy that role due to the death or wounding of male relatives. If it is difficult for women to be seen as heads of households, it will be much more problematic for them to provide for dependents after conflict. For example, ration cards may only be provided to heads of households. If women are not easily seen as heads of households, they may be overlooked in projects meant to reconstruct agriculture and business within the society, such as loans, grants of seeds or fertilizer, education, and job training. If women are unable to provide for themselves or dependents, they often become the prey of traffickers.

If women are marginalized, they will be reluctant in the post-conflict scene to speak up about atrocities that have occurred to them and to other women, for reasons of traditional shame from assaults, such as rape. Women might be cast out from their families if they speak of their atrocities. In honor/shame societies, atrocities against women will go unpunished, for even the woman herself will not admit they occurred. This has stymied several war crimes tribunals attempting to prosecute those who committed rape in war—women will not testify. When war crimes tribunals are headed by officials from honor/shame cultures, they may downplay the importance of actively prosecuting those who committed atrocities against women.

If women are viewed by the society at large as not having a valuable perspective that may be of use in reconstruction and negotiation, then men may be assumed capable of speaking for women. If it is assumed that men are capable of speaking for women, then women will not be included in the councils of decision making during reconstruction, or in peace negotiations. Combatants' voices may carry more weight in peace negotiations, marginalizing women.

It should be noted that the United Nations is in the process of "gender mainstreaming" all of its organizations and operations, including its peacekeeping operations, with an eye to incorporating gender-sensitivity into all stages of planning and management. However, there is considerable distance between objectives and performance. While waiting for the United Nations to practice what it has begun to preach, are there other important paths to acknowledging and improving the gendered reality of the post-conflict period?

Perhaps due to a holistic view of security that includes social and economic issues, incorporating women in political negotiation tends to solidify conflict resolution. Women are often the peace promoters and play an indispensable role in preventing war and sustaining peace.

One important path is to include women in the formal negotiation process. Research indicates that women may be predisposed to certain styles of leadership through socialization. For example, men make more personal attacks and interrupt more often during debates, and the male approach to negotiations is associated with competition, violence, intransigence, and territoriality. Rather than imposing a unilateral solution, women tend to take a more cooperative approach to dispute resolution and are less likely to support the use of violence for dispute resolution. "Despite what they have experienced, many of the women … have been able to rise to the challenge of building a sustainable peace, recognizing that the security and satisfaction of one side can never be based on the frustration or humiliation of the other" (Rehn and Sirleaf 2002: 31).

Girls are encouraged to be empathetic and to learn about others. Perhaps as a consequence, women have an understanding of self in relation to others—on average women have a greater ability for relatedness, emotional closeness, and emotional flexibility. This extends to mutual empowerment and mutual self-esteem. According to scholars, women form mutual relationships, defined as those in which a symbiotic relationship occurs with flexible interaction and both receptivity and active initiative toward the other. According to Newt Gingrich, "Listening does not mean obeying, or even agreeing"; mutual respect is necessary for trust and this stems from "an appreciation and understanding of the other person's point of view. There is no obligation to accept or act upon the advice that is offered. The sole obligation is to understand the other side's perspective" (2008: 69).

Consequently, women may be more cooperative and collaborative because they value the process of communication. Being more likely to communicate than men, they are thus more free to share ideas and create a mutual understanding. Indeed, women tend to define themselves by their connection to others, while men may define themselves as distinct from others.

The degree of violence during a civil war, however, appears to be related to the extent of progress for women in political representation in the aftermath—government collapse offers women a window of opportunity, while gendered violence provides the motivation for political activism.

Perhaps due to a holistic view of security that includes social and economic issues, incorporating women in political negotiation tends to solidify conflict resolution. Women are often the peace promoters and play an indispensable role in preventing war and sustaining peace. Citing examples from Rwanda and Scandinavia, Ramdas argues that "[G]reater female political participation consistently leads to more even handed policy making" (2008: 69). As such, greater female participation may help establish a stable peace.

For example, though women also participate in combat, their primary roles during conflict are focused on support and survival: obtaining food, building homes, caring for and educating children, small-scale production, and other domestic concerns. As a result, women in the aftermath have collectively greater practical experience when it comes to making important decisions concerning the economy, food security, and social programs than men who have spent the previous years traversing the country with guns. In a study of Sierra Leone, Molloy (2004) shows how women tend to discourage "spoilers" by urging men to participate in demobilization programs and calling for punitive action against human rights violators. Molloy argues that women empowered by formal inclusion will address the needs of society or the causes of conflict and avoid narrow agreements focused on the demands of warring parties.

Catastrophic State Failure as Opportunity for Women

We know that third-party intervention in terms of state building does not seem to help or hurt women. The degree of violence during a civil war, however, appears to be related to the extent of progress for women in political representation in the aftermath—government collapse offers women a window of opportunity, while gendered violence provides the motivation for political activism. In trying to explain the success of gender quotas in African parliaments, Britton (2006) finds that female MPs are most influential when they form coalitions based on a "shared identity of subordination and/or a shared belief in the necessity of group mobilization to resist or alter that subordination." Wartime experiences may contribute to such a shared identity. She also suggests that states are more successful in implementing legislative gender quotas in newly constituted governments because there are no incumbents to resist it for fear of losing their seats and few vested party interests. However, this critical window is short and women need to have organized groups ready to go when the conflict ends. According to a study by Sharoni (1995), women were involved in the peace process as a direct result of women's mass political mobilization in Palestine and Guatemala. If women wait until conflict ends, then it is often too late to organize effectively. It must be recognized, however, that in such situations women have suffered horribly, perhaps much moreso than less complete breakdowns in state control. Nevertheless, this horrific situation may be the foundation of more meaningful change for women.

Lack of Data

Unlike the other chapters, data is sparse. Our topic lies at the intersection of two important fields that as yet suffer from a tremendous dearth of data. Precision is logistically impossible: conflict tends to be concentrated in the less accessible parts of the countryside where nobody has means (and few have the desire) to keep careful and unbiased records of violence. Likewise, issues concerning the status of women fall outside the public eye and are often politically charged. Although UN Security Resolution 1325, which notes the need "to consolidate data on the impact of armed conflict on women and girls," invites further research on the subject and requests reporting on progress in involving women in peace processes, no comprehensive dataset recording formal female participation in peace negotiations exists. Rather, such data remain scattered through government documents and news sources and are generally vague and contradictory. If, as the qualitative evidence suggests, women are integral actors in sustainable peace efforts, this lack of data must be remedied.

We have undertaken a review of the literature on peace negotiations and post-conflict reconstruction after serious civil conflict to develop a set of cases. Within that set, we would like to know when women on either side of the conflict were directly involved in negotiations or discussing and drafting the peace agreement, both in terms of the number of women (raw as well as relative to men), and capacity (were women only observers, or was their input ignored in practice?). We also seek to examine the agreements themselves for gender-sensitivity: for example, are issues such as female demobilization explicitly addressed? Armed with these data, we may begin to examine whether peace agreements with higher degrees of female mediation do indeed correspond with longer peace duration.

Importantly, we cannot assume women's involvement to be exogenous; in fact it is very plausible that seeing women in a peace process is itself an indicator of pre-existing trends toward empowering women in that country. However, with better data collection (particularly if states can be encouraged to report appropriately disaggregated data), we would be better able to control for such trends or match countries on similar levels of

Table 9.1 Country Status After Most Recent Peace Process

	Women Not Involved	Formal or Strong Informal Involvement of Women
Functioning of Government: (score is less than 4)	Angola (2002); Cambodia (1991); Chad* (2007); Russia* (Chechnya, 1997); Côte d'Ivoire* (2007); Guinea* (2002); Guinea-Bissau (1998); Tajikistan (1997); Republic of the Congo (1999); Somalia* (2006)	Democratic Republic of the Congo (2002–2003); Sudan (2006)
Functioning of Government: (score is 4 or above)	Bosnia (1995); **Ethiopia (2000);** Nepal* (2006)	**Afghanistan (2002); Burundi (2000);** Colombia (1999–2002); East Timor (1999); El Salvador (1992); Indonesia (2005); Liberia (1996); Mozambique (1992); Northern Ireland (UK) (1998); Philippines (1996); Rwanda (2002); Sierra Leone (1999); South Africa (1991–1996); Uganda (2005–2008)

Peace processes drawn from the UCDP Peace Agreement Dataset unless otherwise noted. Functioning of Government and Rule of Law data drawn from Freedom House 2008.

Table Notes: "Functioning of Government" is scaled from 0 to 12, with 12 denoting a country where elected officials affect policy, corruption is minimal, and the operation of government is open and transparent. A score of 4 is relatively low. The average score in 2008 was 6.56. About 26% of countries received a score below 4, so this measure represents the lowest quartile. "Rule of Law" is scaled from 0 to 16, with 16 denoting an independent judiciary, police under civilian control, and protection from political terrorism, unjustified imprisonment and torture by either the government or insurgents. In 2008 the average score was 8.61. 28% of countries rank below 6, so this roughly represents the lowest quartile. A country's name appears in bold if the Rule of Law score is less than 6.

* For cases missing from the UCDP and for peace agreements after 2005, data were drawn from BBC's country profile timelines (2008).

women's status. We can, however, look at the relationship between women's formal participation in the peace process and whether or not the peace process failed.

Women and Peace Processes: Preliminary Findings

The actual effect of bringing women into official negotiations and peace processes is challenging to measure—eight years after the passage of UN Security Council Resolution 1325, women's involvement continues to be sporadic and primarily symbolic. To complicate matters, the qualitative nature of female involvement varies significantly from case to case, and data from war zones is notoriously difficult to collect; yet some overall trends are visible. While no country has implemented an ideally gender-sensitive peace process, even limited attention to women's issues seems to correlate with positive outcomes. In Tables 9.1 and 9.2, the left column contains peace processes between 1991 and 2008 where women did not participate as negotiators or delegates and there is no evidence that women were strongly organized for peace at the societal level. Since it is hard to gauge the real

Table 9.2 Involvement of Women in Successful and Failed Peace Processes

	Women Not Involved	Formal or Strong Informal Involvement of Women
Failed Peace Processes: Major peace processes where at least one party rejected or defected from the agreement.	Afghanistan (1993, 1996); Angola (1991, 1994); Chad* (1993, 1995, 1999, 2002, 2005, 2007); Russia* (Chechnya, 1997); Côte d'Ivoire* (2004, 2005, 2007); Democratic Republic of the Congo (1999); Guinea Bissau (1998); Liberia (1991, 1993–1994, 1995); Republic of the Congo (1999); Rwanda (1991–1993); Sierra Leone (1996); Somalia* (1993, 1994, 1997, 2006); Sudan (1997)	Colombia (1999–2002); Somalia (2000); Sudan* (2005–2006); Uganda (1994^, 2005–2008†)
Peace Agreements Remaining in Force: Major peace agreements holding through 2008.	**Angola (2002);** Bosnia (1995); **Cambodia (1991); Ethiopia (2000); Guinea* (2002); Nepal* (2003, 2006);** Tajikistan (1997)	**Afghanistan (2002);** Burundi (2000–2003); **Democratic Republic of the Congo (2002–2003);** East Timor* (1999); El Salvador (1992); Indonesia (2005); Kenya (2008); Liberia (1996–2003); Mozambique (1992); Northern Ireland (UK) (1998); Philippines (1996); Rwanda (2002); Sierra Leone (1999–2000); South Africa* (1991–1996); Uganda (2002)

Data drawn from the UCDP Peace Agreement Dataset unless otherwise noted.

Table Notes: Countries appear in bold if some significant unrest or violence continued in the wake of the agreement.

* For cases missing from the UCDP and for peace agreements after 2005, data were drawn from BBC's country profile timelines (2008).

^ CGI 2006.

† Sudan Tribune 2008.

power of formal female participants, all cases where one or more formal participants were female and/or where women in society were strongly organized for peace are located in the second column. One marginal case is Nepal, where the few local-level women's peace initiatives do not coordinate with national women's groups, and one woman participated in peace talks in early 2003 with a very limited role.

Table 9.1 contrasts Freedom House democracy scores from countries with no female involvement in the most recent peace process to those where women acted as negotiators or made some visible efforts to affect the process through civic action, including local meetings, peace marches, and national forums. The "Functioning of Government" score awards higher rankings to governments that are responsive, hold democratic elections, and operate transparently between elections. Corrupt or authoritarian regimes receive lower scores, and a score below four places a country in the lowest quartile of all countries. Although this sets a fairly low threshold, we see that some countries that have recently engaged in serious conflicts, such as Afghanistan, Rwanda, and Uganda, have relatively functional governments. One should note that women are well-represented in the legislatures of these particular states, at 27.7 percent, 56.3 percent, and 30.7 percent, respectively. Scholars have demonstrated that increased numbers of female legislators can aid sustainable peace. On the other hand, most countries where women were excluded entirely from the peace process remain in the lowest quartile even five or ten years later. These results are certainly affected by other factors and it is very possible that countries with a propensity to function well are more likely to include women in peace-building; however, even conflicted Afghanistan—where women's participation was imposed largely by external forces—appears to have benefitted.

Closer examination of various cases confirms that women generally effect positive outcomes for peace duration and social indicators, and that peace agreements are more durable when women formally participate in their negotiation. An ideal peace process would include both grassroots mobilization and formal representation of women.

Table 9.2 uses UCDP (2008) data on peace agreements to determine how women's participation relates to the duration of an agreement. Somewhat strikingly, given the broad range of women's peace-building activities that qualify a country for the right-hand column, most of these agreements are still in force today, and all but two effectively ended major violent conflict within the country. The majority of agreements where women were not involved have come to an end through rejection or defection by one or more parties. Some agreements in this column exist nominally but have failed to bring real peace to the country.

Closer examination of various cases confirms that women generally effect positive outcomes for peace duration and social indicators, and that peace agreements are more durable when women formally participate in their negotiation. An ideal peace process would include both grassroots mobilization and formal representation of women.

Women's groups played an active role in the Angolan independence movement throughout the 1970s and 1980s, but they consistently failed to coordinate non-elite women locally and nationally. Donald Steinberg, the U.S. ambassador to Angola under President Clinton, attributes the breakdown of the 1994 Lusaka Protocol to its failure to account for gender concerns in its implementation (2007). Although the agreement between the rebels and the Angolan government was lauded as "gender-neutral," none of the negotiation teams included women and little or no time was given to discussing population displacement, human rights abuses, or the reconstruction of health and social services. Disarmament and reintegration programs excluded thousands of women who had been kidnapped by rebels to fill "non-combatant" roles as domestic servants or sex slaves. As a result,

Steinberg explains, citizens viewed the peace process as doing little to serve the population at large. When relations between the government and the rebels began to deteriorate in 1998, civil society was not strong enough or invested enough to insist on a peaceful resolution. The ensuing war ended in 2002 after the death of the rebel leader; however, violent conflict continues in some regions. Angolan women have increasingly participated in informal reconciliation across communities and families, and the number of women in parliament jumped from 15 percent to 40 percent in 2008.

Even when women face barriers to formal representation, they benefit from being organized into strong civil associations during the peace process. In Burundi, after men openly opposed women's participation in the peace process on cultural grounds, women directed their influence through other channels, including public education on women's issues through the media. UN Development Fund for Women trained women from all levels of society in conflict resolution in preparation for a women's peace conference in 2000 where women met to finalize their recommendations for the peace accords (Rehn and Sirleaf 2002: 80). Even though women were only allowed into peace talks as observers, "they were able to unite across ethnic, political, and class backgrounds to develop a clear agenda, and almost all of their jointly-made recommendations were included in the Burundi Peace Agreement" (WPS 2002: 62). Additional ceasefire agreements signed in 2002 and 2003 locked in the agreement (UCDP 2008). Despite occasional incidents of rebel violence that continued through 2007, Burundi showed gradual but steady improvement on social indicators, such as literacy, schooling, and health.

On the other hand, when civil society is weak, involving women formally may help to counteract cultural resistance to women's rights and regenerate civic organization. In Afghanistan, the United Nations saw that women actively participated as delegates and advisers throughout the drafting of the Bonn Agreement and the Emergency Loya Jirga that elected the transitional government. In the interim government several ministries are headed by women, including the newly created Ministry of Women's Affairs (WPS 2002: 62–63). Although Kandiyoti notes that some new legal provisions represent a step backwards for women, and most accounts emphasize that there has been slow improvement in women's actual situation, women now have legal rights to vote, hold office, and go to school (2008).

Even when women face barriers to formal representation, they benefit from being organized into strong civil associations during the peace process.

In a final illustrative case, the Ugandan government appointed female parliament minister Betty Bigombe to spearhead peace efforts with the rebel Lord's Resistance Army in 1988. Acting without the military's knowledge, Bigombe initiated personal contact with the rebels in 1993. Once negotiations were under way, she convinced the government that a peaceful settlement was more cost-effective than a military victory, although the military continued its attacks throughout the dialogue. Though the rebel negotiators trusted Bigombe, they were suspicious that the government and the military intended to sabotage the talks or renege on their promises (Bigombe privately expressed similar concerns) and as a result, talks collapsed in 1994 (Conflict Reconciliation 2008). Although women may be more peaceful negotiators, their influence is limited if they are forced to work at cross purposes with the government or military.

Conclusion

In conclusion, we suggest that efforts to involve women in peace processes, both in civil peace-building associations and in formal negotiations improve peace duration and governance. Training in peace-building from NGOs and international organizations appears to strengthen the women's movement in preparation for peace processes. In our analysis, limited as it is to a sample of approximately 30 cases, we find that the formal participation of women is more likely to lead to a sustainable peace. While some countries include a token female on negotiating teams or drafting committees, a single woman does not necessarily represent the interests of all women in a country. Successful peace processes should combine adequate representation of women in official peacemaking with open dialogue that includes the perspectives of women at all levels of society.

However, this preliminary analysis is not an adequate basis for policy-making. There is a crying need for more and more detailed information on the involvement of women in peace negotiations and reconstruction. Only by careful process-tracing of the ways in which women's involvement changes the processes and outcomes of peace negotiation can we make a stronger empirical case that the participation of women is pivotal in achieving a durable peace.

Despite this dearth of data, the United Nations has already crafted guidelines for the involvement of women, and the inclusion of a gendered perspective on post-conflict reconstruction. Detailed checklists have been drawn up to guide UN personnel as they attempt to facilitate peace in these war-torn areas. UN peacekeeping troops are now receiving gender sensitivity training before they take to the field. However, these often fall by the wayside in practice, as "more important" exigencies arise. One of the most significant contributions to be made by scholars is to articulate why there is very little that is more important to sustainable peace than the formal inclusion of women in its creation. Successful peace processes should combine adequate representation of women in official peacemaking with open dialogue between men and women at all levels of society.

10. THE IMPACT OF TRIBUNALS AND TRUTH COMMISSIONS ON POST-CONFLICT PEACE BUILDING

James Meernik, Rosa Aloisi, Angela D. Nichols, and Marsha Sowell

International organizations, governments, and non-governmental organizations have invested substantial resources into repairing the political, social, and economic damages caused in societies that have been rent by civil wars, massive repression, and other forms of unrest and abuse. In 2006 alone the nations of the Organization for Economic Cooperation and Development spent as much as $6 billion in official development assistance and the funding of UN peacekeeping operations.[1] Two vehicles in particular have gained increasing attention from both domestic and international actors—truth commissions and international criminal tribunals. Other forms of transitional justice have been adopted as well and often in concert with these institutions, such as lustration, reparations, and memorialization. In fact, since the creation of the South African Truth Commission in 1994, somewhere between 15 and 20 truth commissions have been established.[2] And since the inception of the ICTY (International Criminal Tribunal for the Former Yugoslavia) in 1993, at least four more (depending on how one counts such institutions) ad hoc international tribunals have been created, in addition to the International Criminal Court. Almost all those involved, from the victims, the vanquished, and the victors, to a wide array of international governmental and non-governmental entities recognize that some form of reckoning with the past will occur as societies seek to repair the social and political damage caused by widespread violence. Indeed, with the end of the Cold War, transitional justice is increasingly used as part of a standard package of measures for rebuilding societies and nations.

The reader might be surprised to learn, however, that despite the popularity and expense of these transitional justice institutions, very little empirical research has been conducted regarding their impact, and virtually no published studies have analyzed why some nations choose such institutions and others do not (see Brahm [2007] for an excellent overview of truth commission research). According to Fletcher and Weinstein (2002: 585), "there have been virtually no studies that systematically have attempted to examine or measure the contribution of trials to reconciliation and social reconstruction." Hayner (1994, 2001) and Freeman (2006) have conducted impressive and rich studies of the political, legal, and social causes and consequences of truth commissions, but few empirical analyses exist on

---

1 As found at *http://www.oecd.org/dataoecd/36/20/39289596.pdf* on October 14, 2008.

2 Different methods of defining and counting such institutions by Freeman (2006), Hayner (1994, 2001), Amnesty International (at *http://www.amnesty.org/en/international-justice/issues/truth-commissions*) and the United States Institute of Peace (at *http://www.usip.org/library/truth.html*) results in these varying estimates.

the contributions of these institutions to peace building. Mendeloff (2004: 375) writes, "truth-telling in post-conflict societies may have some peace-promoting effects, but more systematic research needs to be done before determining its utility" (*cf.* Gibson 2004).

With the end of the Cold War, transitional justice is increasingly used as part of a standard package of measures for rebuilding societies and nations.

The purpose of this chapter is to begin that systematic and empirical exploration regarding why truth commissions and tribunals are established for some nations and not others, and what impact they have on peace building. First, we describe these institutions and examine whether the characteristics of the conflict from which a nation is emerging help predict whether truth commissions or tribunals are established. Second, we analyze several political and economic indicators to assess whether these institutions positively contribute to peace-building efforts. We conclude by evaluating the evidence and advancing suggestions for policymaking.

Truth, Justice, and Peace Building

Before proceeding, we must first define these two institutions we seek to study. Generally speaking, a truth commission is defined as:

> an ad hoc, autonomous, and victim-centered commission of inquiry set up in and authorized by a state for the primary purposes of (1) investigating and reporting on the principal causes and consequences of broad and relatively recent patterns of severe violence or repression that occurred in the state during determinate periods of abusive rule or conflict, and (2) making recommendations for their redress and future prevention. (Freeman 2006: 18)

A criminal tribunal is a "judicial body created to investigate and prosecute individuals accused of violations of human rights or humanitarian law in the wake of violent conflict" (IDEA 2003). Both such institutions are designed to aid nations that have emerged from war, severe repression, and the like. Such institutions look backward to uncover the truth through evidence gathering and testimony and to punish the guilty, although the latter is more often the hallmark of tribunals. They are forward-looking institutions insofar as their intended benefits (e.g., deterrence, reconciliation, and political reform) are supposed to redound to the affected societies in the future. We are concerned here with two principal questions. First, what factors explain why some states become involved in truth commissions or tribunals? Second, and more importantly, how successful are these institutions in facilitating political reform and economic growth, and in helping states avoid the recurrence of civil war?

We acknowledge at the outset the many diverse criteria by which we might evaluate these institutions. Mendeloff (2004: 359–361) finds that the literature suggests multiple beneficial effects that are supposed to result from the work of truth commissions and tribunals in facilitating peace building: 1) social healing and reconciliation; 2) justice; 3) creation of an official historical record; 4) public education; 5) institutional reform; 6) promotion of democracy; and 7) preemption and deterrence. Further, as Brahm (2007) discusses, these effects are intended to register in several ways. Many of these institutions' objectives pertain to individuals and social groups (e.g., reconciliation), while others involve governmental action and the state. This analysis focuses on the national political and economic effects of transitional justice. While an understanding of the impact of transitional justice on individual attitudes, social groups, and society in general is a critical aspect of this research program, we believe that the national-level effects are more accurately identified and defined at present.

To organize our analysis, we focus our attention on those nations that have emerged from civil war as defined by the Uppsala Conflict Data Project/Peace Research Institute of Oslo (PRIO). Their measure of all civil violence in the Armed Conflict Data Set in the period 1976–2004 (v.4, 2008) is used.[3] Our mission focuses on these states for two reasons. First, as Mason (1999) states "since the end of WWII, civil war . . . has been the most frequent, deadly, and persistent form of armed conflict in the international system, regardless of whose count one uses." As well, confining our analysis just to nations that have experienced civil wars ensures that our analysis is limited to a group of similar states whose post-conflict peace building efforts are then distinguished by whether they experienced these forms of transitional justice or not—in effect a quasi-controlled experiment. It is important to note at the outset that not all states that have established truth commissions have done so in the aftermath of war. Many, such as the former East Germany, do so to grapple with prolonged periods of repression. We do not include such cases here. As well, we must note that missing data for some variables cause our analysis to lose some cases. Table 10.1 provides a listing of all nations that concluded a civil war in the 1976–2004 period, but which chose not to establish a truth commission and were not subject to an international tribunal. Table 10.2 provides a listing of all nations that emerged from a civil war in the 1976–2004 period and have been involved in truth commissions and/or international criminal tribunals, and the year in which these institutions were created.

The nations that have been the subjects of truth commissions and international criminal tribunals share at least one common characteristic: their societies have suffered a period of significant violence in the recent past, such as civil war, genocide, a repressive and violent regime, or some combination of these. Yet, despite the horrific violence experienced by many societies, there are important differences in the choices made by these nations to deal with their pasts. What explains this variation?

We acknowledge at the outset that civil wars are wrought with violence, and that systematic human rights violations are a harsh reality of conflict. Although violence and human rights violations are present in almost

---

3 These data are found at *http://www.prio.no/CSCW/Datasets/Armed-Conflict/UCDP-PRIO/*.

Table 10.1 Civil War States Not Involved in Transitional Justice

Country	Year*	Country	Year*
Angola	1992	Mauritania	1979
Azerbaijan	1994	Mexico	1995
Bangladesh	1993	Moldova	1993
Burma (Myanmar)	1989	Mozambique	1993
Burundi	1993	Nicaragua	1980
Cambodia	1978	Niger	1993
Central African Republic	2003	Pakistan	1978
China	1982	Papua New Guinea	1991
Comoros	1990	Philippines	1991
Congo, Republic of	1995	Romania	1990
Congo, Democratic Republic of	1979	Russia	1991
Djibouti	1995	Saudi Arabia	1980
Egypt	1999	Senegal	1991
Equatorial Guinea	1980	Somalia	1979
Eritrea	1998	Spain	1982
Ethiopia	1977	Sudan	1977
Gambia, The	1982	Suriname	1989
Georgia	1993	Syria	1983
Guinea	2002	Tajikistan	1997
Guinea-Bissau	2000	Tanzania	1979
Guyana	1993	Thailand	1983
India	1985	Togo	1987
Iran	1981	Trinidad & Tobago	1991
Iraq	1985	Tunisia	1981
Israel	1997	Turkey	1993
Kenya	1983	United Kingdom	1992
Lebanon	1977	Uzbekistan	2001
Lesotho	1999	Yemen Arab Republic	1980
Malaysia	1982	Yemen People's Republic	1987
Mali	1991	Zimbabwe	1980

* Year for which earliest civil war ended. The earliest ending civil war is recorded for the year in the period 1976–2004 in which there was the first instance of a civil war ending.

all conflicts, the level of intensity varies. In some wars, mass killing is the goal; in others, it is a side effect. The greater the violence, the more likely we would suspect that there would be need for an officially sanctioned method of confronting the past and repairing the breaches in society. However, according to the Uppsala/PRIO data, those nations that choose to establish a truth commission tend to emerge from civil wars in which an average of 0.1 percent of the population was lost, while in those states that chose not to create such institutions, the average percentage of the population that died during their just concluded war is also 0.1 percent. While this finding may seem counterintuitive, as we might expect more violence would cause a greater need for the truth, it is also possible that the people of some societies in which so many have lost their lives find it more difficult to confront the past. There may be too many who are complicit who then resist truth and justice, and too many who have been harmed who prefer to focus on the future rather than the past. The analysis also finds that the percentage of the population killed in war in nations that were subject to international tribunals is 0.3 percent. For such states the violence may be so severe and destructive that international intervention in the form of a tribunal is the more realistic and pertinent method.

The duration of civil wars is also an important determinant of developments in the post-conflict phase (Grant 1992; Mason 1996; Regan 1998; Mason 1999; Balch-Lindsay and Enterline 2000) and has proven to be an excellent predictor of both civil war settlements (Mason 1996; Mason 1999) and of the effect of third-party involvement (Balch-Lindsay and Enterline 2000). Long-lasting civil wars, because of their presumed greater impact on a nation's people and institutions, would seem more likely to create

Table 10.2 Truth Commissions and International Tribunals in Post-Civil War States			
Country	Truth Commission	International Tribunal	Start Year
Bosnia & Herzegovina		●	1993
Croatia		●	1993
East Timor		●	2000
El Salvador	●		1992
Ghana	●		2003
Haiti	●		1994
Indonesia	●		2004
Macedonia		●	1993
Morocco	●		2004
Paraguay	●		2004
Peru	●		2001
Rwanda	●	●	1999, 1994
Serbia & Montenegro	●	●	2001, 1993
Sierra Leone	●	●	2002, 2000
South Africa	●		1995
Sri Lanka	●		1994
Yugoslavia		●	1993

the need for truth telling to repair the long-term damage. We found that among the post-civil war societies that have had a truth commission, the average length of conflict is 5,834 days, while the average for states subject to tribunal was 1,235 days. For those nations that have emerged from civil war and have elected not to pursue such methods of transitional justice, the average civil war length was 3,704 days. Long-running civil wars seem particularly likely to result in truth commissions.

Civil war intensity can be measured by looking at the average deaths per day throughout a conflict. The average number of deaths per day in cases of civil war that were followed by a truth commission is 25.9, and in the case of states subject to tribunals, it is 29.1. The average number of deaths per day for those cases of civil war that were not followed by a truth commission or tribunal is 70. The large difference here suggests that intense and destructive wars are not likely to result in the later adoption of transitional justice. The intensity of the violence would seem to be a hindrance to transitional justice rather than an inspiration.

We also speculate that nations whose civil wars end in settlement might be more likely to enact transitional justice mechanisms as a result of the negotiating process or third-party pressure.[4] We find that 60 percent of

---

4 We use data from Hartzell and Hoddie (2003, 325–326).

post–civil war states that were subject to a tribunal ended their conflict with a settlement, and 40 percent of post–civil war states that were followed by a truth commission ended in a settlement. Only 6 percent of the post–civil war states that neither established a truth commission nor were subject to a tribunal ended their war with a settlement. Clearly, those warring actors that are able to reach a settlement to end the fighting are primed and positioned to become involved in transitional justice. Nations involved in intensely violent wars that result in outright victory by one side or conclusion short of a settlement seem to be the least likely candidates to adopt transitional justice.

The Impact of Truth Commissions and Tribunals on Politics

To evaluate the effects of truth commissions and international tribunals on the affected nations, we look at three factors: human rights abuses, democratization, and political rights. We find that much of the literature suggests that truth commissions can play a role in advancing human rights (Brahm 2007; Hayner 1994). By revealing the truth regarding atrocities, and often placing blame or guilt on the responsible parties, these institutions can help deter future abuses. As well, many truth commissions make numerous recommendations regarding governmental reforms, particularly in the judiciary, the military, and police (Brahm 2007: 27) that can result in significant improvements in human rights protections.

Prior research and transitional justice advocates also contend that a sustainable peace can best flourish in democratic and open political environments. If regimes do not take steps to open up the electoral process and institutions of governance, but merely retain their undemocratic characteristics, the likelihood of renewed violence will increase (see Collier et al. 2003; Fearon and Laitin 2003; Hegre et al. 2001). Political reform is a critical and oft-utilized component of truth commission mandates (Minow 1998; Freeman and Hayner 2003).

Three measures are used to study the effects of truth commissions and tribunals. We measure human rights using the Political Terror Scale data.[5] We measure political rights, using data from Freedom House.[6] For data on states' levels of democracy, we use the Polity 2 measure from the Polity IV data.[7] We provide analyses for states that choose truth commissions and/or were subject to international tribunals after the most recent end to a civil

---

5 The Political Terror Scale evaluates countries and their abuses of human rights and takes the average scores from readings of Amnesty International repors and U.S. State Department reports. The scale measures from 1–5 where "5" is the greatest level of abuse and "1" is the least amount of human rights abuse involving multiple, internationally recognized human rights. Data are available at *http://www.politicalterrorscale.org/*. Site last visited May 1, 2008.

6 The Freedom House measures ranges from "1" (most rights/liberties) to "7" (fewest rights/liberties, although we reverse these numbers). Data are available at *http://www.freedomhouse.org/template. cfm?page=15*. Site visited December 8, 2008.

7 This measure ranges from "-10" (lowest level democratic institutions and elections-essentially and autocracy) to "10" (the highest rating for a democracy). Data are available at *www.systemicpeace.org/ polity/polity4.htm*. Last visited March 1, 2008.

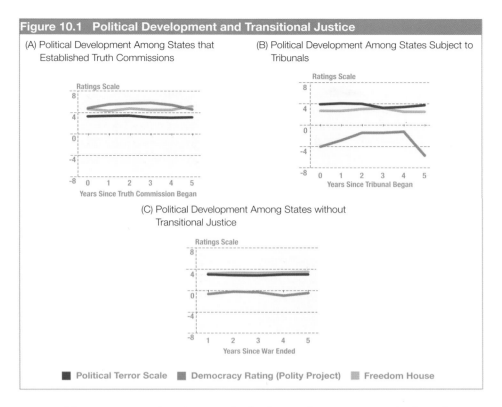

Figure 10.1 Political Development and Transitional Justice

(A) Political Development Among States that Established Truth Commissions

(B) Political Development Among States Subject to Tribunals

(C) Political Development Among States without Transitional Justice

■ Political Terror Scale ■ Democracy Rating (Polity Project) ■ Freedom House

war and beginning in the year in which the truth commission/tribunal came into existence (year 0) and continuing for five more years. To provide a basis of comparison in post-conflict peace building, we also examine nations that emerged from civil wars but were not involved in either form of transitional justice. For these states we begin counting the passage of time with the first year after the just concluded war.

The red lines represent the level of human rights abuse (larger values indicate more human rights abuses) in nations that choose truth commissions (Figure 10.1, graph A); those that are subject to tribunals (Figure 10.1, graph B) and those not involved in transitional justice (Figure 10.1, graph C). Generally, none of the lines exhibits noticeable changes over time. There is incremental improvement (i.e., lower scores) in all three graphs, most noticeably in years three and four, but we are hesitant to conclude that human rights show much improvement in general after civil wars. We note that those nations subject to tribunals appear to commit more human rights violations in general, as their typical scores are somewhat higher than the other two groups of states. Given the small N of the tribunal states, however, we must approach such findings with significant caution.

The most striking evidence regarding political development occurs in the Polity democracy ratings (larger values indicate greater levels of democracy). In particular, we note the substantial differences in absolute scores between the relatively high ratings achieved in nations that choose truth commissions, and the fairly low ratings among states subject to tribunals and states not involved in either form of transitional justice. Truth commission states show a gradual improvement in the Polity scores over time, although the Polity score by year five begins to drop back down. The Polity ratings for nations subject to tribunals follow a similar upward trajectory with a later downturn. However, the Polity ratings for the tribunal states are markedly lower in absolute terms, and reach a nadir in year five of -5.66. The democracy scores for nations not involved in transitional justice are fairly low as well, although not approaching the level of the tribunal states.

These findings are mirrored in the Freedom House scores (larger values indicate more political rights). For truth commission states there is little movement in the direction of greater political rights for the first several years after the truth commission commences, but a significant upturn in year five. Political rights in nations subject to international tribunals exhibit slight increases for several years, before dropping back at the end of the five-year window. The scores for post-civil war states not involved in either form of transitional justice increase noticeably, albeit not dramatically over the five-year period. Once again, the absolute scores for those states that choose truth commissions are significantly higher (in the 4.3–5.2 range) than those states that are subject to tribunals (2.5–3.16) and those involved in neither (3.2–3.4).

Clearly, those states that embark down the path of truth commissions begin the journey with governments that are significantly more democratic and politically open. Indeed, their democratic openness may have led them to choose to create such institutions. Such regimes and their opponents may well have made the difficult choices regarding the creation of truth commissions and democratic polities as part of the peace process ending the war. Yet, it is equally plausible that open, democratic regimes are simply more likely to favor the creation of truth commissions. Further data on regime types and peace settlements in the years immediately prior to and in the aftermath of conflict are needed to better understand whether such speculation can be supported by the evidence.

The Link between Transitional Justice and Economic Health

We next examine the impact of transitional justice on the economic health of post-conflict nations. Truth commissions and international tribunals may be able to help create local and international confidence in the stability and economic fortunes of post-conflict nations by demonstrating that these states take seriously their attempts at peace building. The reconciliation of warring factions and the implementation of institutional reforms are factors that should make those countries more stable and therefore more attractive to foreign investments (Pascoe 2007). For example, the African National Congress (ANC) supported the South Africa Truth and Reconciliation Commission (TRC) in part to help attract foreign direct investment (FDI). As studies suggest (Tuman and Emmert 2004), FDI and other forms of capital flow, which are greatly influenced by a strong potential for growth, should increase with improving political conditions. By removing from power

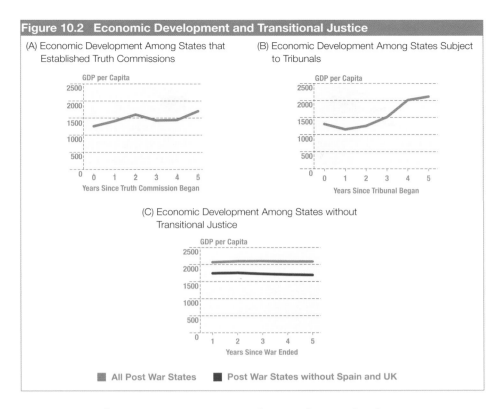

Figure 10.2 Economic Development and Transitional Justice

(A) Economic Development Among States that Established Truth Commissions

GDP per Capita

Years Since Truth Commission Began

(B) Economic Development Among States Subject to Tribunals

GDP per Capita

Years Since Tribunal Began

(C) Economic Development Among States without Transitional Justice

GDP per Capita

Years Since War Ended

■ All Post War States   ■ Post War States without Spain and UK

repressive and corrupt governments that exploit and subvert economies, economic growth can occur more naturally and unhindered. As well, scholars (Tandon 2000) suggest that foreign investors will have a greater incentive to let capital flow toward more open, free, and new democratic countries. In an indirect way, transitional justice can help "create business, trade and reconstruction" (Pascoe 2007).

To evaluate the impact of transitional justice on the economic health of the affected nations, we examine gross domestic product (in constant 2004 U.S. dollars) per capita. We find in Figure 10.2 (graph A and B) that the per capita gross domestic products of truth commission states and tribunal states increase significantly at a fairly steady pace over the course of the post-conflict years. Truth commission states begin this era with an average GDP per capita of $1,259 and conclude at $1,700, while tribunal states begin and conclude these post-conflict years with an average gross domestic product per capita of $1,305 and $2,111, respectively. And while both types of states exhibit considerable economic growth, the tribunal states demonstrate higher growth (61 percent vs. 35 percent) over this six-year period. In contrast, those states that did not experience any form of transitional justice show few signs here that their economies are increasing in size. We note, however, that because both Spain (Basque separatists) and the United Kingdom (Northern Ireland) are in our sample, they might be biasing these estimates because of their substantially larger economies. When we exclude them, we see in graph C that the average gross domestic product for post–civil war states now drops approximately $300, but the flat trend line remains. The overall growth rate for the group of states excluding Spain and the UK is -.02 percent.

Commitment to the rule of law is likely key to investor confidence as it evidences a preference for legalization and predictability.

These results would certainly seem to suggest that states involved in transitional justice demonstrate significantly better signs of economic development than those that are not. However, we must be cognizant of the potential for confounding factors to bias these results. It is possible that those nations that choose truth commissions or are subject to international tribunals are also accorded greater attention and resources by the international community of nations, non-governmental organizations, and governmental organizations. The willingness of truth commission states to undertake reform, coupled with the devastation and violence wrought by war in states under the jurisdiction of international tribunals, may create the visibility and interest so often needed to attract outside support. Such assistance may then mask the true economic growth potential of states. Yet, it is also entirely possible that transitional justice states demonstrate a real commitment to the rule of law, which in turn attracts significantly more investment and external assistance than one would find in states that eschew this sort of peace building. Commitment to the rule of law is likely key to investor confidence as it evidences a preference for legalization and predictability. Undoubtedly, economic factors interact with political stability and greater respect for human rights to produce a more stable and profitable economic climate.

Transitional Justice and the Persistence of Peace

The success of truth commissions and tribunals depends critically on the absence of war. Nations that lapse into renewed violence can hardly be said to be building a foundation for future peace and stability. Yet, we know from extensive research on the subject of civil wars that once nations have become embroiled in one conflict, the likelihood that they will return to war increases considerably (Doyle and Sambanis 2000; Mason and Quinn 2006). Hence, we should expect that if transitional justice does contribute to "peace" building in the most fundamental sense of the term, it should discourage the reoccurrence of war. Our measure of peace building is the absence of civil war conflict in the years after the first recorded instance of the end of a civil war in a given nation. Our data on civil wars derives from the Uppsala Conflict Data Project/Peace Research Institute of Oslo (PRIO) measure we cite earlier. We calculate the percentage of post–civil war states involved in subsequent wars across our three categories of nations—truth commission states, tribunal states, and states involved in neither.

We find that most states that are involved in one conflict subsequently become involved in another war. Graph A in Figure 10.3 shows that among

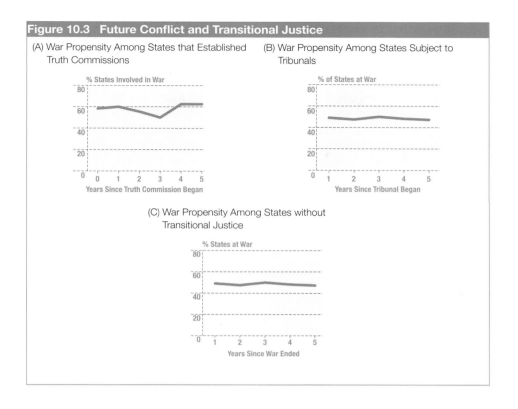

Figure 10.3 Future Conflict and Transitional Justice

(A) War Propensity Among States that Established Truth Commissions

% States Involved in War

Years Since Truth Commission Began

(B) War Propensity Among States Subject to Tribunals

% of States at War

Years Since Tribunal Began

(C) War Propensity Among States without Transitional Justice

% States at War

Years Since War Ended

post-conflict states that establish truth commissions, the percentage of such nations that relapse into war varies from a low of 50 percent in the third year after the creation of a truth commission, to a high of 62.5 percent in years four and five. The number of wars experienced by states subject to international tribunals varies somewhat. However, since the number of all such tribunal states is small, we should avoid reaching any firm conclusions from the data in graph B in Figure 10.3. Interestingly, among those nations that are not involved in either form of transitional justice (graph C in Figure 10.3), the percentage of such states subsequently involved in war is somewhat lower. It reaches a high of 50 percent in year three after war has ended, and a low of 47.3 percent in year five. But while the percentages of war-involved states in graph C are somewhat lower than we find in graphs A and B for the transitional justice nations, they still indicate a sad and substantial likelihood of relapse into war.

It is also possible that some of these conflicts have been ongoing for a number of years and continue despite the ending of other wars. That is, some of these conflicts may be relatively confined to a specific geographic area whose occurrence, in a sense, is not related to the transitional justice enterprise. Perhaps, as well, states and domestic institutions, weakened by previous wars, do not have the resources to resist other conflicts, much as individuals afflicted with life-threatening illnesses find it difficult to fight off secondary infections. In effect, these conducive conditions encourage the strengthening of rebellious actors and the spread of war across a state.

Certainly there are many nations in the world that have suffered multiple, simultaneous conflicts, such as Congo and Indonesia. These findings are in keeping with the works cited above. This research has found that once conditions are ripe for civil war in a nation, the likelihood of additional and subsequent conflicts arising increases substantially. Of all the trends examined here, this indicator of the peace prospects of post-conflict nations provides the least grounds for optimism. Even the tremendous efforts required to create and sustain the institutions of transitional justice would appear to make little difference in the likelihood of future war.

Clearly, more research is needed here to determine why only about half of these post-conflict nations maintain their peace. Whatever the possible causes might be for the relapse into violence, it would seem that future cross national and empirical studies such as this should be combined with focused case study analyses to better determine the deeper and complex reasons behind this phenomenon.

Conclusion

Given the complexities of the events and nations studied here, the inferences made from the analysis must necessarily be qualified. Our findings regarding states that establish truth commissions tend to show that these are nations that have emerged from longer wars that produce significant loss of life. Overall, the intensity of the violence as measured by deaths per day is significantly less than those states not involved in transitional justice. However, the loss of life (as a percentage of the population) experienced in nations that go on to establish truth commissions is approximately the same as those nations that do not choose transitional justice. Nations that become subject to international tribunals experience the most battle deaths per capita and also the shortest conflicts. The relatively short and intensely violent wars that these nations suffer through may well generate the visibility and interest that ultimately leads to the establishment of international justice mechanisms. Perhaps the most striking finding in this section of the chapter was the extremely low percentage of non-transitional justice states whose conflicts ended in a settlement. The inability of the warring factions to agree on terms or perhaps because of the outright victory achieved by one side, may make the establishment of truth commissions difficult or unpopular.

Economically, transitional justice nations demonstrate cause for optimism.

Perhaps the most solid and consistent conclusion we can draw regarding the consequences of transitional justice is that these nations, especially those that adopt truth commissions, appear to begin the post-conflict period with significant advantages in comparison to other post-conflict nations. First, they begin the post-conflict phase in better political health—their scores on indicators of political and civil rights and level of democracy are significantly higher than for all other post–civil war states. Generally, throughout the post-conflict phase we find their scores on these measures are higher than those nations that are not involved in transitional justice as well as those nations falling under the jurisdiction of international tribunals. Nations subject to international tribunals present fairly poor scores on all three indicators of political development, especially the democracy ratings. We suggest that perhaps because these states experienced such devastating human rights catastrophes (which created the need for international justice) their political health may well be at a low ebb. The international tribunals themselves may play a role in such problems because they do not contribute meaningfully to local institutional reform (Drumbl 2007) and their truth-telling work is far removed in distant courts.

Economically, transitional justice nations demonstrate cause for optimism. Both states that have chosen the path of truth commissions and those subject to international tribunals have significantly higher per capita gross domestic products after five years than those states that are not involved in transitional justice. In fact, economic growth among many states without transitional justice is negative over time. Somewhat at odds with our previous findings regarding the problems facing states subject to international tribunals, we see that these very same states have the highest growth rate and reach the highest absolute level of gross domestic product per capita. We suggest that the same international commitment that led to the creation of tribunals may also be playing a role in resuscitating these economies.

If they choose to embark on the path of transitional justice, with "choose" being the operative word, their future prospects look to be significantly bright. Those societies that are unable or unwilling to make this choice to confront the past can expect their political and economic prognosis to be less optimistic.

Ultimately, we surmise that the real heavy lifting of political reform comes in the immediate post-war period in which societies determine to grant more political rights, democratize political institutions and confront the past via truth commissions. Such deep and wide political reform sets the stage for later improvements in human and political rights and may also contribute to economic health. Thus, it may not always be truth commissions per se that are responsible for these political improvements, but rather the political settlement and public commitment for truth, justice, and freedom that set the foundation for these improvements. We stress, however, that not all of these positive trends are set in motion by the wholesale reform of government. There are still likely independent and positive effects felt in those societies that elect to establish truth commissions or are subject to international criminal tribunals. Unfortunately, we also find that all post-conflict states are at significant risk for renewed outbreaks of civil war.

These results suggest that international policymakers should focus on assisting local leaders in post-war societies to end their wars as soon as possible (which contradicts those who would argue that nations are more apt to end their conflicts after they have reached a hurting stalemate [e.g., Luttwak 1999]) and concentrate their efforts on achieving a settlement premised on political reform. The conclusion of war, and for that matter, periods of lengthy and/or severe governmental repression should be the occasion for the wholesale makeover of the political system and the establishment of transitional justice mechanisms that can confront the past in a free and open setting. Absent this societal consensus on a national, political opening and reckoning, the prospects do not appear good for many, if not most, post-conflict states. If they choose to embark on the path of transitional justice, with "choose" being the operative word, their future prospects look to be significantly bright. Those societies that are unable or unwilling to make this choice to confront the past can expect their political and economic prognosis to be less optimistic. In all cases, however, substantial efforts by all parties must be made to prevent civil wars from recurring. Deep, wide, and inclusive political reform is critical.

11. CONCLUSION

J. Joseph Hewitt, Jonathan Wilkenfeld, and Ted Robert Gurr

The elements of the conflict syndrome, a collection of hazards that often operate simultaneously to threaten the stability of states, remain prominent features of the international landscape. First discussed in the 2008 volume of *Peace and Conflict*, these related dangers (heightened risks of political instability, terrorism, ethnic war, mass civilian casualties, and involvement in international crises) have not abated in the intervening years. This is surely one of the important messages to take away from the slate of regularly featured chapters included in *Peace and Conflict 2010*.

The risks for political instability and conflict have increased for those states that were already at high risk, especially states in sub-Saharan Africa and South Asia (from Joseph Hewitt's Chapter 2). The transition of some states to partial democracies is one source of heightened risk. Worsening neighborhood security in some regions due to renewed armed conflict is another (e.g., resurgent fighting in the Democratic Republic of Congo). Amy Pate (Chapter 4) documents trends in worldwide democratization and reports that the number of states that have completed a democratic transition, fully consolidating governing institutions into mature, well-functioning democratic governments, has stalled—with a number of notable retrenchments. At the same time, the number of anocratic regimes—hybrid regimes exhibiting traits of both autocracies and democracies—has increased slightly. This development is a source of concern because anocracies are particularly prone to instability and conflict. Gary LaFree, Laura Dugan, and R. Kim Cragin present analyses from comprehensive and detailed data on all terrorist incidents since 1970 and conclude that there is no discernible upward or downward trend in worldwide terrorism (Chapter 6). For those who worry that terrorism has become a strengthened global menace, this is good news; for those who are assured that the dangers of terrorism are dissipating, the news is not at all favorable. The authors document complicated patterns in the data showing the complex dynamics of terrorism—changes in regional concentrations of activity, a range of weapons and targets, and an evolving collection of targeted states.

Analyses of the most recent data on active armed conflict worldwide indicate that any downward trend in the numbers of such conflicts that began in the early 1990s has certainly leveled off now (Hewitt, Chapter 3). Ten years ago, there were 25 active conflicts worldwide. Since then, the number has shot up significantly, declined significantly, and then returned to today's total of 26. On a positive note, Monica Duffy Toft and Stephen M. Saideman report that the number of armed conflicts for self-determination continues to decline (Chapter 5). Moreover, these conflicts are increasingly settled through negotiated settlements or stalemate/ceasefires rather than through imposed military victory of one side over another. Recognizing that the dangers of conflicts for self-determination remain a persistent form of conflict, the authors offer a number of concrete proposals for addressing the demands for greater autonomy made by groups, so that the lethality and destruction of such conflicts can be mitigated.

One of the starkest findings relates to trends in conflict recurrence. Of the 39 different conflicts that became active in the past ten years, 31 of them were conflict recurrences. Moreover, the number of recently terminated conflicts with a recurrence history is at an all-time high. So, the total picture painted by the data on current armed conflict is indeed a sobering one. The findings on conflict recurrence make it clear why it was important for *Peace and Conflict 2010* to focus on post-conflict recovery with solicited chapters authored by experts in this area.

When armed violence subsides in countries that have endured deadly civil conflict, what types of policies and other actions are most effective in helping the process of reconciliation and reconstruction? This volume's special section on post-conflict transition examines the problem from numerous perspectives. Whether the violence ends by a formal peace agreement, a tentative cease-fire, an imposed military solution, or a leader's abdication of power, the subsequent post-conflict transition marks an opportunity for building a more durable peace. The challenge for the international community is to identify properly the policy responses that capitalize on these opportunities—opportunities that are often all too brief.

The total picture painted by the data on current armed conflict is indeed a sobering one. The findings on conflict recurrence make it clear why it was important for Peace and Conflict 2010 *to focus on post-conflict recovery.*

To understand the many findings reported in these chapters, let us consider the recent experience of Liberia. In this fashion, we hope to illustrate the relationship of the book's findings to policy decisions about post-conflict reconstruction. While hardly an adequate case analysis of Liberia's post-conflict transition, references to some key features of the country's experience since the 2003 peace agreements will prove valuable. Liberia's experience, which has been largely positive, offers numerous examples of how policies that focus on democratization, economic recovery, the role of women, and transitional justice have played a role in post-conflict recovery.

In August 2003, Charles Taylor resigned as Liberia's president and sought exile in Nigeria. He had ruled since 1989, presiding over a period that was largely marred by intense civil warfare. Soon after his departure, the country reached a peace agreement, establishing an interim government that defined a power-sharing arrangement between two rebel factions and party leaders who remained after Taylor fled. As the *New York Times* reported at the time, there was little confidence among observers in the country that this particular agreement would prove very durable. "Peace pacts have been patched together and have fallen apart before during 14 bitter years of civil war and conflict in Liberia; some Western diplomats here said today that this accord's wording is hardly different, and hardly better, than the ones that went before" (Weiner 2003). Indeed, in Liberia's recent past, a period of relative stability that began in 1996 was disrupted when conflict returned in 2000. With a history of conflict recurrence, it was understandable that many were pessimistic about future prospects for peace. Nonetheless, by November 2005, Liberia held presidential elections that propelled Ellen Johnson-Sirleaf into office, making her the first female head of state in Africa. Moreover, since 2003, the level of violence has remained relatively low. In all, despite the pessimism expressed in the immediate aftermath of Taylor's departure, Liberia has witnessed some notable successes.

In Liberia, and elsewhere, successful post-conflict reconstruction depends on breaking some resilient, vicious circles that threaten to ensnare the country in renewed conflict. One vicious circle involves democratization and conflict recurrence. When violence subsides after many years of armed conflict, democratization offers the means to address group differences peacefully. But open political competition often produces unsatisfactory compromises or complete defeats that leave some groups tempted to resort once again to violence to attain goals. Another vicious circle involves economic recovery and conflict recurrence. The ravages of societal conflict leave economies in disrepair, giving both civilians and former soldiers few opportunities to re-enter society as economically productive citizens. Without economic recovery, the risks of conflict recurrence can increase. Policies that help to weaken and break these two vicious circles serve to enhance the chances for successful post-conflict recovery, reducing the risks of conflict recurrence and heightening the potential for a more durable peace. The four chapters focusing specifically on the challenges of post-conflict transitions offer useful guidance in this regard.

Anke Hoeffler (Chapter 7) points to a set of policy responses that address the problems posed by conflict recurrence and economic recovery. She provides an overview of a series of analyses that examine how international aid can support rebuilding the economy in post-conflict societies. There is evidence suggesting that aid is particularly effective in the years immediately following the end of a civil war. More importantly, aid should be sustained for at least four to seven years beyond the end of active fighting.

The research presented by Håvard Hegre and Hanne Fjelde (Chapter 8) also has ramifications for addressing post-conflict vicious circles, specifically the one involving conflict recurrence and democratization. Hegre and Fjelde point out that the same forces that threaten to destabilize a tentative peace agreement (sluggish economic growth, lingering disagreements about power-sharing among society's main ethnic and political groups, and continued opportunities for insurgency) are precisely the forces that undermine democratization. Democratization, by itself, is no guarantee for a successful post-conflict transition. But Hegre and Fjelde offer findings that suggest greater progress in post-conflict societies that have adopted democratic governing institutions. Since the late 1990s, democratic post-conflict societies are less likely to experience conflict recurrences than autocratic or anocratic societies. However, since this relatively recent trend affords only a small sample of observations, it is important to interpret it with caution. Still, seen in light of the research presented by Amy Pate (Chapter 4) that there is less political discrimination against ethnic minorities in democracies, the lower number of conflict recurrences in democracies could be a manifestation of a diminished level of grievance held by groups.

The recent history in Liberia illustrates some of the policy implications drawn from the findings reported by Hoeffler and Hegre and Fjelde. As Hoeffler indicates is the case for many post-conflict societies, the level of foreign aid received by Liberia did indeed jump considerably in the year immediately after active fighting subsided. The 2004 allocation from the United States, the largest donor of foreign assistance to Liberia, was the eighth largest among all recipients of U.S. foreign assistance (Tarnoff and Nowels 2004). In subsequent years, the level of assistance decreased slightly, but in the most recent budget request for Liberia, the U.S. Agency for International Development (USAID) has requested a significant increase in funds.[1] Based on Hoeffler's findings, that pattern of funding in Liberia—sustaining assistance levels for several years after the termination of fighting—is the proper approach for supporting economic recovery and, ultimately, mitigating risks of conflict recurrence.

Beyond foreign assistance levels, other factors are in place in Liberia that recent research would suggest bode well for future prospects. The UN peacekeeping mission in Liberia (United Nations Mission in Liberia, UNMIL) was authorized immediately after the peace agreements in August 2003. Hoeffler links the presence of UN peacekeeping with a sizeable reduction in the risk of conflict recurrence. The mission, which has been authorized to observe and monitor the implementation of the ceasefire agreements, continues to operate today. One of its important functions is to provide support for disarmament, demobilization, and reintegration efforts for all parties who had been actively involved in the fighting. These so-called DDR activities are viewed as crucial steps in moving countries through the period of post-conflict reconstruction. During the post-conflict period, Liberia has reformed its armed forces, relying heavily on extensive vetting of applicants and strengthened efforts to professionalize training (International Crisis Group 2009). With a mass decommissioning of soldiers and upper-level personnel, the size of the military has shrunk considerably—a fact reflected in the steadily declining portion of the GDP accounted for by military spending (Stockholm International Peace Research Institute 2008). In light of research reported by Hoeffler that high levels of post-conflict military spending are associated with greater risks for conflict recurrence, these developments in Liberia are certainly quite positive.

---

1 These figures are based on USAID foreign assistance data for Liberia for the years 2004–2007 (*http://www.usaid.gov/policy/budget/cbj2007/afr/lr.html*, accessed on April 30, 2009) and on figures available from the USAID 2009 Fiscal Year Congressional Budget Justification (*http://www.usaid.gov/policy/budget/cbj2009/*, accessed on April 30, 2009).

Finally, some of the factors that Hegre and Fjelde discuss that can work simultaneously to erode the prospects for successful democratization and continued post-conflict peace seem not to pose grave dangers in Liberia. Political discrimination experienced by ethnic groups in Liberia (e.g., the Mandingo, Gio, and the Mano) appears to be easing since the 2003 peace agreements. According to the most recent annual corruption indices maintained by the World Governance Indicators Project at the World Bank, the level of transparency and accountability in the Liberian government has improved considerably in the last year (Kaufmann et al. 2008). Finally, Liberia has posted very respectable economic growth figures since 2003, including 9 percent growth in 2007 (World Development Indicators 2008). All told, the findings reported in both chapters 7 and 8 indicate that success in each of these areas in Liberia will prove helpful for economic recovery and democratization, suggesting steady progress in its post-conflict transition.

The chapters in Peace and Conflict 2010 *offer an inventory of the range of challenges posed as states emerge from destructive armed conflicts. With rates of conflict recurrence at historic highs, it is clear that constructing durable peace arrangements is just as difficult, if not more so, as bringing the initial fighting to an end.*

The book reports some other promising insights that should inform programs for post-conflict reconstruction. Mary Caprioli, Rebecca Nielsen, and Valerie M. Hudson (Chapter 9) link high levels of involvement for women in peace processes to higher success rates for peace agreements. That is, when mechanisms are put into place that give women a formal role (or strong informal involvement) in the proceedings that produce a peace agreement, that agreement appears to have a longer duration than processes that did not explicitly require participation by women. Policies and programs that strengthen representation of women in civil society peace-building organizations or enhance training for women in conflict resolution (e.g., for work in mediation centers) should receive prioritization in post-conflict reconstruction efforts.

Certainly, the case of Liberia illustrates how high levels of involvement by women can have a dramatic impact on post-conflict circumstances. During the civil war, the Women in Peacebuilding Network mobilized Liberian women to advocate for peace and security in the country. The organization's activities in the months before the 2003 peace agreements are seen as crucial for clearing the way for a negotiated agreement between Charles Taylor and the rebel parties. There is no greater evidence for the important role of women in the post-conflict period than the election of Ellen Johnson Sirleaf to the presidency. Today, women head several of Liberia's key ministries playing roles in the reconstruction of the country (Bekoe and Parajon 2007).

James Meernik, Rosa Aloisi, Angela D. Nichols, and Marsha Sowell (Chapter 10) offer encouraging conclusions about the impact of transitional justice. For instance, states that have engaged in transitional justice have significantly higher per capita GDP after five years than those states that do not. The authors are mindful that the success attributed to transitional justice must be understood in a larger context. When peace agreements establish major political reforms that grant more political rights and democratize political institutions in addition to establishing truth commissions, a foundation clearly exists that supports a broader public commitment for demobilization and reconstruction. These larger forces have much to do with post-conflict success above and beyond transitional justice per se.

Here, again, the case of Liberia is telling. The Truth and Reconciliation Commission of Liberia was launched in 2006. With a mandate to investigate human rights abuses that occurred during the civil war period 1979–2003, the commission has been aggressive about encouraging citizen participation. It has even established mechanisms for people who have fled Liberia during the war to testify (*New York Times*, September 18, 2007). The findings reported in Meernik et al. instruct us to be cautious about ascribing too much direct credit to truth commissions for checking conflict recurrence. Rather, the commission's creation and mandate are a reflection of a broader societal resolve to democratize, expand political rights, and facilitate a meaningful reconciliation. Whether the commission is successful or not depends on the larger political and economic context.

Taken together, the chapters in *Peace and Conflict 2010* offer an inventory of the range of challenges posed as states emerge from destructive armed conflicts. Undoubtedly, with rates of conflict recurrence at historic highs, it is clear that constructing durable peace arrangements and rebuilding war-damaged states is just as difficult, if not more so, as bringing the initial fighting to an end. Part of the reason for this difficulty, as we have noted above, is that two vicious circles stymie post-conflict transitions, complicating the task of identifying appropriate steps for reconstruction. First, a successful post-conflict recovery depends on rebuilding the economy. But civil war often leaves the economy—an economy that was probably not thriving before the fighting began anyway—in shambles. Without economic opportunities for soldiers and civilians to re-enter society, the potential for renewed fighting will remain. Second, democratization opens the door to nonviolent and transparent mechanisms for addressing grievances and resolving conflicts. But the open competition that it invites will produce outcomes that are seldom satisfying to all parties, leading sometimes to the temptation to gain more through violence, particularly in societies that have recently emerged from violence. Clearly, breaking these vicious circles with effective policy responses is crucial. The research featured here takes steps toward that end. By identifying the factors that weaken these vicious circles, the analyses presented here can serve as a basis for informing effective policies that address the difficulties of rebuilding war-torn countries.

APPENDIX

This appendix identifies all major armed conflicts as of December 31, 2007, and tracks their origins as well as changes in the status of these conflicts since the publication of *Peace and Conflict 2008*. To compile this appendix, we have relied almost exclusively on information in the Conflict Database maintained by the Uppsala Conflict Data Program (UCDP) at Uppsala University, Sweden (http://www. pcr.uu.se/research/UCDP/). The brief updates for further developments in 2008 rely primarily on material posted by the International Crisis Group (http://www.crisisgroup. org).

The appendix provides descriptions for the 26 major armed conflicts that were ongoing in 21 countries as of December 31, 2007. These cases have two key characteristics: (a) they were reported as active in 2007 (i.e., at least 25 battle-related deaths were reported for that year), and (b) the accumulated battle deaths in the conflict exceeded 1,000. These 26 armed conflicts include three that had been dormant: Democratic Republic of Congo restarting in 2006, Somalia restarting in 2006, and Peru restarting in 2007. Two conflicts have been added to those that were active in 2005 and continue to be active today: Pakistan (Baluchi separatists) and Ethiopia (OLF in Oromiya). Four major armed conflicts have terminated since the publication of *Peace and Conflict 2008*: Nepal, Burundi, Indonesia, and Azerbaijan.

These 26 conflicts are identified through data provided by UCDP-PRIO for 1946–2007 (http://www.pcr.uu.se/database/). In 2007, UCDP reported a total of 34 active armed conflicts, of which 8 had not exceeded a total of 1,000 battle-related deaths since 1946 (see Harbom and Sundberg 2007).

The Uppsala Conflict Data Program defines an *armed conflict* as a contested incompatibility that concerns government and/or territory where the use of armed force between two parties, of which at least one is the government of a state, results in at least 25 battle-related deaths. A *major armed conflict* is one in which at least 1,000 battle-related deaths have occurred during the course of the conflict. An *incompatibility* can pertain to government (type of political system, the replacement of the central government or a change in its composition) or territory (the status of a specified territory, e.g., a change of the state in control of a certain territory (interstate conflict), secession, or autonomy (intrastate conflict).

Conflict Type and Intensity Scores: Conflicts are classified as *interstate* (between two or more governments), *intrastate* (between a government and a non-government party), or *intrastate with foreign involvement* (the government or opposition party or both receive troop support from other governments). UCDP classifies conflicts into three intensity levels: *minor* (at least 25 battle-related deaths per year and fewer than 1,000 battle-related deaths during the course of the conflict); *intermediate* (at least 25 battle-related deaths per year and an accumulated total of at least 1,000 deaths but fewer than 1,000 in any given year); and *war* (at least 1,000 battle related deaths per year). For purposes of the current study, only conflicts classified as intermediate or war are considered as armed conflicts.

Current Status: The current status of the armed conflicts as of December 2007 can fall into two categories—*terminated* or *ongoing*. A terminated conflict is categorized according to any of the following types: 1) peace agreement; 2) victory; 3) ceasefire agreement; 4) low activity; or 5) no activity (the latter three are sometimes grouped as other outcome); or 6) other.

Afghanistan
Ongoing, Intrastate with the Taliban, with Foreign Involvement

Afghanistan has been at war since 1978. Several factors have converged to make the country a fertile ground for protracted guerrilla war and transregional insurgencies: the existence of distinct tribal identities, a salient religious element, Afghanistan's geopolitical location as a meeting place of three regions, and the country's landlocked and mountainous geography. The two prominent groups at the onset of the insurgency were Jamiat-i-Islammi and Hezb-i-Islami, which have remained among the central warring parties to the present. Both groups aimed at overthrowing the government and declared a jihad (holy war) against the state-power in March 1979. The Soviet invasion in December 1979 added the dimension of a national freedom struggle to the religious war. The Soviet troop withdrawal in February 1989 ended the first phase of the Afghan civil war, after approximately 1 million deaths. As the Soviet troops withdrew, heavy fighting erupted between the Afghan army and Mujahideen forces. The strategic situation on the ground changed in 1992, when parts of the factionalized opposition movement joined forces. The Taliban movement first emerged in 1994 led by Mullah Mohammad Omar; its stated goal was liberating Afghanistan from the corrupt leadership of warlords and establishing a pure Islamic society. On September 28, 1996, the Taliban forces took control of Kabul, proclaimed the Islamic State of Afghanistan, and initiated enforcement of Sharia (Islamic rule). The anti-Taliban opposition formed a political and military alliance in June 1996—the Northern Alliance. The balance of forces changed drastically with the entrance of the U.S.-led multinational coalition into the conflict in response to the 9/11 bombings. The Northern Alliance, backed by U.S. and UK military force took control of Kabul, and on December 7th the last Taliban stronghold of Kandahar fell. Following intense diplomatic pressure, the parties agreed to the creation of a 29-member interim government headed by Hamid Karzai to lead the country for six months, until a broad-based administration could take over. The security situation in Afghanistan deteriorated in 2004. In 2005 the armed conflict between remnants of the ousted Taliban regime and the Afghan government escalated further. The Afghan government remains dependent on the U.S.-led multinational coalition and the NATO led peacekeeping force to provide security. The Afghan insurgency gained further strength in 2006 with fierce military clashes in the southeastern provinces and a rash of suicide bombings in urban areas. The intensity of the Taliban insurgency reached new heights in 2007. Part of the increase in intensity was due to a concerted Taliban effort to establish stable footholds in the country. Violence remained at a high level in 2008.

Algeria
Ongoing, Intrastate with GSPC

Algeria gained independence from France in 1962 after a bloody war. Severe economic problems persisted during the following 27 years of socialist one-party rule under the Front de Libération Nationale (FLN). During the late 1980s, these economic problems led to violent strikes and riots, leading to the introduction of a multiparty system. The Front Islamique du Salut (FIS) became the most potent opposition force in the country, as its anti-regime stance and Islamic values appealed to the urban poor. After the FIS won the first round of parliamentary elections in 1991, the army cancelled the second round. Amid increasing political violence, FIS was outlawed in 1992. Groups that fought the regime with arms came to dominate the struggle and the FIS lost the initiative. In response, the party endorsed MIA's (Mouvement islamique armée) armed struggle in 1993, and its armed wing, Armée islamique du salut (AIS). In 1992, a number of small extremist groups set up the Groupe islamique armé (GIA). The most prominent splinter group was the Groupe salafiste pour la prédication et la combat (GSPC), appearing in 1998. In 1999 Bouteflika won the presidential election after all other candidates withdrew. In the wake of 9/11, the Algerian government has received significant international support, much of it from the United States, for its fight against Muslim extremism. The character of the violence in Algeria has changed dramatically over the years and has expanded to include government officials, representatives of the opposition, foreigners, and journalists. In the mid-1990s the conflict turned into carnage. GIA, issuing a fatwa that charged the whole Algerian society with apostasy, launched a new strategy, specifically targeting the civilian population. The army's countermeasures became increasingly brutal, resulting in accusations of gross human rights abuses. In 2000, the AIS agreed to disband. In a referendum on September 29, 2005, 97.43 percent of the Algerians voted in favor of a government proposal for a partial amnesty for former rebels (and for the security forces). The amnesty came into effect in February 2006 but was soon rejected by the GSPC. Clashes continued throughout the year. In 2007 there was an increase in attacks by GSPC, which in January had changed its name to Al-Qaïda au pays du Maghreb islamique (AQIM). Bomb attacks in 2007 led analysts to suspect that the group was about to change its strategy, relying more on high-impact attacks. In 2008 the conflict continued according to the pattern instigated in 2007.

Chad
Ongoing, Intrastate with MDJT, RDL

Since gaining independence from France in 1960, Chad has been almost continually enveloped in civil war, including immense ethnic diversity, a tradition of factionalism, as well as animosity between the mainly Muslim north and the Christian and animist south. After independence, southerners controlled the central government. The politically marginalized north launched a Libya-backed rebellion, and in 1973 Libya became directly involved by annexing the Aozou Strip on the Chad-Libya border. Forces armées du nord (FAN), a northern anti-Libyan rebel movement led by Hissèn Habré seized power in N'djamena in 1982. During the 1980s, Libyan troops supported the rebels, and France supported the Habré government. Idriss Deby and his former guerrilla group Mouvement patriotique de salut (MPS) came to power in 1990. The latest rebel group to appear was Mouvement pour la démocratie et la justice au Tchad (MDJT), which launched its armed struggle in 1998, seeking to topple the government, accusing it of being authoritarian and corrupt. The U.S. provided extensive support to the earlier Habré regime as a part of its strategy to contain Libya and, if possible, remove Colonel Ghadafi from power. France sent troops in the early 1980s in aid of the Habré regime. Like the United States, France too was aiming to stop Libya from gaining an upper hand in the region. Sudan also supported the rebels, allowing both the Islamic Front and MPS to have rear bases on its territory. Niger, Nigeria, Algeria, Cameroon, and Central African Republic have all harbored rebel groups on their soil. The locus of the violence in the 1990s and 2000s has been changing as regionally based rebel groups have formed and disappeared. The situation in Chad during 2005 was volatile with spillover effects from the western region of Sudan-Darfur to the adjacent eastern part of Chad. On April 13 Front uni pour le changement démocratique (FUCD) tried unsuccessfully to take control of the capital N'djamena. Déby won reelection in 2006 in an election boycotted by the opposition. Sudanese continued to support the Chadian rebels and Chad continued to support the rebels in Sudanese Darfur. Violence continued through 2008 in the eastern part of the country. Tensions with Sudan mounted over N'djamena's alleged backing of a May Darfur rebel attack on Khartoum. Alliance nationale rebels mounted a new offensive against the Deby government in early June, seizing several eastern towns. Chad and Sudan agreed to deploy troops along the border at a mid-November contact group meeting; troops expected on the ground in January 2009.

Colombia
Ongoing, Intrastate with FARC, EPL, ELN

The Colombian government is involved in a long-term armed conflict with several guerrilla organizations. The conflict, which is active throughout the country, causes the death of thousands of people every year—40,000 in the past decade alone. The weakness of the Colombian state in the 1970s resulted in the formation of self-defense groups as private armies for rich landowners and drug lords. Subsequently, lucrative drug trafficking and kidnappings made these paramilitary forces increasingly independent. In 1995 the United Self-defense Forces of Colombia (AUC) was formed as an umbrella organization for several local paramilitary groups. In 2002, President Uribe was determined to fight "outlaws" on both the political left and right. AUC declared a ceasefire in December 2002 and Uribe's hope was that the two main left guerrilla groups FARC-EP (Revolutionary Armed Forces of Colombia—the People's Army—most often referred to as FARC) and ELN (National Liberation Army) would follow AUC's example. In June 2003 the government, AUC, and Catholic Church representatives signed an accord stipulating complete AUC demobilization by December 31, 2005. As of the end of 2005, half of AUC's 20,000 fighters had handed in their arms. Although there were several groups that fought the government at the beginning of the 1990s, today only two groups remain active: FARC and ELN (EPL—People's Liberation Army—has also been active as late as in 2004). FARC is the only peasant-based guerrilla movement. ELN was created by a group of students whose objective was to bring down the government, and declared itself the military wing of the PCML (Communist Party of Colombia Marxist Leninist). The United States has supported Colombia mainly by providing financial support for the government's anti-narcotics policies, expanded to counter-terrorism in 2001. FARC, ELN, and AUC are listed on the U.S. Department of State's Current List of Designated Foreign Terrorist Organizations. Demobilization of the AUC was completed in 2006. Since 2006 the conflict intensity has decreased every year. Both in 2007 and 2008 marches protesting against kidnappings and demanding the liberation of hostages have been organized nationwide. In 2008 FARC lost its two top commanders: Manuel "Shureshot" Marulanda, who died of a heart attack, and Raul Reyes, who was shot by the army on Ecuadorean territory, causing tense diplomatic relations between the two bordering countries. On two separate occasions in 2008, FARC released a total of six high-ranking politicians that it had held hostage.

DRC (Zaire)
Ongoing, Intrastate with CNDP, with Foreign Involvement

Large-scale conflict began in the Democratic Republic of Congo (DRC) in the mid-1990s. Following the genocide in Rwanda, the remnants of the Interhamwe militia responsible for perpetrating the genocide fled to the DRC (then Zaire), where they staged attacks from refugee camps against ethnic Tutsi Banyamulenge. Following the Interhamwe influx, armed Banyamulenge groups joined forces under the banner of the Alliance des forces démocratiques pour la libération du Congo (AFDL) with other rebels opposed to DRC dictator Mobutu. After toppling Mobutu in 1997, AFDL leader Laurent Kabila seized power, quickly alienating his former supporters. Concerned at Kabila's anti-Banyamulenge stance, armed Banyamulenge, joined by loyal Mobutuists, formed the anti-Kabila rebel group Rassemblement congolais pour la démocratie (RCD). Several foreign governments were involved with the conflict in the DRC. Initially, the Rwandan, Ugandan, and Angolan governments aided AFDL as a strike against Mobutu, who allowed rebel groups from all three countries to launch attacks from DRC soil. By the conflict's second phase, alliances had shifted, with Rwanda and Uganda turning on Kabila to support the rebel opposition, and Angola, Chad, Zimbabwe, and Namibia intervening on behalf of Kabila. Peace accords providing for the disarmament of militias and the deployment of a UN peacekeeping force were signed in mid-1999. Little progress was made in implementing the agreement until the 2001 death of Kabila left his more accommodating son in control. In 2006, Joseph Kabila became the DRC's first democratically elected president in 40 years. Dissatisfied with the outcome of the conflict, former RDC rebel Laurent Nkunda launched the Congrès National pour la Défense du Peuple (CNDP). In 2007, violence between the government and CNDP escalated. Negotiations yielded a January 23, 2008, ceasefire agreement that mandated the creation of a UN buffer zone and promised amnesty to militia fighters. Despite this fragile peace agreement, fighting flared up again in August 2008 in North Kivu, amid rumors that CNDP was recruiting and rearming. The violence escalated in October as the combined efforts of the DRC army and UN forces failed to contain major CNDP advances, and tensions continued to mount over Rwandan support for Nkunda. A ceasefire declared by Nkunda on November 16, 2008, has largely held, although it grew increasingly tenuous as talks between CNDP and the government deadlocked in December, prompting CNDP to refuse to recommit to the ceasefire and threaten to advance into the UN buffer zone. On January 23, 2009, Laurent Nkunda was arrested by the Rwandan government during a Rwandan military operation within DRC borders aimed at hunting down the Hutu rebel group FDLR.

Ethiopia
Ongoing, Intrastate with OLF

Since the state of Oromiya fell under Ethiopian control in the late 1890s, the Oromo people have lacked political influence and proportionate representation. In response to a series of repressive government policies targeting Oromo cultural, social, and political movements, the Oromo Liberation Front (OLF) was formed in 1974, with the stated goal of realizing "national self-determination for the Oromo people and their liberation from oppression and exploitation in all forms." Although the OLF has experienced internal tension over the years, particularly between its Christian wing based in the territory's west, and its Muslim and animist backers active in the region's east and south, the group remains intact. The OLF experienced a difficult first decade. To isolate and contain the group, the Dergue regime initiated in the 1970s a series of resettlement, villagization, and collectivization policies that succeeded in limiting the OLF's influence. By the mid-1980s, however, the Oromo population had grown increasingly resentful of these policies, allowing the OLF to rally a larger following. Despite its rising popularity, the OLF remained crippled by the pronounced disparity between its military resources and those of the Ethiopian government. Lacking any outside suppliers, the OLF was forced to build its arsenal of weapons and supplies through surprise raids against government troops—a strategy that proved only marginally successful. Despite a brief pause in the armed struggle while the OLF attempted to negotiate with the Ethiopian People's Revolutionary Democratic Front (EPRDF) government in the wake of its ouster of the Dergue, the OLF continued its low-level anti-government violence throughout the 1990s. Following failed negotiations with the government in 1997, the more militant wing of the group gained traction. The violence escalated in 1999 when Ethiopia's war with neighboring Eritrea provided the OLF with a window of opportunity. Emboldened by arms shipments from Eritrea, the OLF took advantage of the Ethiopian military's preoccupation by intensifying its attacks. In late 2004, the OLF, under intense pressure to participate in the 2005 elections, appeared to be on the brink of a major policy shift, publicly stating its willingness to open negotiations. Ultimately, however, the OLF refused to participate in the elections. The possibility of negotiation completely evaporated when the government brutally put down street protests in Oromiya in late 2005. The conflict continued throughout 2007 and 2008, with intermittent fighting between government forces and the OLF. In 2008, OLF leader Legesse Wegi was killed by police.

Ethiopia
Ongoing, Intrastate in ONLF

In 1984 the Ogaden National Liberation Front (ONLF) was established to struggle for self-determination. In January 1996 armed conflict broke out when ONLF declared a holy war against Ethiopia and launched an attack on Ethiopian government troops with the stated aim of liberating Ogaden from Ethiopian colonial power. ONLF offered the government a negotiated dialogue, but these proposals were turned down. The same year in June ONLF signed a military agreement on an alliance with the Oromo Liberation Front (OLF) although the parties still acted separately. In 1997 the conflict was inactive but erupted again the following year. On August 15, 1997, ONLF and one faction of Afar Revolutionary Democratic Unity Front (ARDUF) signed a document in which the two organizations agreed to cooperate and coordinate their political, diplomatic, and military efforts. Moreover, the ONLF was split into two factions: one that wanted to continue armed operations against the regime in Addis Ababa, and one that saw its fight as within the framework of the Somali regional state (which was now led by one of its officials, Mohamed Maalim). This led to a definite split of ONLF in June 1998 when one of its factions merged with the Ethiopian-Somali Democratic League (ESDL) and formed a new party called the Somali Democratic Party, with the intention of establishing a new regional government. Remaining ONLF continued the armed struggle. The conflict in Ethiopia continued, although accurate information is difficult to locate. An attack on an oil field in a remote Ogaden region on April 24, 2007, killed 74, including 9 Chinese. ONLF claimed responsibility. Joint ONLF and OLF actions against the government continued through 2006 and 2007. ONLF accused the Ethiopian government of punishing civilians for rebel activity in the troubled Ogaden region and alleged attempted genocide. Clashes between government and ONLF continued through 2008.

India
Ongoing, Intrastate with CPI-M

In the late 1960s several elements of the Indian Communist movement revolted against the prevailing communist party of India (CPI-M), accusing it of being counterrevolutionary. This so-called Naxalite movement became a revolutionary party with the establishment of the Communist Party of India (Marxist-Leninist) in 1969. Other groups that formed during this period and later with differing views on the best strategy for agrarian revolutionary struggle included the Maoist Communist Centre (MCC) and the Communist Party of India (M-L) People's War Group (PWG). The MCC and PWG led the Maoist insurgency against the Indian state in the 1990s. The revolutionary aim included the abolition of the feudal order in rural India. The Naxalite organizations have primarily mobilized among the peasantry, particularly among the tribals and landless poor in the jungle districts of Andhra Pradesh, Maharahstra, Madhya Pradesh, and Orissa. The low-intensity conflict between the Indian government and the rebel opposition was only one dimension of the deteriorating security situation in the Naxalite strongholds of Bihar and Andhra Pradesh during the 1990s. During 2004 the MCC and PWG were extending and consolidating their influence in their communist strongholds while also further strengthening cross-border links with Nepalese Maoist cadres. The government in Andrah Pradesh declared a unilateral ceasefire with the PWG in June 2004. Peace talks were initiated in October but ended without any substantial progress. On October 14, 2004, the MCC announced its merger with the PWG to form the Communist Party of India. Negotiations between CPI (Maoist) and the Andhra Pradesh state government broke down in mid-January 2005 after the rebels accused authorities of not addressing their demands for a written truce, release of prisoners, and redistribution of land. CPI (Maoist) continued to consolidate its hold on large rural areas in several Indian states (Andhra Pradesh, Bihar, Jharkand, Chattisgarh, etc.). The conflict escalated in 2006–2008, affecting 13 of India's 28 states. In particular, the formation of a state-sponsored militia, the Salwa Judum, in the state of Chattisgarh catalyzed a sharp increase in violence. With each state responsible for its own security, there is no comprehensive, coordinated approach by the various state governments to the Maoist conflict, resulting in an increase in violence. The central government continues to treat the conflict as purely a security issue and asserts that it will not negotiate with the CPI-M until it agrees to lay down its arms.

India

Ongoing, Intrastate with NSCN-K, with Foreign Involvement

Among the ethnic groups and tribes in the northeast, in 1947 the Nagas were first to seek a separate state. Nagaland was established as a separate state under the Indian constitution in 1963. The Naga National Council (NNC) continued the insurgency, but eventually signed the Shillong agreement in 1975, whereby NNC accepted the Indian constitution and agreed to surrender. In 1978 a new movement was formed, called the National Socialist Council of Nagaland (NSCN), demanding the establishment of a "greater Nagaland." The Konyak tribe, which formed the rank and file of the NSCN, formed a breakaway faction. In 1988, the Tangkhuls continued to dominate the command structure of the NSCN. As part of a deliberate strategy to enforce the vision of a "greater Nagaland," the insurgents have targeted other ethnic groups and forced their violent expulsion from the territory. It has been estimated that the conflict has claimed 20,000 lives during the last four decades. Strong regional linkages have remained between territorial insurgencies in the neighboring Indian states. NSCN has allegedly also received secondary support from regions within Bangladesh, Thailand, Burma, and Myanmar, and training from Pakistan's Inter Service Intelligence (ISI). Improved relations between India and Myanmar led to increased cooperation in fighting against the National Socialist Council of Nagaland-Khaplang (NSCN-K). In early 1997, several factors coincided to put pressure on the National Socialist Council of Nagaland-Isac Muivah (NSCN-IM) and facilitate negotiations for a political solution: the success of the government's counteroperations; the arrest of several prominent NSCN-IM leaders; Myanmar's hostile attitude towards NSCN activity on its territory; Indo-Bangladesh cooperation on preventing rebel activity along their border; and the strengthening of the hostile Khalang faction of the NSCN. The government signed a ceasefire with the NSCN-K in 2000 to limit the occasional cross-border attacks. Ceasefires with NSCN-K and NSCN-IM have been extended on several occasions. There were no talks between the government and NSCN-K, though a formal ceasefire remained in place 2005–2007. This ceasefire did not preclude attacks on NSCN-K by India's ally, Myanmar. The 2005–2007 offensives by Indian-Myanmar forces against NSCN-K bases have been criticized by both factions as a setback in the peace process. By December 2007 virtually all of the fighting took place between NSCN-K and the Myanmar army across the border from Indian Nagaland. Inter-factional fighting between the NSCN-IM and NSCN-K took place throughout 2005–2007. In January 2008, the Nagaland government was removed by Delhi and the state was brought under federal authority.

India
Ongoing, Intrastate with Kashmir Insurgents

The insurgency in Kashmir results from the state's disputed accession to India following partition in 1947. The dispute escalated into full-fledged war with Pakistan in 1948. The UN-mediated ceasefire line that was agreed to in 1949 divided Kashmir between Indian- and Pakistani-controlled sections. Anti-government demonstrations, strikes, and violent attacks on government targets launched in 1988 marked the onset of the Kashmir insurgency. By 1990, as many as 40 different militant groups existed. The main division is between the pro-Pakistani elements favoring accession to Pakistan and the pro-Azadi

elements favoring Kashmir's complete independence. The intrastate conflict has become closely entangled with the interstate relations between Pakistan and India. India has repeatedly accused Pakistan of supporting the Kashmir separatists, while Pakistan has denied these allegations and stated that its support to the insurgents is limited to political, cultural, and diplomatic areas. Positive moves by both parties in mid-2000 and early 2001 raised hope for a political dialogue, but no progress was made. Discussions have been deadlocked by irreconcilable preconditions: the Indian government insists that all talks must take place within the framework of the Indian constitution, while the insurgents demand that any talks must address the Kashmiri's demand for independence. The rebel opposition has demanded that Pakistan participate in the negotiations, but India insists that Kashmir is a purely internal matter. While cross-border infiltration has dipped thanks to the building of a new fence along the Line of Control and the cessation of military hostilities between India and Pakistan, Kashmir insurgents continue to engage the Indian army. The level of battle-related violence in Kashmir continued to drop in 2006, leading to an increase in tourism and development aid projects in the state. At the same time, disturbing indications continued throughout 2006 that civilians were increasingly becoming the target for militant violence, and that some groups were redirecting their energies towards large-scale attacks on soft targets outside of Jammu and Kashmir, such as the Mumbai train bombings of July 2006, which were reportedly committed by the Kashmiri insurgent group Lashkar-e-Toiba. In 2007 there was a sharp decline in battle-related fatalities, as well as in attacks on civilians. Violence grew in India-controlled Kashmir in 2008, as protests sparked by a planned Hindu shrine land transfer resumed. Involvement of Pakistan-based militants in the November 2008 Mumbai attacks prompted a sharp escalation in tensions. Initial investigations pointed to involvement of the Kashmiri group Lashkar-e-Toiba.

Iran
Ongoing, Intrastate with PJAK

The Kurdish Mujahideen e Khalq (MEK) roots are in the early 1960s in a nationalistic, liberal, lay-religious party, called the Liberation Movement. After a failed uprising against the Shah in 1963, many of the movement's leaders were imprisoned, and the younger generation advocated armed struggle. It was the younger members of the Liberation Movement who formed MEK, which became the more religiously oriented, anti-American offspring to the Liberation Movement. The group's potential for violence was developed as members were sent to train in PLO camps in Lebanon and Jordan. In 1971 the group attempted to attack the state, but the operations were foiled, leading to the execution of the founders and the arrest of many members of the group. This led to an influx of new leaders and members with a more Marxist-centered ideology, causing the group to eventually splinter. In the period leading up to the 1979 Islamic Revolution, MEK leaders were released from prison and they managed to become Iran's largest political movement. The Marxist-Leninist splinter group became known as the Paykar Organization during the revolution. MEK ended up opposing the regime through violent means. After a major violent incident in June 1981, leaders of the group fled to Paris. In 1987 most of the group moved to Iraq, where they remain today. Their support of the Iraqi side in the Iran-Iraq war had a negative effect on their popular support in Iran. There was not much activity in the conflict immediately after the Iran-Iraq war, but in 1991 the conflict started again. The capture of the Kurdish leader Abdullah Ocalan by Turkish security forces in 1999 led to protests and demonstrations in the Kurdish parts of Iran. As a result of these protests, Iranian PKK members created a new movement with the name Democratic Union Movement. On April 25, 2004, this movement held its first congress and formed a more structured organization with the name PJAK—The Free Life Party of Kurdistan (Partî Jiyanî Azadî Kurdistan). At this congress PJAK also presented its political motives and goals. PJAK continued its fighting in 2006 and the incidents and number of deaths were around the same as in 2005. In 2007 the rebel activity in Iran was similar to that in 2006 with the two rebel groups PJAK and the new Jondollah group active. Also the intensity of the fighting was similar to that in the previous years.

Iraq
Ongoing, Intrastate with TQJBR, Al-Mahdi Army, Jaish Ansar Al-Sunna, IAI

After Iraq was defeated in the interstate conflict against the United States, UK, and Australia in 2003, forces from a U.S.-led coalition of countries remained in Iraq to support the new government. The situation remains complex, with the Shi'i dominated government still struggling to contain violence among insurgent groups. One of the groups that wanted to overthrow the Iraqi government in the fall of 2003 was Jaish Ansar Al-Sunna (Army of Ansar Al-Sunna) in northern Iraq. As the number of casualties increased in the early months of 2004, the "Military Department" of the Zarqawi group stated their intention to overthrow the government, expel the U.S. forces, and establish a Sunni Islamic state with Sharia law. The group started its activity in 2004 and named itself TQJBR (Tanzim Qa'idat al-Jihad fi Bilad al-Rafidayn, The Organization of Jihad's Base in the Country of the Two Rivers). In early 2004, political discontent grew among the Shi'i population, especially targeting the foreign presence in the country. One of the more outspoken critics was Muqtada al-Sadr, who previously had formed a militia, the Al-Mahdi Army. The Al-Mahdi Army launched coordinated attacks on government positions in southern Iraq as well as in Baghdad in April 2004, and fought the government intensively during that year. In late August, the prime Shi'ite cleric in Iraq, Ayatollah Ali al-Sistani, intervened and negotiated a ceasefire. While some clashes continued, Muqtada al-Sadr focused more on preparing for the elections in January 2005, ultimately winning 30 seats in the new parliament. In 2005, activity by TQJBR and the Jaish Ansar al-Sunna escalated with attacks on civilians and inter-communal violence. The security forces originally also cooperated with paramilitary forces of former rebel groups, such as the Kurdish KDP and PUK forces in the north, and the Badr Brigades in Baghdad and in southern Iraq. By 2007, these had largely been incorporated into the official Iraqi police and army. There was growing discontent among the traditional tribal leadership with the behavior of several insurgent groups. This led to the formation of paramilitary tribal militias that started attacking insurgents locally, in particular in Anbar province. The government encouraged this development and promoted it in other parts of the country as well. The "surge" in 2007 led to an intensification of the conflict. As the conflict eventually became less intense in the capital Baghdad, there was an escalation of fighting further north in Iraq. Towards the end of the year, the number of incidents decreased, even though the number of casualties remained very high, as the insurgents started to focus on fewer, but larger-scale attacks. Violence gradually diminished during 2008 and into 2009, as the impact of the U.S. troop surge took hold. Radical Shi'ite cleric Muqtada Sadr announced a six-month extension of his Mahdi Army ceasefire in February 2008. In November a long-term security pact between United States and Iraq was signed, providing for U.S. troop withdrawal by the end of 2011.

Israel

Ongoing, Intrastate with Fatah, Palestinian Islamic Jihad, Hamas, (Hezbollah 2006)

The roots of the conflict lie in ancient and competing claims for the territory known as Palestine. The UN-mandated partition of Palestine in 1947 led to the establishment of the State of Israel in 1948 and was followed by five interstate wars with Arab countries between 1948 and the present. Two key factors that resulted from the wars and that fed the Israeli-Palestinian part of the Israeli-Arab conflict were Palestinian refugees growing out of the 1948–1949 war and the occupation of the West Bank and Gaza from Jordan and Egypt in 1967. In 1959 Yasser Arafat founded Fatah, which became an important player in the umbrella organization PLO (Palestinian Liberation Organization). Other Palestinian organizations took up arms soon after Fatah. Hezbollah has its origins in the Israeli occupation of southern Lebanon, after its intervention in the Lebanese civil war in 1982. In the West Bank and Gaza, Islamic groups such as the PIJ (Palestinian Islamic Jihad) and Hamas conducted their first attacks during the later half of the 1980s. Local Palestinian leaders in December 1987 initiated violent demonstrations against the Israeli occupation, the so-called Intifada (Uprising). The Oslo Accord, signed on September 13, 1993, called for the establishment of a Palestinian Interim Self-Government Authority and a preparatory transfer of power and responsibilities from Israel to authorized Palestinians, with a final settlement to be reached within five years. The second Intifada began in 2000 and all but ended any chance that the Oslo Accord would be implemented. In early 2005 Israel proceeded with the construction of a security wall roughly along the Green Line separating Israel from the West Bank. Israel's pullout from Gaza and the official ceasefire led to a decrease in conflict activity in 2005. In early 2006 Hamas won legislative elections in the West Bank and Gaza. Violence escalated between Israelis and Palestinians while tensions rose between Hamas and Fatah. Hamas's refusal to recognize Israel and respect previously signed agreements led to an almost complete blockade by western countries. (At the peak of Israeli-Palestinian clashes the conflict with Hezbollah in southern Lebanon reignited in 2006 following the abduction of two Israeli soldiers in July. A fragile UN-brokered ceasefire commenced on August 14.) Israeli-Palestinian "tit-for-tat fighting continued in 2007. In June 2007 Hamas-Fatah hostilities resulted in the break-up of the Palestinian territories into a Hamas-controlled Gaza Strip and a Fatah-controlled West Bank. The first months of 2008 saw a continuation of rocket fire from Gaza towards southern Israel, as well as Israeli targeting of Hamas, with the blockade in force. A six-month ceasefire was reached through Egyptian mediation in June. As the truce ended in December, rocket fire began anew, as did Israeli attacks on rocket-launching crews and activists. On December 27 Israel launched a massive air and then ground assault on Hamas throughout the Gaza Strip. An internationally brokered ceasefire took hold on January 18, 2009.

Myanmar
Ongoing, Intrastate with KNU

The Union of Myanmar (Burma until 1989) consists of several ethnic groups. The Karen's traditional homeland is along the border with Thailand. The KNU (Karen National Union) was formed in 1947. Shortly after independence in 1948, the KNU demanded the formation of an independent Karen state. Tensions continued to grow and in January 1949 fierce fighting erupted between KNU forces and a combination of government troops and affiliated paramilitary forces. KNU has formed alliances with other insurgent groups, especially those in close areas such as the Karenni, Mon, and Pao. Myanmar has accused Thailand of backing the KNU, as the group has been able to retreat

to bases on Thai territory. The KNU had great military success until an internal split, and ensuing government offensive in 1994–1995. In late 1994, disenchantment with the Christian leadership of KNU among a group of Buddhist Karen led to a split in the organization and the formation of the Democratic Kayin Buddhist Army (DKBA). The DKBA quickly signed a ceasefire with the Myanmar government and began an armed struggle against the KNU. The KNU has relied mostly on the tactic of armed attacks on government troops, while the government offensives have been large-scale operations lasting for months. After the fall of the KNU headquarters in 1995 and a tougher stance towards border-crossings from the Thai authorities, KNU has adopted more of a guerrilla strategy. After decreasing clashes in 2003, the KNU and the government announced a "gentleman's agreement" ceasefire in December 2003, although occasional breaches of the ceasefire were reported. In March 2006, counterinsurgency action in western Karen state reportedly forced villagers to flee their homes, bringing the total of internally displaced to 5,000 since January. In April, the army intensified its offensive against Karen communities near the new capital Pyinmana along the Thai border. The comprehensive government offensives launched in 2006 continued throughout the year in 2007. The fighting included joint attacks from the government and the DKBA as well as increased casualties from the non-state conflict between DKBA and the KNU. Thousands of Karen people were displaced and many fled across the border into Thailand. In February 2008, Pado Mahn Shar, leader of the KNU, was shot dead at his home.

Myanmar
Ongoing, Intrastate with SSA-S

The 1947 constitution of the Union of Burma stipulated that the Shan State had the right to leave the union ten years after the country became independent in 1948. Two years later, the Karen rebellion (see above) spread into Shan State as the Karen insurgents were supported by fleeing Chinese Kuomintang (KMT) troops; as a result the Burmese government sent additional troops to the area. With the alleged assistance of the American CIA, the KMT maintained bases in Burma during the next decade in their struggle against the Chinese communist government. They also developed into the largest opium-dealing army in the world. The Shan nationalist movement started gaining strength in the mid-1950s. They managed to take over most of the drug business after the KMT left in 1961. Following the Burmese military coup in 1962, the elected Shan administration came under virtual military occupation by the government. The three largest Shan rebel organizations merged in 1964 as the SSA (Shan State Army). In the late 1980s and early 1990s, most of the Shan insurgent organizations either signed ceasefire agreements with the government or became affiliated (or incorporated) with the MTA (Mong Tai Army). In 1989, several ethnic groups emerged from the disintegration of the Burmese Communist Party (CPB). The strongest militarily was the UWSA (Wa), which signed a ceasefire with the government with the promise to help the government against MTA. Throughout 1995, the members of the MTA split into several different factions. A number of these were involved in fighting against the government, but finally three main groups united as the Shan State Army–South Command (SSA-S.) The SSA-S continued fighting in the Shan conflict, as well as fighting UWSA, which allegedly took over the drug business left by MTA. The SSA-S relied on cross-border attacks from Thailand. The fighting had slowly intensified between the government and SSA-S after a year of almost no conflict activity in 2003. Some small clashes were reported in 2004 as the government increased its military presence in Shan state. In 2005 and 2006, conflict activity increased as the SSA-S established a presence in several areas of Shan state. Limited confrontations continued in 2007 as the SSA-S strengthened its control over its area while the government forces were mainly concentrated in towns and along the highways in Shan state.

Pakistan (Baluchistan)
Ongoing, Intrastate with the BLA

The current conflict in the sparsely-populated but resource-rich Pakistani province of Baluchistan arose from local opposition to government development projects initiated in the region following Pervez Musharraf's ascent to power in 1999. Natural gas pipelines, new railroad and road networks, an international airport, and a deep-sea port were planned, along with the construction of new military bases to provide security for this new infrastructure. The infrastructure projects and heightened military presence soon earned the resentment of local ethnic Baluch, who accused the government of acquiring ancestral land without adequate compensation, displacing thousands from their homes, and failing to provide employment for the local population. In September 2003, the Baluchistan Provincial Assembly unanimously passed a resolution against planned military cantonments in several cities. In the same month, several nationalist Baluch political groups formed Baluch Ittehad (Baluch Unity), whose stated objective was to resist "anti-Baluchistan projects." By the end of 2003, small bombings and incidences of sabotage targeting new infrastructure were frequent. The government responded by increasing its military presence, drawing vehement criticism from the Baluch. By the end of 2005 Baluch Ittehad had declared an autonomous Baluchistan, and large-scale fighting was underway. Following government offensives against Baluch Ittehad and the eventual death of leader Nawab Akbar Bugti in August 2006,

Bugti's successor announced that the struggle against the government would thereafter be directed by the Baluchistan Liberation Army (BLA). Operational since a June 2004 attack against a paramilitary checkpoint, the BLA was officially listed as a terrorist group by the Pakistani government in 2006. Joining forces with the remnants of Baluch Ittehad, the BLA carried out ambushes and rocket attacks directed at government infrastructure. Baluch activists claimed that heavy fighting, including government attacks against civilians in the region, persisted in 2007. In November 2007, the BLA stepped up its attacks against government forces amid rumors of internal discord. On October 26, 2008, the Pakistani government unveiled a road map for the resolution of the conflict, one that emphasized constitutional changes, the rebuilding of institutions, and the redistribution of natural resource revenues. While there is no evidence of foreign involvement in the conflict, the Pakistani government has accused India of backing Baluch groups, and suspects U.S. and British intelligence agencies of aiding the Baluch in an attempt to counter Chinese influence in the region. Both India and the Baluch have denied any such involvement, along with claims that Afghan warlords are among the BLA rebels fighting in Baluchistan.

Peru
Ongoing, Intrastate with Sendero Luminoso

Conflict between the Peruvian government and the Maoist insurgent group Sendero Luminoso (SL) dates back to 1980, when the group began a violent struggle aimed at the destruction of existing Peruvian institutions and the implementation of a peasant revolutionary regime. Violence dramatically declined after the 1992 capture of SL founder Professor Abimael Guzman. Past its 1980s heyday, the group lost much of its momentum as a popular movement, its survival largely dependent on support from coca farmers and drug-trafficking revenue. In 1994, SL re-

portedly split into two separate factions: the "pacificist" supporters of Guzman, who from prison had begun to make public overtures toward peace with the government, and a new "hardliner" group led by Oscar Ramirez Durand. From 2000 onwards, the conflict in Peru was considered terminated, until a 2007 resurgence of violence. By 2006, the hardline SL faction was active primarily in the Apurimac-Ene River Valley (VARE). The SL pacifists were confined to the Hullaga Valley under separate leadership. Following failed negotiations with the Peruvian government, the Hullaga Valley faction decided in 2007 to rejoin the hardline group, resulting in the essential reunification of Sendero Luminoso. Now consisting of several hundred guerillas who stage sporadic ambushes on government security forces and offer armed protection for cocaine traffickers, the group is strengthening its presence in the La Mar Province in Ayachuco. Benefiting SL has been growing frustration on the part of cocaleros over the Peruvian government's anti-narcotics strategy. Aided by peasants reliant on coca-growing for their economic survival who willingly inform on police and military activities, SL also takes advantage of local anti-government sentiment by inciting protests aimed at further inflaming tensions. On January 11, 2008, SL rebels killed 12 soldiers and a civilian in the Huancavelica province in what constituted the group's deadliest attack in years. The next day, another SL attack ended with the deaths of four police officers in San Martin. A truth commission formed in 2001 to investigate human-rights abuses perpetrated by both leftist rebels and the Peruvian government found SL responsible for more than half of the 69,280 deaths resulting from over two decades of government-leftist fighting. In 2007, the Peruvian government provided monetary compensation to hundreds of communities in the highland and jungle regions worst affected by the government's 20-year conflict with SL.

Increasing criticism of U.S. involvement in Filipino affairs led to the formation of several protest groups in the early 1960s. Inspired by the successful revolutions in China, Cuba, and Vietnam, younger members of the Partido Komunista ng Pilipinas (PKP) were eager for the party to resume the type of armed activity that had characterized the party immediately after World War II. In 1968 the Huk established the CPP (Communist Party of the Philippines). The CPP looked to the Maoist idea of an agrarian revolution, and developed plans for a military struggle. CPP's military wing, the NPA (New People's Army), was established in 1969. In the following years, the NPA kept expanding, and in 1972 President Marcos declared countrywide martial law to suppress the "state of rebellion" caused by the Communists, as well as the increasing communal conflicts between Moros and Christians in Mindanao. Several factors led to a decrease in fighting between the CPP and the government in the early 1990s. The military was preoccupied with internal struggles. Changes also occurred within the CPP, namely, there was diminishing international political support as well as internal divisions on what tactics to pursue. As a consequence, several factions left the CPP to pursue urban guerrilla warfare. Conflict activity decreased as more formal peace negotiations were held in the mid-1990s. Under President Estrada in 1998 peace negotiations stalled. The economic crisis of 1998–1999 also led to widespread criticism of the government, and the different factions of the CPP seemed to unite, with the conflict escalating in 1999–2002. Since the CPP tactics were to connect with rural support and establish strongholds in the two largest islands, Luzon and Mindanao, it has been able at times to control substantial territory. The conflict continued unabated in 2005 and 2006, with the CPP's armed wing NPA active in 69 of the country's 79 prov-

inces. In 2006 President Arroyo announced a policy of all-out war against the rebels. The rebels responded by calling for an intensification of the struggle. The violence persisted in 2007. As in previous years, Arroyo ordered the military to "crush" the CPP-NPA, calling them the number one threat to national security. In 2008, the NPA rebels continued to inflict losses on Philippine's Armed Forces as well as on civilians.

The government of the Philippines has long been involved in fighting communist and Muslim (Moro) insurgencies in Mindanao. The term "Moro" is more specific than the universal "Muslim" since it denotes the political identity of the local Muslims. During the 1970s, the Moro National Liberation Front (MNLF) and its military wing engaged in armed struggle against the central government, leading to as many as 120,000 deaths. Under pressure from the Organization of the Islamic Conference, in 1976 the MNLF dropped its demands for independence and settled for autonomy. The agreement provided for the granting of autonomy to 13 of the 23 provinces in Mindanao, Sulu, and Palewan islands. When the MNLF dropped its demand for independence, breakaway factions emerged, including the Moro Islamic Liberation Front (MILF). Hostilities resumed and continued into the early 1980s. In the early 1990s, increased international attention was directed towards Mindanao, resulting from several high-profile kidnappings. The Abu Sayyef Group (ASG) was responsible for several attacks on civilians. In 1996 the Final Peace Agreement was signed, and fighting decreased in the following years. After formal negotiations had resumed, the government launched an "all-out war" policy against the Moro groups in 2000, leading to an escalation in conflict and the breakdown of peace talks. In 2003, the conflict between the government and MILF escalated again. During the second half of 2003 several attempts to start peace talks were made. The ceasefire lasted for much of 2004 as well. However, sporadic clashes continued in 2004 and 2005 amidst fresh peace talks. In 2006, negotiations continued between MILF and the government; however, the Abu Sayyaf Group continued to carry out attacks and bombings. In August 2006 the Philippine government launched a major offensive against the rebels on Jolo. In 2007 the MILF became active again as a negotiation deadlock between the warring parties persisted. A new dyad also became active in 2007 when a MNLF faction under Habier Malik declared jihad on the government. Further, the ASG showed a tendency for greater tactical and logistical cooperation with other armed Moro groups in 2007 and carried out several attacks with MILF, mainstream MNLF, and the new MNLF faction separately. Clashes between government troops and both MILF and Abu Sayyef in Mindanao continued throughout the 2008, amid sporadic but unsuccessful attempts at negotiation.

Russia
Ongoing, Intrastate with Republic of Chechnya

During the Soviet era, the Autonomous Republic of Chechen-Ingush was under the authority of the Russian Republic. After the Soviet Union was dissolved in 1991 and the Russian Federation was formed, the new Russian government considered Chechen-Inguish to be one of the federated states. The Chechens aspired to political as well as cultural independence—Chechnya declared independence in 1991. In 1994 the conflict escalated radically when the Russian army launched a large-scale military intervention into Chechnya. During the first war, from 1994 to 1996, the Yeltsin government's intervention in Chechnya was unpopular in Russia. The second war broke out in 1999 and is still ongoing; President

Putin has consistently referred to the Russian action in Chechnya as a "campaign against terrorism." This approach has enjoyed both strong popular and political support in Russia. During both conflict phases, "the Republic of Chechnya" has been obstructed by an internal power struggle. From the outset of the conflict, the fighting took the form of violence against civilians and indiscriminate killings. In 2004, the conflict escalated as the rebels instigated attacks in neighboring republics such as Dagestan, Ingushetia, and Northern Ossetia, with terrorist acts reaching as far as Moscow. During the course of the conflict, few serious efforts have been made to negotiate a solution. In the second phase, the Russian government's approach was a refusal to recognize "President" Maskhadov's authority. As of the end of 2005, Russia maintained a certain degree of control over the Chechnya territory. The Russian leadership also dictated Chechnya's political future through Alu Alkhanov and his puppet government. Nevertheless, the rebels continue to be an active threat both for Chechnya and for the neighboring areas. The conflict continued to be active in 2006 and 2007, but with a significantly lower number of battle-related deaths than in 2004 and 2005. The rebels appeared to have been severely weakened and did not carry out any spectacular terrorist attacks or participate in any large-scale attacks. A reason for this could be the deaths of key figures within the Chechen leadership, not least the rebel military commander Shamil Basayev in 2006. As of the end of 2007, Russia maintained a certain control over the Chechnya territory. The Russian leadership also controlled Chechnya's political status through the local administration. Low-level violence continued into 2008.

Somalia
Ongoing, Intrastate with SICS, with Foreign Involvement

Since the 1991 ouster of dictator Siad Barre, armed factions have been struggling over control of Somalia. Between 1997 and 2000, there existed no effective government in Somalia, as fighting raged between rival clan-based militias. In 2000, a Transitional National Government (TNG) was elected by clan elders at a peace conference boycotted by many opposition parties. Armed conflict continued in 2001 between the TNG and an umbrella organization of armed resistance groups calling itself the Somali Reconciliation and Restoration Council (SRRC). A ceasefire agreement brokered by the Inter-Governmental Authority on Development (IGAD) led to the 2004 creation of an Interim Charter, which outlined a five-year transition for Somalia from factionalized near-anarchy to federation. In 2005, the new Transitional Federal Government (TFG) suffered a temporary geographic split between factions in Mogadishu and the safer city of Jowhar. By early 2006, the government factions had agreed on a compromise seat of power in Baidoa. By this time, the Mogadishu faction of the TFG had been forced out of the city by a growing network of local Islamic courts. Having gained control of Mogadishu, the courts militia declared itself the Supreme Islamic Council of Somalia (SICS), and proceeded to consolidate its power in southern Somalia. The Ethiopian government, fearing the rise of a nationalist Islamic state on its border, sent troops in late 2006 to help prop up the TFG. The SICS was pushed back to Mogadishu, which the group subsequently abandoned, dissolving its administrative wing and retreating to the south where fighting continued. In January 2007, the U.S. launched airstrikes targeting al-Qaeda operatives reportedly fighting alongside SICS. Throughout 2007, SICS and affiliated clan militias waged a guerila-style war in the streets of Mogadishu against government targets and Ethiopian troops. In late 2007, SICS was absorbed by the newly formed anti-TFG, anti-Ethiopian umbrella group the Alliance for the Re-Liberation of Somalia (ARS). Despite the August 2008 signing by the TFG and ARS of the UN-brokered Djibouti Agreement, violence continued through the end of 2008. Disputes over the implementation of the agreement continue, and the peace process has been rejected not only by extremist Islamic groups outside the ARS umbrella, but by hardline camps within both the TFG and ARS. As of December, Islamist militias controlled almost all of south-central Somalia's major towns, with the exception of Mogadishu and Baidoa, where the almost-defunct TFG was holding onto tenuous control. In January 2009, the resignation of TFG president Yusuf, coupled with the withdrawal of Ethiopian troops, fueled fears of government collapse and increasing violence.

Sri Lanka
Ongoing, Intrastate with LTTE

Tamil militancy in Sri Lanka arose when the Tamils expressed fear that the unitary constitutional arrangements of the new state in 1948 would not give minorities adequate protection against the possible discriminatory consequences of majoritarian Sinhalese rule, including the constitutional stipulation of the primacy of Sinhala and Buddhism—the language and religion of the Sinhalese majority. The constitutional status of the predominantly Tamil area in the northeast of the island has remained the core of the conflict. The Liberation Tigers of Tamil Eelam (LTTE) was established in 1976 as a purely military organization, pursuing separatist demands. The LTTE initiated regular fighting by 1983, with an estimated 65,000 killed and 1.8 million displaced (as of 2003). The Indian–Sri Lankan accord of 1987 provided for the establishment of a regional provincial council in the Tamil areas and the disarming of Tamil militants. The Indian Peace Keeping Force (IPKF) was subsequently deployed on the island to guarantee the implementation of the political solution and the cessation of hostilities. When IPKF troops withdrew from Sri Lanka in 1990 full-fledged fighting resumed. Intense inter-factional fighting exhausted the previously Indian-backed more moderate Tamil alliance and left the LTTE unchallenged. The most violent phase of the conflict began in 1995, aimed at eliminating the military capacity of the LTTE. By late 2000 war fatigue led the Tamil Tigers to declare a unilateral ceasefire. The LTTE and the government signed a memorandum of Cessation of Hostilities in 2002. In 2006, after four years of relative peace, military conflict again broke out between the government and LTTE. Human rights abuses and political killings were carried out with impunity by both sides. Talks in February and October 2006 failed to restart discussion of a political settlement. The armed conflict continued unabated in 2007. A series of major ground offensives by the Sri Lankan army during the first half of the year brought the eastern part of the country back under government control for the first time since 1994. LTTE was severely weakened by the government offensive. In spite of heavy fighting, the ceasefire agreement remained officially in place throughout the year, as none of the parties wanted to be blamed for its demise. On January 2, 2008, however, the government announced that it had decided to abrogate the ceasefire agreement with LTTE as of January 16, 2008. Military operations intensified with heavy losses. The government announced on January 2, 2009 the capture of the de facto LTTE capital of Killinochchi after months of fierce fighting and heavy casualties; an estimated 250,000 to 300,000 civilians were displaced and trapped in the shrinking area of LTTE control.

Sudan
Ongoing, Intrastate with SLM/A, JEM

In early 2003, while the government and SPLM/A were negotiating a settlement of the conflict in southern Sudan, another conflict broke out in Darfur, western Sudan. The Sudan Liberation Movement/Army (SLM/A) declared that it would fight the government to change the political system in Sudan. It demanded a united democratic Sudan based on equality, the separation of religion and the state, complete restructuring and devolution of power, more equitable development, and cultural and political pluralism. Subsequently another opposition group, JEM (Justice and Equality Movement), also launched an armed struggle against the government, fighting for a federal system with autonomy for all states, a rotating presidency, and an equal distribution of natural resources. The two groups have cooperated both militarily and politically, despite internal disagreement and fighting between them. Negotiations between the government of Sudan and SLM/A and JEM (jointly and separately) were held throughout the 2003–2005 period, but stalled on power-sharing and security arrangements. Besides the fighting between the two rebel groups and the army, a government-aligned militia called Janjaweed has been burning villages, looting, and killing. Armed conflict continued in Darfur during 2005, albeit at a significantly lower level. The lower level of conflict is due to the presence of AMIS (African Union Mission in Sudan) forces, the flight of most of the population to internally displaced person and refugee camps, pressure by the international community, and consolidation of areas of control by the warring parties. Eritrea, Chad, and Libya have supported SLA and JEM. An estimated 180,000 to 300,000 people have died in Darfur since the civil conflict erupted in 2003, with some 2.6 million civilians left homeless. 2006 was characterized by an increased level of violence, a deteriorating humanitarian situation, and fragmentation among the rebel groups. Clashes between the government and the rebels increased in intensity during 2006. Most of the fighting took place between the government and an alliance formed in the beginning of July, named the National Redemption Front (NRF). This higher level of violence led to a worsening of the humanitarian situation. Fragmentation among the rebels continued into 2007. An umbrella movement called URF (United Resistance Front) was ultimately formed and unification of some SLM/A commanders took place. The situation in Darfur also heavily influenced the situation in neighboring Chad. In 2008, serious clashes between government and rebel forces continued, despite the arrival of rhw United Nations' African Union Mission in Darfur (UNAMID) forces. Clashes also occurred between government forces and the SPLA. Signing of Status of Forces Agreement in February on operating rules removed major barriers to deployment of UN-AU hybrid peacekeeping force. The International Criminal Court charged Sudanese President Bashir with genocide, crimes against humanity, and war crimes.

Turkey
Ongoing, Intrastate with PKK

Abdullah Öcalan founded the PKK (Kurdistan Workers' Party) in 1974 as a Marxist-Leninist group with the goal of establishing an independent and democratic Kurdish state. In August 1984 PKK forces began ambushing Turkish troops on Kurdish territory. Unlike many other Kurdish organizations, such as the Kurdish Democratic Party of Iran (KDPI) in Iran and the Kurdistan Democratic Party (KDP) and Patriotic Union of Kurdistan (PUK) in Iraq, the PKK originally demanded an independent Kurdish state instead of Kurdish autonomy. After Öcalan was arrested and tried in 1999, he gave up the idea of a Kurdish state and convinced the PKK's Presidential Council to drop the word

"Kurdistan" from the names of PKK's military and political wings (ARGK and ERNK). The PKK retained its sizeable "Public-defense Force." Syria, Greece, and Iran have provided the PKK with shelter, training grounds, and/ or financial support. Northern Iraq has been a safe-haven for PKK fighters. In April 2002 the PKK changed its name, announcing that it had fulfilled its historical mission and that it was now dissolved. At the same time the Congress for Freedom and Democracy in Kurdistan (KADEK) announced its establishment to continue PKK's struggle for the liberation of the Kurds through dialogue and democracy rather than violence. KADEK was dissolved after the summer of 2003 and a new Kurdish group intended to attract broader support, KONGRA-GEL (People's Congress of Kurdistan), was formed. The group reverted to its original name PKK in 2005. In that same year a sharp increase in clashes was reported. On August 19, 2005, the PKK unilaterally declared a ceasefire after Prime Minister Erdogan announced that his government wanted more reforms for the Kurds. Attacks decreased but nevertheless continued, indicating the ceasefire was not recognized or adhered to by either side. The PKK's ceasefire appeared to be an effort to get their case heard during sensitive negotiations leading up to Turkey's October 3rd date for the start of entry talks with the European Union. On several occasions, the PKK has declared unilateral ceasefires (in August 2005, September-October 2006, June 2007). However, the ceasefires did not hold, and armed clashes as well as the planting of bombs and landmines by the PKK continued throughout the year. The bulk of the fighting took place in the PKK stronghold areas of southeastern Turkey and northern Iraq. In late 2007, the Turkish government stepped up its military action against the PKK, with parliament authorizing operations against PKK headquarters in northern Iraq. Cross-border air-strikes as well as ground incursions continued in 2008.

Uganda

Ongoing, Intrastate with LRA and ADF

Uganda's history since independence in 1962 has been characterized by violence, much of it based on regional interests. The current conflict with the Lord's Resistance Army (LRA) has its roots in 1986, when Museveni seized power and the National Resistance Army (NRA) forces began to commit human rights abuses throughout the Acholi region. Acholi soldiers from Obote's defunct national army and youths fleeing from NRA operations either hid or crossed the border into Sudan to take up arms. In August 1986, these fighters, under the name Uganda People's Democratic Army (UPDA), launched the first attack against NRA troops. UPDA signed a peace agreement with the government in 1988. Meanwhile, an Acholi woman named Alice Auma claimed to have been possessed by an alien Christian spirit and in 1986 began raising an army. In November 1986 Uganda Democratic Christian Army (UDCA) began attacking NRA units stationed in Acholi. The UDCA has its roots in both of these movements and is led by Joseph Kony. In 1992 Kony formed the Lord's Resistance Army. The Khartoum regime until the early 2000s supported LRA, providing bases, weapons, and military training. In return, LRA fought alongside Sudanese government forces against SPLA/M. Zaire/DRC has also supported rebels opposing Musevni's government. However, in 1998 the DRC switched sides in the conflict. The Uganda's Peoples' Defense Force (UPDF) subsequently received permission from Sudan to fight LRA in southern Sudan. The rebels came under even further military pressure when Sudan struck a deal with Uganda, allowing UPDF to go even further into Sudan. During the last two months of 2004, a ceasefire was respected and peace talks were initiated. The peace agreement between the Sudanese government and SPLM/A meant that LRA came under increasing pressure in southern Sudan. In August 2006, the government and the LRA reached a ceasefire agreement. A revised cessation of hostilities agreement was signed November 1, but talks were later suspended. By 2007, the conflict between LRA and the Ugandan government was no longer active, although a final peace agreement has yet to be signed. And in late 2008 yet another massacre was attributed to the LRA. The Alliance for Democratic Forces (ADF) arose in 1996 in western Uganda. ADF was a conglomeration of at least three earlier groups: remnants of the separatist Rwenzori movement, the National Army for the Liberation of Uganda (NALU), and extremist elements from the Tabliq Muslim community. The movement claimed to be fighting against what they perceive to be a one-party state. Sudan has provided support to ADF, as have Zaire/DRC and Rwanda. ADF initially used bases in Zaire and launched attacks across the border. Like LRA, ADF attacked indiscriminately, killing and abducting large numbers of civilians. In 1998 Uganda intervened in the DRC war, ostensibly to destroy ADF's bases and to prevent the group from receiving supplies in the future. From 2000 on, the government managed to destroy several ADF bases in eastern DRC and the activity of the group subsequently diminished. In 2007 remnants of the group reappeared, briefly engaging the army again. In early 2008, the army launched a crackdown on suspected collaborators with ADF in the west. ADF requested peace talks in July 2008 to end the12-year insurgency, and the government agreed.

United States

Ongoing, Intrastate with al-Qaeda, with Foreign Involvement

The conflict between the United States and al-Qaeda constitutes a nontraditional case of internal conflict with most of the activity taking place outside of the United States and including armed forces from over 20 different countries. U.S. airbases in Saudi Arabia caused much criticism of the United States and its regional allies. Al-Qaeda had been formed in 1988 by volunteer forces that were fighting alongside the rebels in the Afghanistan conflict (see Afghanistan above). Encouraged by the 1989 withdrawal of Soviet troops that had supported the Afghan government in that conflict, al-Qaeda declared its intent to continue the jihad in defense of Islamic movements. Al-Qaeda's founder Osama bin Laden from Saudi Arabia became increasingly critical of the United States and its presence in the Islamic world. On September 11, 2001, al-Qaeda launched attacks on the Pentagon in Washington, DC, and civilian targets in New York City. The goal was to force the United States to abandon its involvement overseas, and specifically in the Middle East. Following these attacks, U.S. President Bush declared "war on terror" and al-Qaeda. Several other countries quickly supported the United States. In October–November 2001, troops were deployed from the United Kingdom, Canada, Australia, Germany, France, Poland, Italy, and Turkey while other countries offered other types of support. By March 2002, more than 17,000 military personnel from 17 countries had been deployed together with U.S. forces as the "coalition of the willing." U.S. demands that the Taliban extradite the al-Qaeda leaders were rejected. The U.S.-led "Operation Enduring Freedom" that started in October 2001 then targeted suspected al-Qaeda bases in Afghanistan, but also the Taliban regime itself for its support of al-Qaeda. With the defeat of the Taliban government, the U.S. attacks on al-Qaeda intensified. Most surviving al-Qaeda operatives fled across the border into Pakistan in 2002–2003, while others regrouped in Saudi Arabia. When the conflict resumed in 2004, almost all the activity took place in the Pakistani tribal areas of South Waziristan and in Saudi Arabia. Between 2005 and 2007 most of the activity in the conflict took place in the border region between Afghanistan and Pakistan. In March 2006 the Pakistani army launched a heavy military offensive in the border areas. Anger at civilian casualties caused by international forces continued. At the beginning of the Obama Administration in 2009, the United States plans to drastically increase its troop levels in Afghanistan.

REFERENCES

Asal, Victor, and Amy Pate. 2005. "The Decline of Ethnic Political Discrimination, 1950–2003," in Ted Robert Gurr and Monty Marshall (eds.), *Peace and Conflict 2005*. College Park, MD: Center for International Development and Conflict Management.

Baker, Raymond W. 2005. *Capitalism's Achilles Heel: Dirty Money and How to Renew the Free-Market System*. Hoboken: John Wiley & Sons.

Balch-Lindsay, Dylan, and Andrew J. Enterline. 2000. "Killing Time: The World Politics of Civil War Duration; 1820–1992." *International Studies Quarterly* 44:615–642.

Barry, Ellen. 2007, September 18. "From Staten Island Haven, Liberians Reveal War's Scars." *New York Times*. Retrieved April 28, 2009, from: *http://www.nytimes.com/2007/09/18/nyregion/18liberians.html*.

Bekoe, Dorina, and Christina Parajon. 2007. "Women's Role in Liberia's Reconstruction." United States Institute of Peace. Retrieved April 29, 2009, at *http://www.usip.org/pubs/usipeace_briefings/2007/0530_liberia_women_reconstruction.html*.

BMZ (Federal Ministry for Economic Cooperation and Development). 2007. *Transforming Fragile States—Examples of Practical Experience*. Baden-Baden: Nomos.

Brahm, Eric. 2005. "Patterns of Truth: Examining Truth Commission Impact in Cross-National Context." Paper presented at the International Studies Association Annual Meeting, Honolulu, HI.

———2007. "Uncovering the Truth: Examining Truth Commission Success and Impact." *International Studies Perspectives* 8:16–35.

Brancati, Dawn. 2006. "Decentralization: Fueling the Fire or Dampening the Flames of Ethnic Conflict and Secessionism." *International Organization* 60(3):651–685.

Britton, Hannah. 2006. "Gender Quotas, Electoral Strategies, and State Feminism in Africa." The International Studies Association Annual Meeting.

Burnside, Craig, and David Dollar. 2000. "Aid, Policies and Growth." *American Economic Review* 90:847–868.

Carment, David, Patrick James, and Zeynep Taydas. 2006. *Who Intervenes?: Ethnic Conflict and Interstate Crisis*. Columbus: Ohio State University Press.

Cetinyan, Rupen. 2002. "Ethnic Bargaining in the Shadow of Third-Party Intervention." *International Organization* 56(3):645–678.

Chauvet, Lisa, and Paul Collier. 2009. "What are the Preconditions for Turnarounds in Failing States?" *Conflict Management and Peace Science*. forthcoming.

Chauvet, Lisa, Paul Collier, and Anke Hoeffler. 2006. *The Cost of Failing States and the Limits to Sovereignty.* UN-WIDER WP.

Chen, Siyan, Norman V. Loayza, and Marta Reynal-Querol. 2008. "The Aftermath of Civil War." *The World Bank Economic Review Advance Access* February 10, 2008.

Clague, Christopher, Philip Keefer, Stephen Knack, and Mancur Olson. 1996. "Property and Contract Rights in Autocracies and Democracies." *Journal of Economic Growth* 1(2):243–276.

Colaresi, Michael and Sabine C. Carey. 2008. "To Kill or to Protect: Security Forces, Domestic Institutions, and Genocide." *Journal of Conflict Resolution* 52(1):39–67.

Collier, Paul. 1999. "On the Economic Consequences of Civil War." *Oxford Economic Papers—New Series* 51(1):168–183.

———2000. "Doing Well Out of War: An Economic Perspective." In Mats Berdal and David M. Malone (eds.), *Greed and Grievance: Economic Agendas in Civil Wars* (91–111). Boulder: Lynne Rienner.

———2007. *The Bottom Billion: Why the Poorest Countries are Failing and What Can Be Done about it.* Oxford: Oxford University Press.

Collier, Paul, V. L. Elliott, Håvard Hegre, Anke Hoeffler, Marta Reynal-Querol, and Nicholas Sambanis. 2003. *Breaking the Conflict Trap: Civil War and Development Policy.* Washington, DC: The World Bank.

Collier, Paul and Anke Hoeffler. 2004a. "Conflicts." In Bjørn Lomborg (ed.) *Global Crises, Global Solutions* (pp 129–156).

———2004b. "Greed and Grievance in Civil War." *Oxford Economic Papers* 56:663–695.

———2004c. "Aid, Policy and Growth in Post-Conflict Countries." *The European Economic Review* 48:1125–1145.

———2006. "Military Expenditure in Post-Conflict Societies." *Economics of Governance* 7(1):89–106.

Collier, Paul, Anke Hoeffler, and Dominic Rohner. 2009. "Beyond Greed and Grievance." *Oxford Economic Papers.* 61:1-27.

Collier, Paul, Anke Hoeffler, and Måns Söderbom. 2004. "On the Duration of Civil War." *Journal of Peace Research* 41:253–273.

———2008. "Post-Conflict Risks." *Journal of Peace Research* 45:461–478.

Crisis Management Initiative (CMI). 2006. "The Aceh Peace Process: Involvement of Women." http://www.cmi.fi/files/Aceh_involvement_of_women.pdf.

de Rouen, Karl, and David Sobek. 2004. "The Dynamics of Civil War Duration and Outcome." *Journal of Peace Research* 41(3):303–320.

Doyle, Michael W., and Nicholas Sambanis. 2000. "International Peacebuilding: a Theoretical and Quantitative Analysis." *American Political Science Review* 94(4):779–801.

Drumbl, Mark A. 2007. *Atrocity, Punishment and International Law*. Cambridge UK: Cambridge University Press.

Dugan, Laura, Gary LaFree, Kim Cragin, and Anna Kasupski. 2008. "Building and Analyzing a Comprehensive Open Source Data Base on Global Terrorist Events." Final report for National Institute of Justice Study.

Elbadawi, Ibrahim A., Håvard Hegre, and Gary Milante. 2008. "The Aftermath of Civil War." *Journal of Peace Research* 45(4):451–459.

Epstein, David L., Robert Bates, Jack Goldstone, Ida Kristensen, and Sharyn O'Halloran. 2006. "Democratic Transitions." *American Journal of Political Science* 50(3):551–569.

Esty, Daniel C., Jack Goldstone, Ted Robert Gurr, Barbara Harff, Marc Levy, Geoffrey D. Dabelko, Pamela T. Surko, and Alan N. Unger. 1999. *The State Failure Report: Phase II Findings*.

Fearon, James D. 2004. "Why Do Some Civil Wars Last So Much Longer Than Others?" *Journal of Peace Research* 41(3):275–301.

Fearon, James D., and David D. Laitin. 2003. "Ethnicity, Insurgency, and Civil War." *American Political Science Review* 97:75–90.

Fletcher, Laurel E. and Harvey Weinstein. 2002. "Violence and Social Repair: Rethinking the Contribution of Justice to Reconciliation." *Human Rights Quarterly* 24(3):573–639.

Flores, Thomas Edward, and Irfan Nooruddin. 2009. "Democracy Under the Gun. Understanding Post-Conflict Economic Recovery." *Journal of Conflict Resolution* 53(1):3–29.

Fortna, Virginia Page. 2004. "Does Peacekeeping Keep Peace? International Intervention and the Duration of Peace after Civil War." *International Studies Quarterly* 48(2):269–292.

Freeman, Mark. 2006. *Truth Commissions and Procedural Fairness*. Cambridge: Cambridge University Press.

Freeman, Mark, and Priscilla B. Hayner. 2003. "Truth-Telling." In Bloomfield (ed.) *Reconciliation after Violent Conflict: A Handbook*. Stockholm: International Institute for Democracy and Electoral Assistance.

Gates, Scott. 2002. "Recruitment and Allegiance: The Microfoundations of Rebellion." *Journal of Conflict Resolution* 46(1):111–130.

Gates, Scott, Håvard Hegre, Mark P. Jones, and Håvard Strand. 2006. "Institutional Inconsistency and Political Instability: Polity Duration, 1800–2000." *American Journal of Political Science* 50(4):893–908.

Gates, Scott, and Kaare Ström. 2009. "Power-Sharing, Agency and Civil Conflict." Policy brief, Center for the Study of Civil War.

Gibson, James. 2004. *Overcoming Apartheid*. New York: Russell Sage Foundation.

Gingrich, Newt. 2008. "Lend Them Your Ear." *Foreign Policy* 164:69.

Gleditsch, Nils Petter, Håvard Hegre, and Håvard Strand. 2009. "Democracy and Civil War". In Manus Midlarsky (ed.), *Handbook of War Studies III*. Ann Arbor: University of Michigan Press.

Gleditsch, Nils Petter, Peter Wallensteen, Mikael Eriksson, Margareta Sollenberg, and Håvard Strand. 2002. "Armed Conflict 1946–2001: A New Dataset." *Journal of Peace Research* 39(5):615– 637.

Goldstone, Jack A., Robert H. Bates, Ted Robert Gurr, Michael Lustik, Monty G. Marshall, Jay Ulfelder, and Mark Woodward. 2005. "A Global Forecasting Model of Political Instability." Presented at the Annual Meeting of the American Political Science Association, Washington, DC. September 1–4.

Gurr, Ted Robert. 1993. *Minorities at Risk : A Global View of Ethnopolitical Conflicts*. Washington, DC: United States Institute of Peace Press.

————2000. *Peoples versus States : Minorities at Risk in the New Century*. Washington, DC: United States Institute of Peace Press.

Hartzell, Caroline, Matthew Hoddie and Donald Rotchild. 2001. "Stabilizing the Peace after Civil War: An Investigation of Some Key Variables." *International Organization* 55(1):183–208.

Hartzell, Caroline, and Matthew Hoddie. 2003. "Institutionalizing Peace: Power Sharing and Post-Civil War Conflict Management." *Journal of Political Science* 47(2):318–332.

Hayner, Priscilla B. 1994. "Fifteen Truth Commissions-1974 to 1994: A Comparative Study." *Human Rights Quarterly* 16:597–655.

————2002. *Unspeakable Truths*. New York: Routledge.

Hegre, Håvard. 2003. "Disentangling Democracy and Development as De-terminants of Armed Conflict." Paper presented at the 44th Annual Convention of the International Studies Association, February 26–March 1, Portland. http://folk.uio.no/hahegre/Papers/DisentanglingWB.pdf. 20

Hegre, Håvard, Ibrahim Elbadawi, and Gary Milante. 2007. "How Civil War Alters the Chance of Democratization and Democratic Stability." Paper presented to the conference on Management of Post-Conflict Transition:

The Challenges of Insitutional Reform in Sudan, Khartoum, January 22–24, 2007.

Hegre, Håvard, and Nicholas Sambanis. 2006. "Sensitivity Analysis of Empirical Results on Civil War Onset." *Journal of Conflict Resolution* 50:508–535.

Hegre, Håvard, Tanja Ellingsen, Scott Gates, and Nils Petter Gleditsch. 2001. "Toward a Democratic Civil Peace? Democracy, Political Change, and Civil War, 1816–1992." *American Political Science Review* 95 (1):33–48.

Hewitt, J. Joseph. 2008. "Trends in Global Conflict, 1946–2005." In J. Joseph Hewitt, Jonathan Wilkenfeld, and Ted R. Gurr, *Peace and Conflict 2008*. Boulder: Paradigm Publishers.

Hoddie, Matthew, and Caroline Hartzell. 2005. "Power Sharing in Peace Settlements: Initiating the Transition from Civil War." In Philip G. Roeder and Donald Rothchild, *Sustainable Peace? Power and Democracy after Civil Wars*. Ithaca and London: Cornell University Press.

Hoffman, Bruce, and Donna Kim Hoffman. 1998. "The Rand-St. Andrews Chronology of International Terrorist Incidents, 1995." Reprint from *Terrorism and Political Violence*. Santa Monica: RAND.

Höglund, Kristine, Anna Jarstad and Mimmi Söderberg Kovacs. 2009. "The Predicament of Elections in War-Torn Societies." *Democratization* June(3).

Hudson, Valerie M., Mary Caprioli, Bonnie Ballif-Spanvill, Rose McDermott, and Chad F. Emmett. 2009. "The Heart of the Matter: The Security of Women and the Security of States." *International Security* 33(3):7–45.

Human Security Report Project. 2008. "MiniAtlas of Human Security." http://www.miniatlasofhumansecurity.info/en/access.html. (Accessed December 12, 2008).

Huntington, Samuel P. 1991. *The Third Wave: Democratization in the Late Twentieth Century*. Norman and London: University of Oklahoma Press.

International Crisis Group. 2009. "Liberia: Uneven Progress in Security Sector Reform." http://www.crisisgroup.org/library/documents/africa/west_africa/148_liberia___uneven_progress_in_security_sector_reform.pdf. (Accessed April 29, 2009).

Jarstad, Anna, and Desiree Nilsson. 2008. "From Words to Deeds: The Implementation of Power-Sharing Pacts in Peace Accords." *Conflict Management and Peace Science* 25(3):206–223.

Jenne, E. K., S. M. Saideman, and W. Lowe. 2007. "Separatism as a Bargaining Posture: The Role of Leverage in Minority Radicalization." *Journal of Peace Research* 44 (5):539–558.

Jenne, Erin K. 2007. *Ethnic Bargaining: The Paradox of Minority Empowerment*. Ithaca: Cornell University Press.

Kandiyoti, Deniz. 2008. "The Politics of Gender and Reconstruction in Afghanistan." In Donna Pankhurst (ed.) *Gendered Peace: Women's Struggles for Post-War Justice and Reconciliation* (pp.155–286). New York: Routledge.

Kaufmann, Daniel, Aart Kraay, and Massimo Mastruzzi. 2008. "Governance Matters VII: Aggregate and Individual Governance Indicators, 1996–2007." World Bank Policy Research Working Paper No. 4654.

Keefer, Philip. 2007. "Clientelism, Credibility, and the Polity Choices of Young Democracies." *American Journal of Political Science* 51(4):804–821.

King, Gary, and Langche Zeng. 2001. "Improving Forecasts of State Failure." *World Politics* 53:623–658.

Kreutz, Joakim. 2010. "How and When Armed Conflicts End: Introducing the UCDP Conflict Termination Dataset." *Journal of Peace Research*. forthcoming.

LaFree, Gary and Laura Dugan. 2007. "Introducing the Global Terrorism Database." *Political Violence and Terrorism* 19:181–204.

————2009. "Tracking Global Terrorism, 1970–2004." In *To Protect and to Serve: Dilemmas in Policing Terrorism and Serving the Public*. forthcoming.

LaFree, Gary, Laura Dugan, and Susan Fahey. 2008. "Global Terrorism and Failed States." In J. Joseph Hewitt, Jonathan Wilkenfeld, and Ted Robert Gurr, *Peace and Conflict 2008*. Boulder: Paradigm Publishers.

LaFree, Gary, Laura Dugan and Raven Korte. 2009. "The Impact of British Counter Terrorist Strategies on Political Violence in Northern Ireland: Comparing Deterrence and Backlash Models. Criminology." forthcoming.

LaFree, Gary, Sue-Ming Yang, and Martha Crenshaw. 2009. "Trajectories of Terrorism: Attack Patterns of Foreign Groups that Have Targeted the United States, 1970 to 2004." *Criminology and Public Policy*. forthcoming.

Marshall, Monty, and Keith Jaggers. 2008. "Polity IV Project: Political Regime Characteristics and Transitions, 1800–2007." Center for Systemic Peace: Severn, MD. http://www.systemicpeace.org/inscr/inscr.htm. (Accessed January 27, 2009).

Mason, T. David, and Patrick Fett,. 1996. "Stop the Killing: How Civil Wars End: A Rational Choice Approach." *Journal of Conflict Resolution* 40(4):546–568.

Mason, T. David, and Jason Quinn. 2006. "Sustaining the Peace: Stopping the Recurrence of Civil Wars." in T. David Mason and James Meernik (eds.) *Conflict Prevention and Peace Building in Post-War Societies*. London, New York: Routledge Press.

Mason, T. David, Joseph P. Weingarten, and Patrick J. Fett, "Win, Lose, or Draw: Predicting the Outcome of Civil Wars," *Political Research Quarterly* 50(2):239–268.

Mendeloff, David. 2004. "Truth-Seeking, Truth-Telling, and Post-Conflict Peacebuilding: Curb the Enthusiasm?" *International Studies Review* 2004(6): 355–380.

Minorities at Risk Project. 2009. "Minorities at Risk Dataset." College Park, MD: Center for International Development and Conflict Management. http://www.cidcm.umd.edu/mar/data.asp.

Minow, Martha. 1998. *Between Vengeance and Forgiveness: Facing History after Genocide and Mass Violence*. Boston: Beacon Press.

Molloy, Desmond. 2004. "The Gender Perspective as a Deterrent to Spoilers: The Sierra Leone Experience." African Centre for Constructive Resolution of Disputes (ACCORD).

Mueller, Jerry Z. 2008. "Us and Them: The Enduring Power of Ethnic Nationalism." *Foreign Affairs* 87(2):18–35.

Mukherjee, Bumba. 2006a. "Does Third Party Enforcement or Domestic Institutions Promote Enduring Peace after Civil Wars? Policy Lessons From an Empirical Test." *Foreign Policy Analysis* 2006(2):405.

———2006b. "Why Political Power-Sharing Agreements Lead to Enduring Peaceful Resolution of Some Civil Wars, But Not Others?" *International Studies Quarterly* 50:479–504.

Muller, Edward N., and Erich Weede. 1990. "Cross-National Variations in Political Violence: A Rational Action Approach." *Journal of Conflict Resolution* 34(4):624–651.

Murdoch, James C., and Todd Sandler. 2002. "Economic Growth, Civil Wars and Spatial Spillovers." *Journal of Conflict Resolution* 46:91–110.

Nilsson, Desiree. 2006. In the Shadow of Settlement. Multiple Rebel Groups and Precarious Peace (Ph.D. thesis, Department of Peace and Conflict Research, Uppsala University).

Olzak, Susan. 2006. *The Global Dynamics of Racial and Ethnic Mobilization*. Palo Alto: Stanford University Press.

Paris, Roland. 2004. *At War's End: Building Peace after Civil Conflict*. New York: Cambridge University Press.

Pascoe, Daniel. 2007. "Regan, Patrick. 1996. "Conditions of Successful Third-Party Interventions in Intrastate Wars." *Journal of Conflict Resolution* 40(2): 336–359.

Przeworski, Adam, Michael E. Alvarez, José Antonio Cheibub, and Fernando Limongi. 2000. *Democracy and Development. Political Institutions and Well-Being in the World, 1950–1990*. Cambridge: Cambridge University Press.

Quinn, David. 2008. "Self-Determination Movements and Their Outcomes." in J. Joseph Hewitt, Jonathan Wilkenfeld, and Ted Gurr (eds.) *Peace and Conflict 2008*. Boulder, Colorado: Paradigm Publishers.

Quinn, J. Michael, T. David Mason, and Mehmet Gurses. 2007. "Sustaining the Peace: Determinants of Civil War Recurrence." *International Interactions* 33(2):167–193.

Ramdas, Kavita. 2008. "A Woman's Worth." *Foreign Policy* 164:69.

Regan, Patrick M. 2000. *Civil Wars and Foreign Powers: Outside Intervention in Intrastate Conflict*. Ann Arbor: University of Michigan Press.

Rehn, Elisabeth, and Ellen Johnson-Sirleaf. 2002. *Women War Peace: The Independent Expert's Assessment*. New York: United Nations Development Fund for Women.

Reilly, Benjamin, 2008. "Post-War Elections: Uncertain Turning Points of Transition." In Anna Jarstad and Timothy Sisk (eds.), *From War to Democracy. Dilemmas of Peacebuilding*. New York: Cambridge University Press.

Reinikka, Ritva, and Jakob Svensson. 2004. "Local Capture: Evidence from a Central Government Transfer Program in Uganda." *The Quarterly Journal of Economics* 119:679–705.

Roeder, Philip G. 2007. *Where Nation-States Come From: Institutional Change in the Age of Nationalism*. Princeton: Princeton University Press.

Roeder, Philip G., and Donald Rotchild. 2005. "Power Sharing as an Impediment to Peace and Democracy." In Philip G. Roeder and Donald Rotchild (eds.), *Sustainable Peace? Power and Democracy after Civil Wars*. Ithaca and London: Cornell University Press.

Rost, Nicolas, and John A. Booth. 2008. "Determinants of Regime Type in Newly Independent States." *European Journal of Political Research* 47:635–664.

Saideman, Stephen M. 2001. *The Ties that Divide: Ethnic Politics, Foreign Policy, and International Conflict*. New York: Columbia University Press.

———2002. "Discrimination in International Relations: Analyzing External Support for Ethnic Groups." *Journal of Peace Research* 39(1):27–50.

Saideman, Stephen M., and R. William Ayres. 2000. "Determining the Causes of Irredentism: Logit Analyses of Minorities at Risk Data from the 1980s and 1990s." *Journal of Politics* 62(4):1126–1144.

———2008. *For Kin or Country: Xenophobia, Nationalism, and War*. New York: Columbia University Press.

Sambanis, Nicholas. 2002. "A Review of Recent Advances and Future Directions in the Quantitative Literature on Civil Wars." *Defense and Peace Economics* 13:215–243.

————2003. *Breaking the Conflict Trap: Civil War and Development Policy.* Washington, DC: World Bank.

————2004. "What Is a Civil War? Conceptual and Empirical Complexities of an Operational Definition." *Journal of Conflict Resolution* 48:814–858.

Schmid, Alex. 2004. "Statistics on Terrorism: The Challenge of Measuring Trends in Global Terrorism." *Forum on Crime and Society* 4:49–69.

Shain, Yossi. 2007. *Kinship and Diasporas in International Affairs.* Ann Arbor: University of Michigan Press.

Sharoni, Simona. 1995. *Gender and the Israeli-Palestinian Conflict: The Politics of Women's Resistance.* Syracuse: Syracuse University Press.

SIPRI Yearbook 2008: *Armaments, Disarmament and International Security.* Stockholm International Peace Research Institute.

Snyder, Jack. 2000. *From Voting to Violence. Democratization and Nationalist Politics.* New York and London: W. W. Norton.

Söderberg Kovacs, Mimmi. 2008. "When Rebels Change Their Stripes: Armed Insurgents in Post-War Politics." In Anna Jarstad and Timothy Sisk (eds.), *From War to Democracy: Dilemmas of Peacebuilding.* New York: Cambridge University Press.

Steinberg, Donald. (2007, April 25). "Failing to Empower Women Peacebuilders: A Cautionary Tale from Angola." PeaceWomen E-News.

Stockhold International Peace Research Institute. 2008. *SIPRI Yearbook: 2008.* New York: Oxford University Press.

Strand, Håvard. 2007. *Retreating from a Civil Democratic Peace? Revisiting the Relationship between Political Institutions and Civil War.* Political Science Department, University of Oslo and Center for the Study of Civil War, PRIO.

Tandon, Yash. 2000. "Root Causes of Peacelessness and Approaches to Peace in Africa." *Peace and Change* 25(2):166–187.

Tarnoff, Curt, and Larry Nowels. 2004. "Foreign Aid: An Introductory Overview of U.S. Programs and Policy." Congressional Research Service Report for Congress.

Toft, Monica Duffy. 2003. *The Geography of Ethnic Violence: Identity, Interests, and the Indivisibility of Territory.* Princeton: Princeton University Press.

————2009. *Securing the Peace: The Durable Settlement of Civil Wars.* Princeton: Princeton University Press. forthcoming.

United Nations Inter-Agency Task Force on Women, Peace and Security (WPS). 2002. "Women, Peace, Security." United Nations.

United States Agency for International Development (2005). "Measuring Fragility: Indicators and Methods for Rating State Performance." Washington, DC.

Uppsala Conflict Data Program. 2008. "Peace Agreement Dataset v. 1.0, 1989–2005." Uppsala University. www.ucdp.uu.se/database.

Uppsala/PRIO Armed Conflict Database. 2008. Data File as described in Gleditsch, Nils Petter; Peter Wallensteen, Mikael Eriksson, Margareta Sollenberg, and Håvard Strand, 2002. "Armed Conflict 1946–2001: A New Dataset." *Journal of Peace Research* 39(5):615–637.

Wallensteen, Peter. 2007. *Understanding Conflict Resolution: War, Peace and the Global System.* London: Sage Publications, 2nd edition.

Walter, Barbara E. 1997. "The Critical Barrier to Civil War Settlement." *International Organization* 51:335–365.

———1999. "Designing Transitions from Civil War." *International Security* 24(1):127–155.

———2002. *Committing to Peace: The Successful Settlement of Civil Wars.* Princeton: Princeton University Press.

———2004. "Does Conflict Beget Conflict? Explaining Recurring Civil War." *Journal of Peace Research* 41(3):371–388.

Wantchekon, Leonard. 2004. "The Paradox of "Warlord" Democracy: A Theoretical Investigation." *American Political Science Review* 98(1):17–33.

Weiner, Myron. 1971. "The Macedonian Syndrome." *World Politics* 23(4):665–683.

Weiner, Tim. 2003, August 20. "In Ruined Capital, Liberians Fear for Shaky Peace." *New York Times.* Retrieved April 28, 2009 from: *http://www.nytimes.com/2003/08/20/world/in-ruined-capital-liberians-fear-for-shaky-peace.html.*

World Development Indicators. 2008. Computer File.

Acknowledgments

We are extremely grateful to many people who played a large role in this project. It simply would not have been possible to pull all of the elements of this book together without the hard work and energy from many of our colleagues. First and foremost, we would like to thank Jennifer Knerr at Paradigm Publishers. She has been tireless in her support and enthusiasm for this project. Kimberly Stites provided research and administrative support in the early stages of the project. Chantal Russell provided very valuable research assistance, including the preparation of some of the updates for entries in the Appendix on active armed conflicts. We are also very grateful to Tjip Walker, Senior Conflict Advisor in the Office of Conflict Management and Mitigation at the US Agency for International Development. His comments and guidance about various chapters in the book have proven very valuable. We are especially indebted to Sarah Long, who served as the primary research assistant for the book. She was responsible for most of the production aspects of the book, including graph and table designs. Dependable and unflappable, she worked many long hours helping us sort through the myriad details of this project. Finally, Elizabeth Kielman, CIDCM's Deputy Director, was critical to the whole enterprise. All along the way, she forcefully pushed us to make improvements. For that, we are especially grateful.

About the Authors

Ted Robert Gurr (University of Maryland) is Distinguished University Professor at the University of Maryland. He is the founder of the Polity project and the Minorities at Risk project. His most recent book is *Peoples versus States: Minorities at Risk in the New Century* (United States Institute of Peace Press 2000). Professor Gurr has been a core member of the Political Instability Task Force since its inception in 1994 and has written or edited twenty other books and monographs including the award-winning *Why Men Rebel* (Princeton 1970) and *Ethnic Conflict in World Politics* (Westview 1994, 2003 with Barbara Harff).

J. Joseph Hewitt (University of Maryland) is Assistant Director and Director of Government Relations at CIDCM. His particular responsibilities for the center include projects funded by government contracts and grants. His research focuses on the causes of armed interstate conflict, conflict early-warning, international crisis bargaining, and the connections between government attributes and conflict behavior.

Jonathan Wilkenfeld (University of Maryland) is Professor in the Department of Government and Politics and Director of the Center for International Development and Conflict Management. He is also Co-Principal Investigator for the Center for the Study of Terrorism and Responses to Terrorism. His research focuses on international conflict and crisis, foreign policy decision making, experimental and simulation techniques in political science and, most recently, the role of third-party mediation in international disputes.

About the Contributors

Rosa Aloisi is a doctoral student in the Department of Political Science at the University of North Texas. Her research focuses on international criminal justice, state behavior regarding international law and international institutions.

Mary Caprioli is an Associate Professor of Political Science at the University of Minnesota, Duluth and serves on the Board of Directors for WomanStats. Her research interests focus on linking the security of women to the security of states.

R. Kim Cragin is a senior policy analyst athe RAND Corporation and Adjunct Professor at the University of Maryland. She focuses on terrorism-related issues, spending three months on General David Petraeus's staff in 2008. In addition to Iraq, Kim has conducted fieldwork in the West Bank and Gaza Strip, Lebanon, Egypt, Djibouti, Colombia, Northern Ireland, northwest China, Sri Lanka, southern Thailand, Indonesia, Malaysia, and the southern Philippines. Her most recent RAND publications include *The Dynamic Terrorist Threat* (2004), *Dissuading Terror* (2005), and *Sharing the Dragon's Teeth: Terrorist Groups and the Exchange of New Technologies* (2007).

Laura Dugan is an Associate Professor in the Department of Criminology and Criminal Justice at the University of Maryland. She is an active member of the National Center for the Study of Terrorism and Responses to Terrorism, the National Consortium on Violence Research, and the Maryland Population Research Center. Her research examines the causes of and policy responses to terrorism. She also designs methodological strategies to overcome data limitations inherent in the social sciences.

Hanne Fjelde is a doctoral student in the Department of Peace and Conflict Research at Uppsala University and a research affiliate with the Centre for the Study of Civil War at the International Peace Research Institute, Oslo. Her dissertation is on the association between political institutions, the quality of governance, and civil war, with a particular focus on Africa.

Håvard Hegre is an Associate Professor in the Department of Political Science at the University of Olso. He also serves as Research Professor and working group leader in the Centre for the Study of Civil War at the International Peace Research Institute, Oslo. Hegre has published in a number of leading academic journals, and is co-author of the World Bank Policy Research Report *Breaking the Conflict Trap*. His current research interests include the relationships between democracy, socio-economic development, and militarized conflict.

Anke Hoeffler is a research officer at the Centre for the Study of African Economies. She is also a research associate at the International Peace Research Institute, Oslo. Her research focuses on the macroeconomics of developing countries, the economics of conflict, and political economy. She has published on the causes of war, military expenditure, post-conflict economies, the effect of aid, and the problems of democracy in low-income and natural-resource–rich societies. Her most recent publication is the co-authored article "Beyond Greed and Grievance: Feasibility and Civil War" in

Oxford Economic Papers, 2009 (with Paul Collier and Dominik Rohner).

Valerie M. Hudson is Professor of Political Science. Her research foci include foreign policy analysis, security studies, gender and international relations, and methodology. Hudson's articles have appeared in *International Security, Journal of Peace Research, Political Psychology*, and *Foreign Policy Analysis*. She is the author or editor of several books, including (with Andrea Den Boer) *Bare Branches: The Security Implications of Asia's Surplus Male Population* (MIT Press, 2004), which won the American Association of Publishers Award for the Best Book in Political Science and the Otis Dudley Duncan Award for Best Book in Social Demography. Hudson is one of the Principal Investigators of the WomanStats Project.

Gary LaFree is Director of the National Consortium for the Study of Terrorism and Responses to Terrorism (START) and Professor of Criminology and Criminal Justice at the University of Maryland. His recent research deals with national and international macro-level trends in violent crimes and terrorism. LaFree is the author of *The Changing Nature of Crime in America* (National Institute of Justice 2000) and *Losing Legitimacy: Street Crime and the Decline of Social Institutions in America* (Westview 1998).

James Meernik is Professor of Political Science and Interim Associate Dean for Administrative Affairs in the College of Arts and Sciences at the University of North Texas. He was Chair of the Department of Political Science from 2002–2008. Meernik specializes in research on United States foreign policy and post-conflict peace building, with an emphasis on the role of transitional justice and international law. From 2003–2008 he was associate editor of the journal, *International Studies Quarterly*. He has published over forty articles and several books on these topics.

Angela D. Nichols is a doctoral student in the Department of Political Science at the University of North Texas. Her research interests include transitional justice, post-conflict peace, NGOs, and human rights.

Rebecca Nielsen is a doctoral student at Yale University in the Department of Political Science where she studies development, gender, and political participation in the aftermath of civil conflict. She is a former employee of the WomanStats Project at Brigham Young University.

Amy Pate is research director of the Minorities at Risk project at the University of Maryland. Her research focuses on ethnic conflict in the context of democratization, ethnically based terrorism, and state stability. Her recent projects include conflict early-warning analysis (primarily for the US Agency for International Development) and research on the tactical choices of militant ethnopolitical organizations in the Middle East and North Africa.

Stephen M. Saideman is Canada Research Chair in International Security and Ethnic Conflict and Associate Professor of Political Science at McGill University. His publications include *The Ties That Divide: Ethnic Politics, Foreign Policy and International Conflict* (Columbia 2001), *For Kin or Country: Xenophobia, Nationalism and War* (with R. William Ayres, Columbia 2008), and *Intra-State Conflict, Governments and Security: Dilemmas of Deterrence and Assurance* (co-edited with Marie-Joëlle Zahara, Routledge 2008). He has published a number of articles on the international relations and comparative politics of ethnic conflict.

Marsha Sowell (University of North Texas) is a McNair Scholar in the Department of Political Science. Her research interests include international human rights, international conflict, and civil war.

Monica Duffy Toft is an Associate Professor of Public Policy and the Director of the Initiative on Religion in International Affairs at Harvard University. She was a research intern at the RAND Corporation and served in the U.S. Army in southern Germany as a Russian voice interceptor. Her research interests include international relations, religion, nationalism and ethnic conflict, civil and interstate wars, the relationship between demography and national security, and military and strategic planning. She is the author of *The Geography of Ethnic Violence: Identity, Interests, and Territory*, an edited volume, *The Fog of Peace: Strategic and Military Planning Under Uncertainty*, and a third on civil war termination: *Securing the Peace*.

CIDCM

Center for International Development and Conflict Management

The Center for International Development and Conflict Management (CIDCM) is an interdisciplinary research center at the University of Maryland. CIDCM seeks to prevent and transform conflict, to understand the interplay between conflict and development, and to help societies create sustainable futures for themselves. Using the insights of researchers, practitioners, and policy makers, CIDCM devises effective tools and culturally appropriate pathways to constructive change.

For almost thirty years, scholars and practitioners at the Center have sought ways to understand and address conflicts over security, identity, and distributive justice. CIDCM's programs are based on the belief that "peace building and development-with-justice are two sides of the same coin" (Edward Azar, CIDCM founding director). CIDCM's accomplished scholars, its expertise in data collection and analysis, and its direct involvement in regional conflict management efforts make the Center a unique resource for discovering enduring solutions to the world's most intractable conflicts.

Research Data Collections

CIDCM collects, analyzes and links data relevant to the study of the dynamics of societal conflicts. The aim is to expand data capabilities to facilitate cross-disciplinary research among scholars and policy analysts concerned with aspects of societal conflict, state failure, and minority rights. The Center hosts several major international databases on societal conflict, including Minorities at Risk and International Crisis Behavior.

Training and Education

The Center provides on-the-ground training for parties to specific conflicts, as well as programs that feature conflict resolution training for students and government officials. The Partners in Conflict program has provided training in citizens' diplomacy and conflict resolution in more than 15 countries, and the ICONS Project creates interactive tools for teaching and training in negotiation, leadership, and conflict management techniques. CIDCM also offers an undergraduate Minor in International Development and Conflict Management.

Policy Analysis

Strategically located at the nexus of theory and practice, CIDCM seeks to foster a conversation among scholars and policy makers, and to use global analyses as a basis for concrete recommendations for the policy community. Extensive field experience, subject matter expertise, and command of both quantitative and qualitative methods provide CIDCM researchers with a strong foundation for advancing cutting edge policy analysis. In this regard, its biennial publication *Peace and Conflict* reports major global and regional trends in societal conflict, development, and governance issues. Other recent examples of analyses offered by the center's researchers include assessments of policy regarding the use of information technology in development, democratization, strategies for conflict mitigation and resolution, and approaches for sustainable development and peace.

In addition, two CIDCM endowed chairs, the Anwar Sadat Chair for Peace and Development and the Baha'i Chair for World Peace, seek to bridge the gap between the academic and policy worlds and develop alternatives to violent conflict.

To learn more about CIDCM, please visit the web site at http://www.cidcm.umd.edu

Jonathan Wilkenfeld
Director

Paul Huth
Research Director

J. Joseph Hewitt
Director of Government Relations